ITQ Handbook

Levels 1 and 2

Marie Claire Williams

D0256323

Heinemann

Inspiring generations

Heinemann Educational Publishers
Halley Court, Jordan Hill, Oxford OX2 8EJ
Part of Harcourt Education

Heinemann is the registered trademark of Harcourt Education Limited

Text © Marie Claire Williams, 2006

First published 2006

10 09 08 07 06
10 9 8 7 6 5 4 3 2 1

British Library Cataloguing in Publication Data is available from the British
Library on request.

10-digit ISBN: 0 435462 23 7
13-digit ISBN: 978 0 435462 23 9

Edited by Alex Gray
Typeset by TexTech International
Original illustrations © Harcourt Education Limited, 2006
Cover design by Wooden Ark Studio
Printed in the UK by Scotprint
Cover photo © Alamy

Websites
Please note that the examples of websites suggested in this book were up to
date at the time of writing. It is essential for tutors to preview each site before
using it to ensure that the URL is still accurate and the content is appropriate.
We suggest that tutors bookmark useful sites and consider enabling students
to access them through the school or college intranet.

Tel: 01865 888058   www.heinemann.co.uk

Contents

Acknowledgements

Every effort has been made to contact copyright holders of material reproduced in this book. Any omissions will be rectified in subsequent printings if notice is given to the publishers.

Microsoft product screenshots reprinted with permission from Microsoft Corporation.

Page 1; page 23; page 181 – Alamy
Page 29 (Figure 3.1) – Tek Image/Science Photo Library
Page 30 (Figure 3.2) – istock/Roorda
Page 31 (Figure 3.4) – Gareth Boden
Page 32 – (*top*) istock/KFB; (*bottom*) istock/Dennys Bisogno
Page 33 (Figure 3.5) –
Page 33 (Figure 3.6) – PhotoDisc/Siede Preis
Page 33 (Figure 3.7) – istock/David Freund
Page 34 (Figure 3.8) – istock/Andresr
Page 34 (Figure 3.9) – istock/Mike McCune
Page 41 (Figure 3.17) – Marie Claire Williams
Page 42 (Figure 3.18) – PhotoDisc/Siede Preis
Page 45 (Figure 3.22) – istock/Andrzej Tokarski
Page 46 (Figure 3.23) – istock/Adam Wallczez
Page 46 (Figure 3.24) – Getty Images/PhotoDisc
Page 106 (Figure 5.1) – Gareth Boden
Page 171 (Figure 8.3) – Pallava Bagla/Corbis

Introduction

ITQ is the name for the new NVQ for IT Users.

What is an NVQ?

An NVQ (National Vocational Qualification) is a standard that has been set by the Sector Skills Council that specifies the competencies required to carry out a job at each of the levels. The skills requirements for IT are set by e-Skills UK.

ITQ is designed for anyone who is using IT in their day-to-day work. The aim of these qualifications is to recognise the application of a range of IT user skills and knowledge in the workplace. ITQ is a new and very flexible National Vocational Qualification that will enable you to gain credit for the IT skills that you need for your specific job.

The qualification consists of one mandatory unit that you must achieve through evidence assessed from a real workplace. You then choose an appropriate selection of optional units that reflects your needs and opportunities. These optional units can be assessed in a number of ways.

The level of the mandatory unit decides the overall level of the qualification. You can achieve some of the optional units at a different level but at least fifty percent must be at the level of the mandatory unit. There is a helpful calculator available on the e-Skills UK website which you can use to help you work out which units to take (www.e-skills.com).

You will need to achieve a total of 40 unit values to achieve the full NVQ at Level 1.
You will need to achieve a total of 100 unit values to achieve the full NVQ at Level 2.

The following table shows the values given to each unit at Level 1 and Level 2.

	Unit values	
	Level 1	Level 2
Mandatory unit		
Make selective use of IT	15	25
Optional units		
Operate a computer	10	20
IT maintenance for users	5	15
IT troubleshooting for users	5	15
IT security for users	5	15
Artwork and imaging software	10	20
Internet and intranets	5	15
E-mail	5	15
Word-processing software	10	20
Spreadsheet software	10	20
Database software	10	20
Website software	10	20
Presentation software	10	20
Specialist or bespoke software	10	20
Evaluate the impact of IT	5	15
Use IT systems	5	15
Use IT to exchange information	5	15
Sector-specific unit	10	20

Many of the optional units may be achieved through a contributory qualification; the agreed list is published on the e-skills website www.e-skills.com. Where one or two contributory qualifications or units have been used to achieve an optional unit, assessment of the mandatory ITQ unit must involve the skills from these optional unit(s). Where more than two optional units are gained in this way then at least two of these units must be included in the assessment of the mandatory unit, and application of the other units must be demonstrated either in the workplace or through simulation. Practical assessments for these contributory units will be accepted as simulation.

The table below shows how the unit numbers for both OCR and City & Guilds map to the National Occupational Standards. The ITQ qualification is also awarded by the British Computer Society.

	OCR		City & Guilds	
	Level 1	Level 2	Level 1	Level 2
Mandatory unit				
Make selective use of IT	1A	2A	101	201
Optional units				
Operate a computer	1B	2B	102	202
IT maintenance for users	1C	2C	104	204
IT troubleshooting for users	1D	2D	103	203
IT security for users	1E	2E	105	205
Artwork and imaging software	1F	2F	112	212
Internet and intranets	1G	2G	106	206
E-mail	1H	2H	107	207
Word-processing software	1I	2I	108	208
Spreadsheet software	1J	2J	109	209
Database software	1K	2K	110	210
Website software	1L	2L	111	211
Presentation software	1M	2M	113	213
Specialist or bespoke software	1N	2N	114	214
Evaluate the impact of IT	1O	2O	115	215
Use IT systems	1P	2P	117	217
Use IT to exchange information	1Q	2Q	118	218

The standards for the qualification are written as Areas of Competence. At each level of a unit there is a summary of what a competent person can do. With this there is a list of the knowledge and understanding needed to underpin the competence and a list of skills and techniques that you are required to be able to demonstrate. For each item listed, known as a component of both knowledge and skills, there is a detailed list of what needs to be covered at each level.

What form can the evidence take?

There are two main types of evidence: performance and supplementary.

1   Performance evidence results from doing a task and will consist of:

- End products – e.g. plans, hard copy, disk files, etc.
- Observation of activities – your tutor/assessor/supervisor will need to watch you carrying out some of the tasks that you include in your portfolio of evidence.

Performance evidence is best if it comes from real work. For the mandatory unit, Make selective use of IT, it must be from real work, but for all the other units it can be from simulation of real work.

For each unit you will need to include a number of work-related tasks. The minimum required for each unit is:

	Level 1	Level 2
Mandatory unit	Straightforward tasks	Comprehensive tasks
Make selective use of IT	3	4
Optional units		
Operate a computer	2	2
IT maintenance for users	2	2
IT troubleshooting for users	2	2
IT security for users	2	2
Artwork and imaging software	2	2
Internet and intranets	2	2
E-mail	2	2
Word-processing software	2	2
Spreadsheet software	2	2
Database software	2	2
Website software	2	2
Presentation software	2	2
Specialist or bespoke software	2	2
Evaluate the impact of IT	2	2
Use IT systems	2	2
Use IT to exchange information	2	2

2   Supplementary evidence may include:

- Questions and answers (written and oral) – your tutor/assessor/ supervisor may sit down and ask you questions or may give you a worksheet to complete.
- Statements by yourself, supervisors and colleagues.
- Previous certificates of competence, e.g. CLAiT.

Collecting your evidence

You will need to put together your portfolio of evidence. This is often put together using a ring binder or lever arch folder. However, particularly as this is an IT qualification, you may be able to compile your portfolio electronically.

Your portfolio will need to include the recording systems required by your awarding body. For each item of evidence, you will need to show:

- which **units, component, knowledge and understanding,** and **skills and techniques** it is evidence of
- who has assessed it
- when, where and under what conditions it was carried out.

Your portfolio of evidence needs to be well organised and easy for others to work through. Each unit should have a separate section and every item of evidence should have a unique reference number to help you to identify it. You will need to compile an index to help you to cross-reference your documents.

Some of the work that you do may provide evidence for more than one of the units. You will need to make sure that you have clearly identified the components that it demonstrates so that it can be correctly cross-referenced.

As this NVQ is about working with new technology, you should be well-equipped by the time you are completing your qualification to use many of the techniques of the software to enhance the presentation of your evidence.

The evidence you compile in your portfolio is assessed by an NVQ assessor and this assessment is confirmed by an internal verifier. An external verifier from the awarding body will also check a sample of the assessments.

The e-skills Passport

The e-skills Passport is a simple and easy-to-use online tool that can be used to find out your current IT skills, identify any gaps, and be used to set your learning targets. You can record your achievements and then re-visit your Passport again and again to keep it up to date as your skills improve.

The e-skills Passport is linked closely to the ITQ Standards and may be available for you to use. You will need to ask your supervisor and workplace assessor.

Mandatory unit

1 Make selective use of IT

1 Make selective use of IT

Introduction

This is the mandatory unit that you must complete to achieve the qualification. All the evidence for the unit must come from the workplace, it cannot be obtained through simulation.

In this unit you will demonstrate the application of your knowledge, understanding, skills and techniques for at least two software application optional units. You will need to show that you can choose the right hardware and software to carry out a particular job in the most effective way. You will need to explain what you have done and the reasons for your choices.

- At level 1 you will need to provide evidence from at least three tasks. These tasks will be simple, straightforward activities that arise naturally in your job.
- At level 2 you will need to provide evidence from at least four comprehensive tasks. They will be tasks of a more complex nature.

What the correct terms for IT hardware, software and particular tasks are and how to use them

Information technology (IT) has its own set of technical terms for the various items of hardware and the different tools and techniques associated with the software. Part of being competent in the use of IT includes being able to use this language correctly.

What you need to know and understand

- What and how to use the correct terms for types of hardware being used
- What and how to use the correct terms for tools and techniques in software being used

What and how to use the correct terms for types of hardware being used

You need to know the correct names for all the hardware that you use. This will include both the particular items, such as mouse and keyboard, and the main cables and connectors that join them together to make up the complete system.

Basic hardware

The IT system that you work with will usually include the following hardware:

- CPU (central processing unit) – the processor and memory housed in the main computer casing.
- Mouse – the pointing device that you use to navigate around the graphical interface.
- Keyboard – usually the main input device.
- Monitor – also referred to as a VDU (visual display unit).
- Hard disk – the main storage of the system.
- Removable storage – CD, DVD, memory stick, floppy disk.
- Printer – this will usually be a laser or inkjet printer.
- Modem – the device used to connect the computer to the Internet.

Other hardware

You will also need to have some knowledge of a wide range of other hardware that might be used to carry out more specialist functions. Although you may not use all of these, you will need to have an understanding of what they do and how they are used.

- Light pen – a pen-shaped input device which is pointed at the screen to make selections or to create images.
- Scanner – used to capture images and text from the printed page.
- Joystick – another device for moving the pointer on the screen, requires less fine control and therefore may be more suitable than a mouse for people with disabilities.
- Camera – digital images can be downloaded directly and saved to the computer system.
- Sound card – used to produce high-quality sound.
- Plotter – used to produce high-quality drawings using a selection of different coloured pens.
- Network card – to enable connection to a computer network.
- Webcam – a web camera is a digital camera that delivers images through a website, continuously or at regular intervals, and is frequently used to provide a visual enhancement to web chat.

Check it yourself

Create a glossary of terms to explain the hardware terms for the equipment that you use. You could check that you have the correct meaning by looking in the 'Operate a computer' unit of this book, searching on the Internet, using a computer dictionary, or using the onscreen helper of your system.

What and how to use the correct terms for tools and techniques in software being used

Tools and techniques

There are a number of basic tools and techniques that apply to all the different types of software that you may use, although exactly how you use them may vary from one application to another.

- Open – to start the file or application.
- Close – to shut down the file or application.
- Save – to create a permanent store of your work.
- Print – to produce a hard copy of your document.
- Delete – to permanently remove a file or part of the work.

You will also use tools and techniques that are specific to the applications that you are working with. These are covered in more detail in CLAiT, ECDL and e-Quals books, but Table 1.1 lists the tools and techniques you will need to cover as a quick reference guide.

Application	Level 1	Level 2
Word processing	<ul><li>Create and edit text using word wrap, insert, delete, cut, copy, paste, drag and drop, find and replace.</li><li>Format text using size, font (typeface), colour, bold, underline and italic; paragraphs using alignment, bullets, numbering, line spacing, borders, shading, tabs and indents; lines using spacing, alignment and breaks; pages using size, orientation, margins, page numbers, date and time.</li><li>Layout using simple tables, use existing templates.</li><li>Combine information using insert, size and position.</li><li>Check using spellcheck, grammar check and word count.</li></ul>	<ul><li>Create and edit text using size and sort, special characters and symbols, mail merge.</li><li>Format text using tabs, columns, styles, headers and footers, page breaks; working within organisational house style; change file formats to RTF and HTML.</li><li>Layout; inserting and editing tables, add and delete columns, modify width and row height, add borders and shading; select, change and use templates.</li><li>Combine information from same and different software types; spreadsheet, images, database, web page.</li><li>Check using proofreading; line, paragraph and page breaks, consistent heading and subheading format.</li></ul>
Spreadsheet	<ul><li>Enter and edit data using add and delete rows and columns, clear cells, cut, copy, paste, drag and drop, find and replace.</li><li>Format cells for numbers, decimal place, font, alignment; rows and columns for height, width, borders and shading; charts with titles and labels; pages using size, orientation, margins, page numbers, date and time.</li><li>Formulae and functions including SUM, arithmetic operators (add, subtract, multiply and divide).</li><li>Analyse and interpret using sub-totals, sort and list.</li><li>Combine using insert, size and position.</li><li>Present simple data using tables, bar graphs, pie charts.</li></ul>	<ul><li>Enter and edit data using absolute and relative cell references, add data and text to a chart, change the type of chart.</li><li>Format cells using colour, shading and borders, move and resize charts; format pages using headers and footers, adjust page set up for printing.</li><li>Formulae and functions including mathematical, statistical, financial and relational.</li><li>Analyse and interpret using filters.</li><li>Combine information including copying spreadsheet graphs to word-processed documents and database data to a spreadsheet.</li><li>Present data using a wide range of graphs and charts.</li></ul>

Application	Level 1	Level 2
Database	• Enter data by updating fields, create new records. • Queries using single selection criterion, sort data. • Reports using menus, shortcuts.	• Create fields for entering data with field characteristics; name, type, size, format. • Modify single-table non-relational database structure by name, type, size. • Queries using multiple criteria. • Format reports for page size, page orientation, page numbering, headers and footers, margins; sort data. • Set up shortcuts.
E-mail	• Send to individuals, carbon copy, address book. • Receive, forward, reply, reply to all, reply with history. • Send and receive attachments. • Format by changing font, type size and colour, using alignment, bullets, numbering and indents. • Exchange information using 'netiquette'.	• Send to group list, add a signature, set priority. • Receive and store in folders and subfolders. • Compress and decompress messages and attachments. • Format using RTF, HTML and plain text. • Exchange information using FTP or http.
Presentation	• Produce simple presentations. • Edit including inserting, manipulating text and pictures; adding lines and simple shapes. • Format slides for text alignment, bullets, numbering, line spacing, colour, fonts, size, background. • Combine information using insert, and then size and position. • Check using spellcheck, grammar check, word count. • Present as slide show, print as handouts; reorder slides.	• Produce complex presentations that include animation. • Edit by inserting objects; resizing images; changing the position and orientation of objects. • Format slides by changing colour schemes or using organisational house style; use and adjust templates. • Check using proofreading techniques. • Present slide shows and speaker's notes.

Application	Level 1	Level 2
Web page	• Plan using web design template; include features such as background, sound, frames, action buttons, links, hotspots. • Create and edit simple web pages using insert and delete, cut, copy, paste, drag and drop, find and replace. • Format fonts, type style, image, chart, size, orientation. • Combine information using insert, size and position. • Check text using spellcheck, grammar check, word count; images for size, alignment, orientation; files for suitable file format.	• Plan and produce multi-page website using links within the page, linking pages, hyperlinks to other websites and alter simple coding. • Edit and format characters, lines, paragraphs and pages, colour, fonts, background, pictures; insert and change text, resize, align, rotate, flip and arrange images; layout using tables and frames. • Combine information such as simple information from a database.
Artwork and imaging	• Create images using lines, boxes, arrows. • Insert and manipulate: align, rotate, flip and arrange objects; cut, paste, crop, trim and resize objects and pictures; insert text and change font, text and colour.	• Create images using painting, drawing and DTP manipulation software. • Insert and manipulate; group and ungroup; use filters to create special effects, edit existing templates.
Internet and intranets	• Use search engine to find and select. • Use bookmarks and favourites; send web pages and web links via e-mail.	• Use meta-search engines, wild cards, AND or NOT (Boolean notation). • Use FTP or HTTP to exchange information; use interactive websites. • Customise browser settings. • Demonstrate awareness of 'nettiquette' when using e-mail and other Internet communication.

Table 1.1 A quick reference guide to the tools and techniques you will need to know

How to produce information that is clear and appropriate

What you need to know and understand

- Know who and what the information is for, where it will be used and when it is needed
- **Level 2** How to produce information that communicates clearly and accurately with the audience, where and when it is needed

Know who and what the information is for, where it will be used and when it is needed

When you carry out a task in the workplace, you do it to meet an identified need. You may be producing a letter, making a slide for a presentation, or a simple budget spreadsheet, but whatever you are doing it will be for a specific purpose. In order to do this well you need to have some understanding of what the finished product will be used for.

Every task that you do will have some sort of deadline. Deadlines are very important in the world of work. Someone else will often use the documents that you produce. If you are late then they will be kept waiting and may not be able to meet their deadlines. If customers do not get a timely response from an organisation, they are likely to go elsewhere in the future.

Check it yourself

For each document that you produce for your qualification you will need to show that you know who and what the information is for. You should complete the task sheet (on page 22) which you can attach as part of your evidence.

For a task that you are working on at the moment, complete the first section of the task sheet. Every task needs to be identified with a name – e.g. 'Late payment of invoice letter'. What type of activity will you do? – e.g. word processing, spreadsheet, etc? It is helpful to write a brief description of what it is – e.g. standard one-page letter printed on headed paper. Who is going to receive this document? – this could be someone within the organisation or someone outside, such as a customer. When is this task due to be completed?

How to produce information that communicates clearly and accurately with the audience, where and when it is needed

The finished product – the letter, presentation slide, or budget – needs to be presented so that the information it is providing can be easily found and used. The layout and style used will need to be suitable for the intended audience – the person who is going to use it.

You need to be able to produce information that is accurate. There will usually be tools such as a spellchecker to help you with this. For each software application there is a range of different formats available. The page setup will enable you to create the best layout, selecting the paper orientation and margins to suit the task.

You will have choices as to what medium to use for the finished product. Do you need to print it out on paper or should it be sent electronically, possibly as an attachment to an e-mail? A presentation may be needed in electronic format stored on removable storage such as a CD or USB (universal serial bus) memory stick, but you may also need to print the individual slides on acetates and also print out handout copies on paper.

Skills Finding and evaluating

What you need to do

- Choose the source that is most likely to provide the information needed
- Locate information from various sources
- **Level 2** Choose and use appropriate methods of searching for relevant information
- Choose information that is appropriate for what is needed
- **Level 2** Review sources and information to help choose the most relevant, and decide when enough has been found

It is important that the information you use to carry out a task is what is required, is accurate and fit for purpose. You will need to know where to get information from – the source, and the methods you can use to find it.

Choose the source that is most likely to provide the information needed

When you are given a task to do you are not always given the precise information that you need and may have to find it before you can do the job. The sources of your information will need to be the right ones to give you exactly what is required.

Locate information from various sources

Information is available in many different forms and from a variety of different places. Some information will be on paper – it could be another document that has been produced within the organisation, a letter from a customer, a price list in a supplier's catalogue, a company's details in an article in a magazine or newspaper, and many more. Sometimes the information will already be in an electronic format – data in a database that you can access from your computer system, information that can be downloaded from the Internet, an attachment received in an e-mail, etc. You will need to use a range of skills to find this electronic information depending upon the software application being used. See Table 1.2.

Choose and use appropriate methods of searching for relevant information

The search methods that you will use will depend upon the application you are working with. Table 1.2 is a quick reference guide for doing this.

Practical task

For the task that you are working on at the moment, complete section 2 of the task sheet on page 22. Identify each source of information that you use and the search method that you used to find the specific information needed for the task.

Keep a note of how you did the task and include screenshots where possible.

Choose information that is appropriate for what is needed

Once you have found the information, you then need to select only the information that is actually needed. Very often a search, particularly on the Internet, will give you far more information than you actually need. To be able to do this correctly you will need to understand the task in hand (see 'Know who and what the information is for, where it will be used and when it is needed' on page 8).

Application	Level 1	Level 2
Word processing	• Use the text search facilities to locate information in a text document which is about five pages long.	• Use the text search facilities to locate information in a large text document.
Spreadsheet	• Search for cells and groups of cells that contain data of a particular type.	• Search for cells and groups of cells that contain data of a particular type or within a given range.
Database	• Carry out a search using a single selection criterion, e.g. all customers that are located in Swindon.	• Carry out a search using multiple selection criteria, e.g. all customers that are located in Swindon that have placed an order in the last six months.
E-mail	• Search for e-mails in current folders that have been received from or sent to a specific recipient.	• Search for e-mails in current folders and archives that have been received from or sent to a specific recipient, or are about a common theme.
Presentation	• Use search facilities to locate suitable content for the presentation, such as information, images etc.	• Use search facilities to locate suitable content for the presentation, such as information, graphics, animations etc.
Web page	• Use search facilities to locate suitable content for the web page, such as information, simple images etc.	• Use search facilities to locate suitable content for the web page, such as information, graphics, animations etc.
Artwork and imaging	• Use search facilities to locate suitable image files – ClipArt, photographs etc.	• Use search facilities to locate suitable image files – ClipArt, photographs etc.
Internet and intranets	• Search for information on one subject using simple search criteria.	• Search for information on a given theme and with a minimum amount of information.

Table 1.2 Quick reference guide for search methods you will need to use

When you are working with images and graphics files you will need to choose information that is of the right size and in a suitable format.

Review sources and information to help choose most relevant, and decide when enough has been found

There is so much information freely available it is sometimes quite difficult to decide whether you have selected the most suitable.

Skills Organising

What you need to do

- Choose and use an appropriate format for organising information
- **Level 2** Use a variety of software tools and techniques to structure information to suit tasks and audience needs

This is about the processes you need to use to produce the final piece of work. You have collected all the information that you are going to use and now you will need to use the appropriate software tools and techniques to bring it all together in the required format.

Choose and use an appropriate format for organising information

The format that you decide to use for each piece of work will take into account the type of information you are using and who it is intended for. Again, you will need to fully understand the task you are carrying out and the purpose for which the information is going to be used. See Table 1.3.

Most organisations will have a set of standards, a house style, and you will need to make sure that the way you present your information meets this. There will usually be different house styles for internal and external documents and it is always important to follow these.

Use a variety of software tools and techniques to structure information to suit tasks and audience needs

The software that you use will have a range of tools and facilities to help you organise and structure your information so that it can be used easily. These will be dependent on the software you are using and the tasks that you carry out. See Table 1.3.

Application	Level 1	Level 2
Word processing	• Arrange information into a simple format in a word processing document. • Organise the files into a simple file structure.	• Produce a letter, information sheet, etc. and present it in a non-routine format for a specific audience, e.g. high contrast or large print for partially sighted readers.
Spreadsheet	• Enter data and present it in a suitable format. • Organise files into a simple file structure.	• Enter data and present it in a suitable format.
Database	• Organise database queries into a logical sequence and correlate reports.	• Format fields and enter data in an organised fashion.
E-mail	• Arrange e-mails into groups. • Maintain address book entries.	• Arrange e-mails into themed groups. • Arrange address book entries, create mailing list groups, and organise multiple e-mail accounts.
Presentation	• Create a presentation so that the slides are in the correct order, it can be controlled by the user and is easy to find. • Organise files into a simple file structure.	• Create a presentation so that the slides are in the correct order, animations function correctly, it can be controlled by the user, and is easy to find.
Web page	• Create single web pages that function correctly, are simple to use and easy to read, e.g. appropriate font, contrast etc.	• Create multiple web pages that function correctly, are simple to use and easy to read, e.g. appropriate font, contrast etc.
Artwork and imaging	• Create documents containing simple artwork and other images that are ordered and formatted correctly. • Organise files into a simple file structure.	• Create documents containing simple artwork and other images that are ordered and formatted correctly.
Internet and intranets	• Select and organise bookmarked pages into groups.	• Select and organise bookmarked pages into themed groups. • Set browser displays to cater for different needs such as high contrast or large font.

Table 1.3 Examples of how you need to show that your information is organised

For the task that you are working on at the moment, complete section 3 of the task sheet on page 22. Identify each software tool or technique that you used to create this piece of work. You need to include the name of the particular tool, for example search and replace, and then include a brief description of what it does and how you used it.

Keep a note of how you did the task and include screenshots where possible.

What the purposes for using IT are and how to judge whether the IT system and software chosen was appropriate

What you need to know and understand

- Why the IT system and software that was used was appropriate for the task
- **Level 2** How using the IT system and software was an appropriate way of carrying out the task

Why the IT system and software that was used was appropriate for the task

You will need to show that you have thought about what you have done, what software you have used, and why. Would another piece of software have been as good? You will need to show that you have thought about whether the particular task would be done better using a word-processing or desktop-publishing package; or can you do this work using a database or a spreadsheet?

Many tasks that you carry out could be done using several different software packages.

- Word-processing software has many of the capabilities of a desktop-publishing program. You can create high-quality documents that integrate text and images very effectively with word processing. However, if you need to manage the page layout, particularly for folded documents and multi-page booklets, then you need to use the specialist features that the desktop-publishing software will provide.

- If you need to create a simple set of data that needs simple sorting and searching you may decide to use the database capabilities of a spreadsheet rather than the use the more complex structure of a database package.

- Many software applications, including spreadsheet, presentation and word-processing packages, have tools to help you produce graphs and charts. You will need to select which one to use based upon the specific requirements of the task, the skills you have and how the data is stored.

- There is a wide variety of software packages that you can use to create pictures and images. Some very specialist packages require a high level of skills while many good images can be created using simple tools within word-processing applications.

Think about it

When you are given a task or job, how do you decide which application software to use?

Word processing software can be used to produce all kinds of documents. Why should you use a desktop publishing package such as MS Publisher rather than a word processor? What tools and features are available in DTP that a standard word-processing package cannot offer?

How using the IT system and software was an appropriate way of carrying out the task

You also need to ask the question 'Are there other ways of doing it?'. You need to be able to justify why using IT systems and the appropriate software will give you what is required. You also need to ask the question 'Is it always best to use a computer?' There will be times when the answer is 'No', and you need to be able to explain why.

What do you think about to help you decide how you are going to do the task? How will using IT help you to do the job better? What will be better? Will you be able to do it more quickly? Or will the result be more accurate? Or will using IT let you present the information better?

Think about it

When you are given a task or job, do you always use your computer?

E-mail has become the standard way for a lot of internal communication in many organisations. It is quick and you can keep records very easily. But you might decide to use a different method of communication such as a memo or the telephone.

Think of some tasks you have carried out where you decided not to use e-mail. Why? And was it more effective?

Skills Explaining (use of IT)

What you need to do

- Describe what you are doing
- Give simple reasons for choosing and using software tools and tasks that match tasks and uses
- **Level 2** Explain which software tools were chosen and how effectively they were used for particular tasks and uses

It is important that you are able to describe and explain what you have done as well as actually doing it. This will help you to show your understanding of the particular task in hand and how you have carried it out.

Describe what you are doing

You will need to produce a clear description of how you carried out each task you submit as part of your portfolio of evidence. One way of doing this is to produce a document that shows, step by step, the actions you carried out to produce the final product. This kind of document can also be a very useful reference sheet which you can use to help remind you how to do it when you carry out similar activities again.

Practical task

Write and send an e-mail to a friend to tell them about the ITQ qualification that you are doing.

Now create a simple step-by-step description of what you did. Make sure that you describe each part of the task including:

- opening the e-mail software
- entering the e-mail address
- entering the subject
- entering the information
- checking it
- sending it.

Could you make this description more helpful? You might want to also include information about the following:

- Do you always only send e-mails to one person? – include information about how to send a copy to another person.
- How do you make sure the information is accurate? – include information about using the spellchecker.
- How do you know that the recipient has read the e-mail? – include information about requesting a receipt.
- Do you keep a copy of the e-mails that you send? – describe how to do this and how to find them later.

Keep a note of how you did the task and include screenshots where possible.

Give simple reasons for choosing and using software tools and techniques that match tasks and uses

You will need to say why you used each software tool for a piece of work, highlighting the particular features of that tool. See Table 1.4.

Practical task

For the task that you are working on at the moment, complete section 3 of the task sheet on page 22. For each software tool or technique that you used to create this piece of work briefly describe the reason for using this particular tool for this particular task.

Keep a note on how you did the task and include screenshots where possible.

Explain which software tools were chosen and how effectively they were used for particular tasks and uses

It is possible to use a number of different software applications to carry out a particular task. Most word-processing packages have quite sophisticated drawing tools, but there will be some graphic and artwork activities that would be better suited to a specialist application. When carrying out a task, you should be able to explain what you chose to use and to justify your choice having considered alternative tools and software. See Table 1.4.

Skills Reviewing

What you need to do

- Identify the effect that own mistakes have on other people at work, with help and advice from other people
- **Level 2** Evaluate own strengths and weaknesses in using IT
- **Level 2** Take account of feedback from other people about own use of IT

This is where you need to review the effectiveness and appropriateness of your own use of IT. You will need to look at the tasks you have completed and review whether the end product was well produced and whether you were able to meet all the requirements. You will also need to demonstrate that you are aware of what you do well, and what you are not so good at, and how to improve your skills and knowledge where necessary.

Application	Level 1	Level 2
Word processing	• Explain why you used word-processing software to produce simple documents.	• Explain the main features of the word-processing software you used and contrast these with alternatives available.
Spreadsheet	• Explain why you used spreadsheets to record, analyse and present the data.	• Explain the main features of the spreadsheet software you used and contrast these with alternatives available.
Database	• Explain what databases are used for and describe the basic features that you used.	• Explain the main features of the database software you used and contrast these with alternatives available.
E-mail	• Explain the basic e-mail facilities and how you used them.	• Explain the advanced facilities you used, including formats and secure forms.
Presentation	• Explain the features of the presentation software that make it more suited to the task than alternatives such as word processing or image and animation software.	• Explain the advanced features of the presentation software that make it more suited to the task than alternatives such as word processing or image and animation software.
Web page	• Explain the features of the software you used to enable simple web pages to be produced in a given format.	• Explain the features of the software you used to enable multiple web pages to be produced in a given format.
Artwork and imaging	• Explain the features of the software you used that make it suitable for producing simple artwork and images.	• Explain the features of the software you used that make it suitable for producing artwork and images and that distinguish this software from non-specialist software (e.g. word processing).
Internet and intranets	• Explain the basic connection methods available and the one that you used. Explain the browser functions that you used.	• Explain the differences between Internet and intranet. Explain the features of the intranet that you used.

Table 1.4 Examples of how you need to show that the tools and tasks you have chosen are effective

Identify the effect that own mistakes have on other people at work, with help and advice from other people

There are very few people who can claim to have never made a mistake. What is important is that when you do make a mistake, you acknowledge that you have and are aware of how this might affect others. Most jobs that you carry out will be linked to work that others are doing. A letter to a customer to confirm a meeting with the Sales Manager that has the wrong date on it will cause considerable problems for the Sales Manager as well as the customer.

Practical task

Choose a task that you have carried out recently. Make a list of all the different types of errors that could have occurred. For each of these possible errors, write down next to it the other people at work who might be affected by this error. In a third column, list the actions that you can take to reduce the likelihood of this particular error occurring.

Evaluate own strengths and weaknesses in using IT

You need to reflect and review the skills and limits of what you can do. A useful way to do this is to carry out an evaluation of your strengths and weaknesses. You should start by listing the strengths. Ask yourself the questions 'What am I good at?' 'What IT skills do I already have?' You then need to think about which skills you still need to develop. What do you still need to learn to do?

Level 2 practical task

What are you good at? Make a list of all the IT skills you have and how you use them. Try to group them into types of skills such as word processing, file management, etc.

For each type of skill listed, make a list of the things you can't do, or need to improve. You need to prioritise this list. Which of these skills are most important for you to acquire?

Take account of feedback from other people about your own use of IT

We can all learn by our mistakes. When you have completed a task it is always advisable to ask someone what they think of it; most colleagues are keen to look at what you have done. You should ask the person for whom the work has been produced to suggest improvements or changes that they would recommend. It is important to listen to another viewpoint and to take this feedback into account the next time you carry out such a task.

Level 2 practical task

Choose a task that you have carried out recently. Evaluate this piece of work. What is done well and what could be improved?

Now ask your supervisor or a colleague to look at this piece of work and evaluate it. Then ask them to give you feedback.

Case study

Sunshine Travel uses computers throughout the organisation. Most staff have access to computers throughout the working day. All the computers and printers are connected to a local area network which is maintained by the technical support team. Some staff have laptops which they take to customers' premises. The company has a website to promote and market its goods and services. Staff have access to the company's intranet where all standard documents and procedures are available.

In the **directors' offices** they use:

- spreadsheets to produce budgets and management information

- word-processing software to produce company reports and letters

- e-mail as the main internal communication method, and more and more for external communication

- presentation software when promoting the company

- the Internet to keep up to date with the market and competitors.

1 A presentation needs to be set up for the Managing Director for a meeting with a very important prospective client. The data is available in a spreadsheet, although it will need to be summarised to give the type of information needed. What applications could be used to produce these charts and which would be the most appropriate?

2 A brochure needs to be produced with information about the key personnel in the organisation. There are images available in bitmap format on the company's intranet. Should this document be put together using a word-processing package or could a more effective application be selected to carry out the task? What would be the benefits of using an alternative package rather than the word-processing one?

3 A large number of e-mail communications are sent and received in the Directors' offices. How could the staff improve the organisation of the address book to use the facilities more effectively?

Task sheet

Section 1 – Requirements	
	Task name
	Type of activity
	Description
	Who is it for?
	Date due

Section 2 – Sources of information	
	Source 1
	Search methods
	Name
	Source 2
	Search methods
	Source 3
	Search methods

Section 3 – Software tools and techniques

Tool	How used	Reasons

Optional units

2
Use IT systems

Introduction

This unit is particularly suitable if you have a job that requires you to use IT as part of your work. The tasks can probably be produced as you use your computer to carry out simple work tasks for any of the IT software units that you are doing.

All the competencies for knowledge, understanding, skills and techniques in this unit are included in other units of the qualification.

Types of computer hardware

What you need to know and understand

- Common types of computer hardware and how to use them
- How to start up a computer
- **Level 2** What storage media are available

See Unit 3: Operate a computer, page 28.

Skills Setting up

What you need to do

- Turn on (login if on a network) and use a personal computer (PC)
- Using a printer
- Change basic settings, such as sound volume, date and time
- **Level 2** Connect up a computer with other hardware and storage media safely

See Unit 3: Operate a computer, page 35.

Skills Accessing

What you need to do

- Filenames
- Folders and subfolders
- Accessing files on a computer hard drive or local storage media
- **Level 2** Accessing files on a local area network (LAN) or a wide area network (WAN)

See Unit 3: Operate a computer, page 47.

Hardware and software errors

What you need to know and understand

- Common hardware and software errors and how to sort them out
- Information about errors necessary to help expert give advice
- **Level 2** Correcting errors and problems from experience

See Unit 4: IT troubleshooting for users, page 79.

Health and safety issues

What you need to know and understand

- What health and safety laws and guidelines affect the use of IT
- Health and safety risks to self in using IT
- **Level 2** Ways to keep risks to people to a minimum
- Health and safety risks to others from common hardware
- **Level 2** Ways to keep risks to hardware to a minimum

See Unit 3: Operate a computer, page 63.

Day-to-day security risks

What you need to know and understand

- Risks to data from people
- Risks to data from hardware or software not working properly
- Risks of receiving and opening attachments from e-mail
- **Level 2** Risks of downloading software from the Internet

See Unit 6: IT security for users, page 131.

Skills Protecting

What you need to do

- Using a login identity (ID) and password to access computer systems
- Store personal data and software safely
- Back up data following guidelines
- Use ant-virus software to protect applications
- **Level 2** Set password levels on software and data
- **Level 2** Make backups of operating systems data
- **Level 2** Download software patches to fix any security flaws
- **Level 2** Take appropriate action to keep risks to a minimum

See Unit 6: IT security for users, page 138.

What advice is available

What you need to know and understand

- Recognising there is a problem
- How to contact an IT help desk or service
- How to follow verbal instructions from an IT expert
- Recognise the limits of own understanding of skills
- **Level 2** Where and how to find advice on common errors with most hardware and software

See Unit 4: IT troubleshooting for users, page 94.

3
Operate a computer

Introduction

To operate a computer requires the ability to carry out the initial steps in using an IT system: to turn on a personal computer (PC) and use a mouse to navigate around a screen; to operate hardware and software day to day (e.g. a PC or personal digital assistant (PDA)); to select operating systems and software that are suitable for the task in hand.

This unit covers the general knowledge, understanding, skills and techniques that you need to use a computer. It is likely that the evidence you need to produce for the unit will arise from the tasks you carry out for other units. You will probably not need to produce extra evidence, but demonstrate that the existing evidence also meets the requirements of this unit.

Although using a personal computer (PC) is not a requirement for this qualification, most candidates are likely to use one, although you may be using an Apple Macintosh. Whatever computer is used it will be either a standalone (single) or part of a network. For much of the qualification, and indeed for the majority of users, for most of the time it is not important.

You will be using a wide range of different software application packages, usually decided by company or department policy, to complete this qualification. Again, it should not make any difference to your work for this qualification as long as the particular computer setup is capable of carrying out the required activities. You are not required to produce all your evidence using the same equipment or software. What is important is that you know what equipment you are working with and are aware of which packages and versions of the software you are using.

Types of computer hardware

What you need to know and understand

- Common types of computer hardware and how to use them
- How to start up a computer
- **Level 2** What storage media are available

Common types of computer hardware and how to use them

Processor

The processor (Figure 3.1) is the part of the computer that carries out all the software program instructions. It is often described in the model number; part of the description will include information about its speed, for example you may be using a Pentium 4 or an AMD 64-bit machine. As models and speeds of processors change frequently, you need to find out what is the current 'entry-level' model. Computer magazines, such as *Computer Weekly*, *PC World* and *Computer Shopper*, are good sources of such information.

Figure 3.1 A processor

Memory

There are various parts of memory within a computer, each of which carries out a different function. The part that you, the user, need to be most aware of is called RAM (random access memory). This is the part of the computer that temporarily holds the programs and instructions you are using and the data that you are inputting. This part of the computer's memory is usually 'volatile', that is, when you switch the computer off anything that has not been stored will be lost.

Storage

Computers are used to store data and programs so that you can retrieve (recall) and amend them later. For this you need a storage system, such as a hard disk, floppy disk, CD (compact disk) or DVD (digital versatile disk), or USB (universal serial bus) memory stick. (Figure 3.2)

Figure 3.2 Storage devices

Keyboard

This is one of the main input devices and probably needs little explanation. The keyboard is used for entering, inserting, changing and deleting data into the computer. However, it is important to note that there are some special keys on a computer keyboard.

There are usually two Shift keys, one on each side of the keyboard. When you hold down the Shift key and press a letter key it will give you the upper case letter, if you press any other key it will give you what is written at the top of the key, for example the number 3 will give you the £ symbol.

There will also be two Control (Ctrl) keys. They are both used for the same purpose, but it is convenient to have one on each side of the keyboard. The Control key is similar in concept and use to a Shift key: it is used together with another key to send a different code to the computer, for example if you hold down the Control key and press the s key in most applications the file will be saved.

Then there is the Alternate (Alt) key, which is another modifying key, like the Shift and Control keys; the use of the Alt key increases the number of commands that are available to a software application.

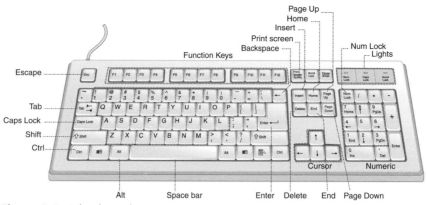

Figure 3.3 A keyboard

Across the top of the keyboard (Figure 3.3) you will find a set of function keys (F1–F12); these are used in different ways by different packages and programs; for example, in PowerPoint the F5 key can be used to start the running of a presentation; in Excel the F4 key is used to convert a cell reference to an absolute reference.

There is also the Escape (Esc) key which is again used in different ways by different programs, but is frequently used to cancel an action. For example, in Excel, you can use the Escape key to cancel data input to a cell up to the point where you press the Enter key.

Many keyboards have a numeric keypad on the right-hand side and also a set of cursor control keys. This numeric key pad makes it easier and quicker to enter numeric data. This keyboard is known as an extended or 102-key keyboard.

There will be a set of cursor control keys, with arrows on them, to help you move the cursor around a document; you will be able to move left, right, up and down. There will also be keys to move to the Top (start) and End (bottom) of a document.

Mouse

A mouse (Figure 3.4) is also an input device. Using it effectively is a skill in itself and one that you need to acquire.

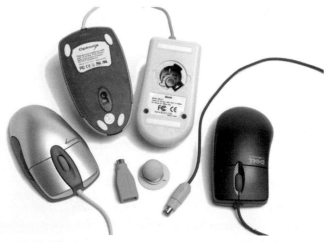

Figure 3.4 Mice

The mouse (Figure 3.4) is used to position the cursor in a document, and can be used in graphics applications to draw. You can single-click with the left mouse button to select a position or object on the screen and sometimes you will need to double-click, for example when clicking on the Microsoft Word icon on the desktop when you want to start using Word. The right mouse button will often be used to display a menu of tools or commands, which can be quicker than going through the standard toolbar at the top of the screen.

Printers

Printing is still the most frequently used form of permanent output. The printer is used to output data in paper form. The printer may be attached to a standalone computer or linked to a network of computers.

Most local printers (not on a network) attached to PCs are either laser printers or inkjet printers. Laser printers produce high-quality paper output at a reasonable price, however colour printing is still relatively high. Inkjet printers can produce good quality colour printing at a lower cost. Table 3.1 lists the advantages and disadvantages of both types of printer.

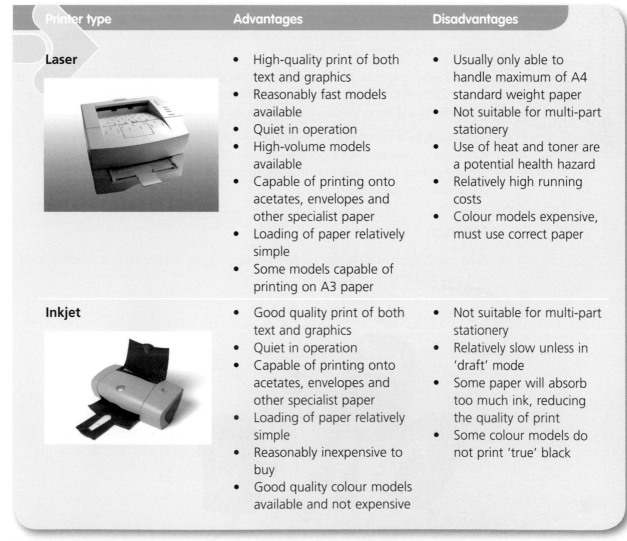

Printer type	Advantages	Disadvantages
Laser	• High-quality print of both text and graphics • Reasonably fast models available • Quiet in operation • High-volume models available • Capable of printing onto acetates, envelopes and other specialist paper • Loading of paper relatively simple • Some models capable of printing on A3 paper	• Usually only able to handle maximum of A4 standard weight paper • Not suitable for multi-part stationery • Use of heat and toner are a potential health hazard • Relatively high running costs • Colour models expensive, must use correct paper
Inkjet	• Good quality print of both text and graphics • Quiet in operation • Capable of printing onto acetates, envelopes and other specialist paper • Loading of paper relatively simple • Reasonably inexpensive to buy • Good quality colour models available and not expensive	• Not suitable for multi-part stationery • Relatively slow unless in 'draft' mode • Some paper will absorb too much ink, reducing the quality of print • Some colour models do not print 'true' black

Table 3.1 Advantages and disadvantages of laser and inkjet printers

Other peripherals

The term 'peripherals' is used to describe any device that is attached to your computer to expand its potential for inputting, outputting and storing data. There may be a number of other types of input, output and storage devices that can be attached as peripherals to your computer. These are some of the most common ones:

Input devices

- **Light pen**   A pen-shaped device that you point at a screen to make selections or to create images.

Figure 3.5 A light pen

- **Scanner**   A device used to capture images and text from a printed page.

Figure 3.6 A scanner

- **Graphics tablet**   A flat board connected to the computer on which you can draw, with a special pen or 'puck', images which are displayed directly on the VDU (visual display unit) and which can be stored in the computer.

Figure 3.7 A graphics tablet

- **Digitiser** A generic name for an input device used for converting data in its current form into digital data which can be processed by the computer; for example, a scanner is a digitiser and a graphics tablet can be used as a digitiser.

Output devices

- **Sound card** A circuit board which enables high-quality sound to be produced on the computer – essential when using multimedia software.

Figure 3.8 Sound card

- **Plotter** An output device used to produce high-quality graphics data. The image is created using a number of different coloured pens which are picked up and put down by an 'arm' which moves across the paper. This type of printing is often used for CAD (computer-aided design) applications.

Figure 3.9 A plotter

Check it yourself

Find out what other equipment is attached to your computer and enter the details in section 3 of the Computer hardware checklist on page 75.

How to start up a computer

When using computer equipment, it is extremely important to follow the guidelines of the manufacturer and/or the supplier. If the equipment is not set up according to instructions, it may not function correctly; it could also be unsafe! Do not attempt to connect or disconnect any equipment for which you are not trained or which is outside your authority. If you have not done a task before, such as connecting the mouse, get technical support and advice if necessary, but always read the instruction manual first.

Skills Setting up

What you need to do

- Turn on (login if on network) and use a personal computer (PC)
- Using a printer
- Change basic settings, such as sound, volume, date and time
- **Level 2** Connect up a computer with other hardware and storage media safely

Turn on (login if on network) and use a personal computer (PC)

Check to make sure that all the connections have been set up correctly before switching on the power. Start up the computer using the on/off button on the main unit. You will also need to turn on the monitor. The system will go through a series of internal checks, lights will usually flash on the keyboard, and your operating system will start up.

Whether you are working on a standalone or a network computer, you will usually have to complete a start-up procedure – in a Windows environment this will involve holding down the Ctrl, Alt and the Del keys at the same time. To continue, you need to input your username and password.

Most computer systems are set up to work from a number of shortcuts (icons that start your software) on the desktop.

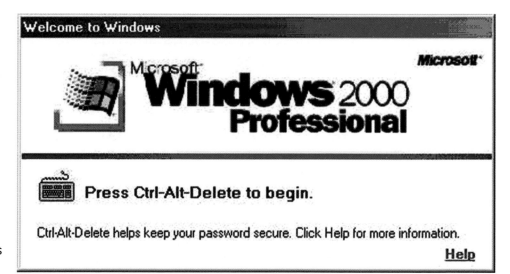

Figure 3.10 Windows login

Using a printer

To use the printer, you need to make sure that you know how to do the following:

- Locate the on/off switch. Remember this normally should not be used to stop a print run as it may cause a paper jam, cancel any software settings for the font or paper orientation, or clear all the print instructions from the print queue.

- Find out which port it is connected to. This will probably be called LPT1 or something similar, or it could be a USB connection.

- Load the paper tray or feed for continuous stationery. Paper for laser and inkjet printers must be loaded the right way up (there should be an arrow on the paper's packaging to indicate this). Continuous paper should be properly clipped on to the sprockets.

- Connect to a different printer. If you are working on a network you will need to know the software commands. If several users share a number of printers through the use of a cross-over or T-switch, you will need to take the other users into consideration.

- Load letter-headed paper. You will need to load it the right way up and the right way round; do not forget to take it out when you have finished.

- Use special paper and acetates. You must make sure that the correct paper or acetates are being used. The wrong type of acetate can cause an awful mess inside a laser printer! Paper that is too thick or the wrong size can jam inside the printer.

- Use sheets of labels. As with special paper, use the correct labels for your printer and check how to load them.

- Print on envelopes. Most laser and inkjet printers are capable of printing on to envelopes, and there is usually a special way to load them.

Change basic settings such as sound volume, date and time

You need to be able to change some basic settings on your computer to personalise it and make it better suited to you and your working environment.

Date and time

Your computer has a clock with the current date and time. This is useful information that you can use automatically in many of your applications. It is therefore important to set it correctly.

In Windows, you can change these settings using the **Control Panel**. You need to identify which time zone you are working in – in the UK you will need to be set to Greenwich Mean Time (GMT); you can also set the time so that it will be automatically adjusted for daylight saving.

Some computer systems are synchronised so that the date is always correct. This may be done through the network you are connected to, or you could set up the computer to an Internet server that updates the information regularly. The following takes you through setting the date and time in Windows XP.

You need to follow these steps to set up the date and time in Windows XP.

Step 1   Go to the **Control Panel** through the **Start menu**.

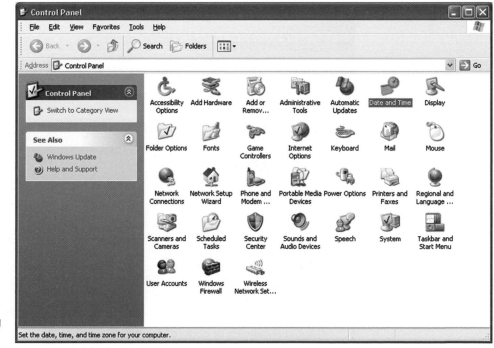

Figure 3.11 Start menu

Step 2   Select **Date and Time** on the Control Panel.

Figure 3.12 Choosing
the date and time

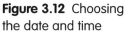

Step 3 Select the **Date & Time** tab. You can change the date on the calendar and the time on the digital clock.

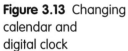

Figure 3.13 Changing calendar and digital clock

Step 4 Select the **Time Zone** tab to set the time zone, for example GMT, and choose to have the clock automatically updated for daylight saving.

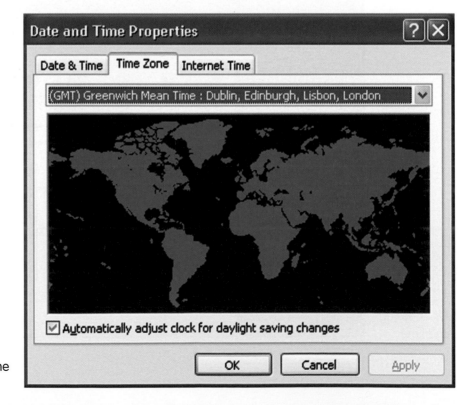

Figure 3.14 Time Zone tab

Monitor – brightness and contrast

Set your monitor so that it is comfortable for you to use. For this you will need to know how to adjust the contrast and brightness levels. To do this you need to go through a menu system that is operated by buttons on the front of the monitor. There is no standard for this and it will vary from monitor to monitor. You will usually have a button to display the monitor menu and from this you can select the brightness and contrast controls. There will be one button to adjust up, often with a + symbol, and one to adjust down with a – symbol.

On a laptop, which has an integral screen, you can access controls to adjust contrast and brightness from the Control Panel. There will be an icon for the settings of monitors which can be found in Windows XP in the **Printers and other hardware** category.

Figure 3.15 Pick a category

Sound

You will need to decide whether sound is appropriate; there will be situations where having the sound on will interfere with the working environment. Make sure that the sound levels are appropriate for your working environment and the types of applications you use. You will probably need to have the volume set differently for your computer at work, where you may need to make sure that others are not disturbed. You may have speakers built into your monitor or a separate set of speakers with their own volume control. The control for built-in speakers is often through buttons on your keyboard but can be managed through the Control Panel.

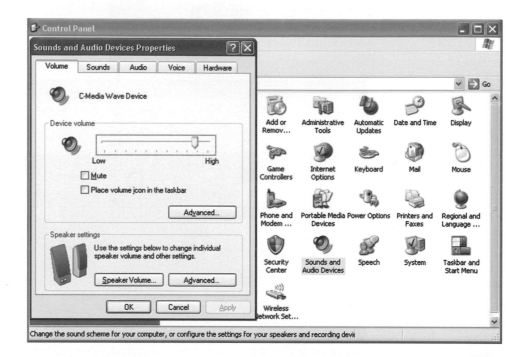

Figure 3.16
Control Panel for managing sound

Practical task

- Check the date and time setting of your computer and correct it if necessary.
- Adjust the contrast and brightness of your computer.
- Adjust the volume of the sound for your computer.

Keep a note of how you did the task and include screenshots where possible.

Connect up a computer with other hardware and storage media safely

Connectors

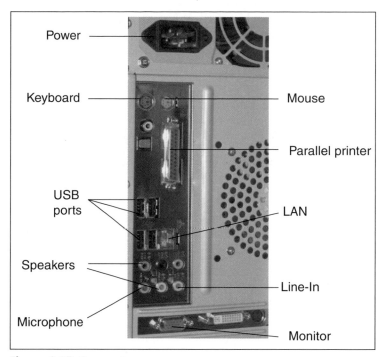

Figure 3.17 Connectors

Connecting up a personal computer is a relatively straightforward process. The workstation you and your colleagues use will probably be a PC which may be connected to a network.

The main computer box, the system unit, is what the other devices are connected to. You will find most of the connectors at the back of the system unit; they will be labelled, either with words or images, to assist you in the process. If you have not connected up parts of a system before, it is a good idea to do it, for the first time, with an expert who can observe, advise and encourage.

Keyboard

The keyboard is connected to the system unit using a permanently connected cable which ends in a round 5-pin connector. This is connected to the round female connector in the system unit. The connector has a tag indicating that it can only go in one way.

Mouse

Your mouse may have a range of different connectors. A serial mouse is usually connected to the COM1 serial port at the back of the system unit using a 9-pin 'D' connector. Sometimes you will connect to the second serial port, but this may require an adapter. The cable will be permanently fixed to the mouse. Many systems now have a PS2 connector which is similar to the keyboard connector. Alternatively, you may have a USB (universal serial bus) connection for your mouse. You will usually have several USB ports on your computer, often at both the back and the front of the computer case.

Power supply

The system unit, printer and monitor will each have a separate power cable, and these should be the last connections that you make. Each plug should be connected to a separate power socket; you should not use multi-way adapters.

Printer

Most printers are connected to the system unit using the parallel printer port, although some printers may use a serial connection. The printer cable will not be permanently connected to the printer. The connector on the cable to be plugged into the printer will be a 25-way **male** connector which connects to a 25-way **female** socket on the printer. The other end of the cable will have a 25-pin connector which connects to a 25-pin **female** socket on the systems unit.

Many printers now use a USB connector, which provides much faster data transmission and speeds up the process.

Monitor

LCD (liquid crystal display) monitors are based on TFT (thin film transistor) technology, resulting in flicker-free viewing. These are much slimmer than **CRT** (**cathode ray tube**) monitors, give off about a third as much heat and produce virtually no electromagnetic emissions. They are capable of high resolutions and can display many millions of colours. They are also extremely compact and energy-efficient, and are now, increasingly, replacing CRT monitors.

The monitor is connected to the system unit using a data cable, which is permanently attached to the monitor and will have a 'D' connector at the end. The cable is plugged into the matching 'D' connector, which will be labelled 'Monitor', or something similar. The shape of the connector ensures that you plug it in the right way round.

Figure 3.18 A TFT monitor

Storage media

The main storage of your computer will be inside the main unit. Other storage devices, such as CD and DVD readers and writers, are usually also internal. However, sometimes you will need to connect removable storage devices such as a memory stick or pen. These are connected through one of the USB connectors on your computer. There is a correct procedure you must follow to remove your USB removable storage device from the computer to avoid losing or damaging the data.

To safely remove a USB memory stick follow this procedure.

1 Single-click on the icon 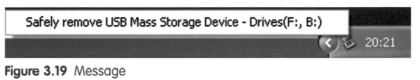 in the task bar at the bottom of the screen.

2 Click on the message.

Safely remove USB Mass Storage Device - Drives(F:, B:)

Figure 3.19 Message

3 Safely remove the device.

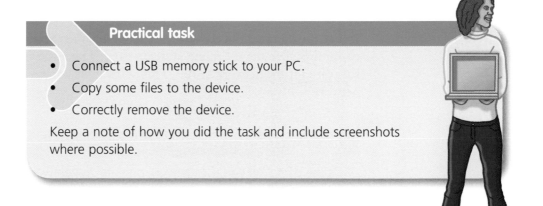

(i) Safe To Remove Hardware

The 'USB Mass Storage Device' device can now be safely removed from the system.

Figure 3.20 Remove device

Practical task

• Connect a USB memory stick to your PC.
• Copy some files to the device.
• Correctly remove the device.

Keep a note of how you did the task and include screenshots where possible.

Modem

You need a modem (**mod**ulator **dem**odulator) to connect to the Internet using a telephone line. Many computers have an internal modem, however you can attach one externally to the computer. This is usually done using one of the USB connectors. If you connect to the Internet with a high-speed broadband connection you will not have a modem but a router.

Sound

There are connectors for attaching devices to a computer to input and output sound; these are usually located at the back of the computer. A microphone can be connected for inputting speech, and high-quality speakers can be connected to enhance the output of sound.

Network

Many people use a standalone PC, however in many cases, such as in the workplace, the PCs used are linked together to work as part of a network. Among the advantages of this are:

- The users on the networked PCs can communicate with each other.
- It will often only be necessary to have one copy of the software stored centrally which all the users can access – see the section on licences (page 150).
- Peripherals, such as printers, can be shared by a number of users, thus making better use of resources.
- Fast, high-volume data storage systems can be used with users being allocated their own private space.
- Users can share data.
- Backup procedures (see page 116) can be carried out centrally.

Computers can be networked together in a number of ways. You do not need to know much about the technical side of this, however it is useful to know the basics of how your system is set up.

Just as the computer needs software to enable the various parts to communicate – the operating system – so it is necessary to have software for the network to run. This software is known as the network software.

Check it yourself – Level 2

Is the computer you usually work on part of a network? What network software is used to run the system? What version number are you using at the moment? If the computer is part of a network, enter this information in section 3 of the Software specification checklist on page 77.

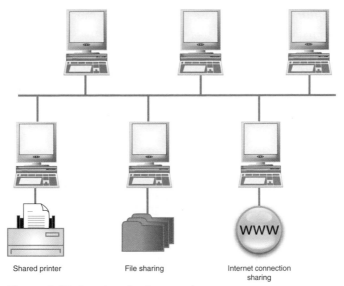

Shared printer   File sharing   Internet connection
sharing

Figure 3.21 A network of computers

What storage media are available

The hard disk (Figure 3.22) is the main high-capacity disk in a computer; it is usually permanently inside the computer. All the programs and packages necessary to make your computer work are stored on this disk; you may also use it to store data you wish to keep. The disk's capacity is large; it is usually measured in gigabytes. Computers connected to a network (see above), in which they share the central resources, will not have their own hard disk drive.

Figure 3.22 A hard drive

The floppy-disk drive (Figure 3.23) has a much smaller capacity than the hard disk, usually 1.44 Mb. The disk is not permanently inside the computer, but is removed when not in use. This means that you can use different disks to store different sets of data. Newer, higher capacity, removable devices are rapidly replacing floppy disks.

Figure 3.23 A floppy disk drive

A CD-ROM (compact disk-read only memory) is a compact disk capable of holding high volumes of data (approximately 650 Mb). This disk can only be written on once and is therefore not appropriate for data that needs to be changed. However, the speed with which data can be accessed is about 10 times slower than that from a hard disk. There are now both write-once CD-Rs and rewritable CD-RWs. CD-ROMs are often used to supply software, games and reference material.

Figure 3.24 CD/DVD device

The digital versatile disk (DVD) is a development of the CD. Unlike a CD, both sides can be recorded on and they can also have two layers. This, together with a much greater recording density, means that up to 17 Gb of data can be stored. DVD writers are now widely available on PCs.

Memory pens or sticks (also known as flash memory) are readily available and are becoming the standard form of removable disk storage. Many users use these rather than floppy disks. They are available in sizes from 256 Mb to several gigabytes.

Skills Accessing

What you need to do

- Access files on a computer hard drive or local storage media
- **Level 2** Access files on a local area network (LAN) or a wide area network (WAN)

Access files on a computer hard drive or local storage media

Information to be kept for future use will need to be saved in a file. The file must be given a name. This name must be unique to the storage area, directory or folder. It usually consists of only letters and numbers – it is better to avoid any other characters as many of the other characters on a keyboard have a special meaning in a filename.

Filenames

Filenames have two parts. The first part is given by the user and can include spaces and have up to 255 characters. The end of the first part of the name is indicated by the use of the full stop (.). The second part is sometimes called the extension or suffix. This consists of up to three characters. It will often be given automatically by the specific application software, for example word processing documents may have the suffix **doc**.

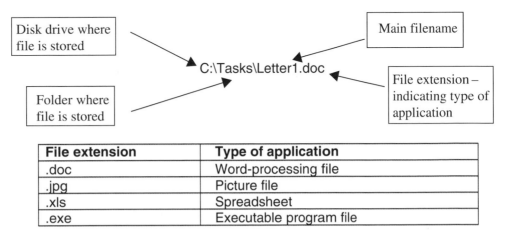

| Disk drive where file is stored | | Main filename |
| Folder where file is stored | C:\Tasks\Letter1.doc | File extension – indicating type of application |

File extension	Type of application
.doc	Word-processing file
.jpg	Picture file
.xls	Spreadsheet
.exe	Executable program file

Figure 3.25 Examples of file extension types

The complete filename is recorded in a directory, or folder, and is used to access the file. The directory contains details about the file, usually the date and time it was created or last updated, where it is located on the disk, and what size (in bytes) it is.

As with any filing system, you should regularly maintain your computer files. In particular, you should delete files you no longer need as they can occupy considerable amounts of disk storage space.

The main commands you will need to be familiar with are:

Save	You will need to use this to save a file with the current filename.
Save As	You will need to use this version of the save command when you need to give a new filename, for example when you want to save a different version of the same file.
Copy and Paste	If you want to store a copy of a file in another storage area you will first need to make a copy of it, and then paste the copy in the area you want it in.
Delete	You will need to use this if you want to permanently remove a file.

Table 3.2 Main commands

Folders and subfolders

The first time a disk is used in a computer it has to be set up – this known as formatting. Part of the disk is set up to hold the directory information necessary to locate the files on the disk. This is known as the root directory and is referenced by the drive letter, a colon (:) and the back slash (\). For example, the root directory of the first floppy disk drive is referenced by **A:** . As it is possible to have a large number of files on any one disk, it is vital to organise them into sub-directories (folders) so that you can find them easily.

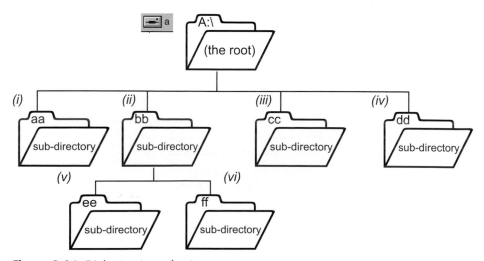

Figure 3.26 Disk structure chart

The system of folders is hierarchical. This is illustrated in Figure 3.26. The paths are written as (i) A:\aa, (ii) A:\bb, (iii) A:\cc, (iv) A:\dd, (v) A:\bb\ee and (vi) A:\bb\ff. So, if all your documents relating to a sports and social club are stored on a floppy disk in folder cc, you would find the minutes of the last committee meeting at A:\cc\mins2005.

An operating system has a utility that enables you to see your folders and files. It will also enable you to carry out housekeeping tasks to keep your files organised.

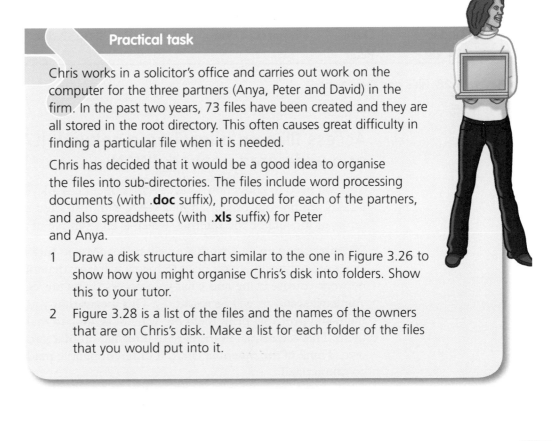

Figure 3.27 Folder and file display

Practical task

Chris works in a solicitor's office and carries out work on the computer for the three partners (Anya, Peter and David) in the firm. In the past two years, 73 files have been created and they are all stored in the root directory. This often causes great difficulty in finding a particular file when it is needed.

Chris has decided that it would be a good idea to organise the files into sub-directories. The files include word processing documents (with **.doc** suffix), produced for each of the partners, and also spreadsheets (with **.xls** suffix) for Peter and Anya.

1. Draw a disk structure chart similar to the one in Figure 3.26 to show how you might organise Chris's disk into folders. Show this to your tutor.

2. Figure 3.28 is a list of the files and the names of the owners that are on Chris's disk. Make a list for each folder of the files that you would put into it.

Filename	Owner	Filename	Owner	Filename	Owner
letta1.doc	Anya	reporta1.doc	Anya	letta13.doc	Anya
costp3.xls	Peter	reportd2.doc	David	lettp21.doc	Peter
costa2.xls	Anya	lettd3.doc	David	lettd21.doc	David
letta5.doc	Anya	lettp2.doc	Peter	costa12.xls	Anya
lettp7.doc	Peter	lettp5.doc	Peter	costa20.xls	Anya
costa4.xls	Anya	lettd4.doc	David	costp21.xls	Peter
lettd10.doc	David	reportp4.doc	Peter	lettd25.doc	David
reporta3.doc	Anya	reporta6.doc	Anya	lettd26.doc	David
costp4.xls	Peter	costa3.xls	Anya	reporta20.doc	Anya
lettd8.doc	David	lettp6.doc	Peter	lettp22.doc	Peter
reportp1.doc	Peter	reportp5.doc	Peter	lettp23.doc	Peter
letta15.doc	Anya	costp13.xls	Peter	reportd22.doc	David
letta20.doc	Anya	reportd21.doc	David	lettd28.doc	David
lettd23.doc	David	letta21.doc	Anya	letta24.doc	Anya
reportd18.doc	David	letta23.doc	Anya	lettd29.doc	David
lettd24.doc	David	costa22.xls	Anya	costa23.xls	Anya
letta26.doc	Anya	lettd27.doc	David	reporta22.doc	Anya
reporta21.doc	Anya	reportp23.doc	Peter	lettp25.doc	Peter
costp22.xls	Peter	letta25.doc	Anya	letta27.doc	Anya
lettd30.doc	David	reportp24.doc	Peter	reportd24.doc	David
lettp26.doc	Peter	reportd25.doc	David	costa24.xls	Anya
lettd31.doc	David	costa25.xls	Anya	lettp27.doc	Peter
reporta23.doc	Anya	costp23.xls	Peter	lettp28.doc	Peter
lettd32.doc	David	reporta24.doc	Anya	lettd32.doc	David
costp24.xls	Peter				

Figure 3.28 Files and their owners

Access files on a local area network (LAN) or a wide area network (WAN)

You will need to know how to access files on a network. This network could be a LAN within your organisation, a WAN with restricted access that you can log on to, or it could be the Internet, which is an example of a WAN.

When working on a network you will have access to files that are shared. The exact procedures that you need to follow will vary depending on the type of network you are using and what your access rights are. Some of the files that you have access to will be read-only. This means that you will be able to open them and probably print them but will not be able to make any changes to them. This is essential in the case of information that you share rather than own. Think of the potential chaos if different people made changes to this common data!

Level 2 practical task

- Log on to a network that you have access to.
- Identify an area of shared files that you are able to access, and produce a structure chart to show the folders and files that are available to you.
- Identify which files, if any, are read-only and why.

Keep a note of how you did the task and include screenshots where possible.

Skills Storage media

What you need to do

- **Level 2** Use common storage media
- **Level 2** Identify the best way to transfer files to different types of storage media
- **Level 2** Archive data to make the most of the storage space available

Use common storage media

You will need to demonstrate the use of a wide variety of storage media. This should include floppy disks, CDs, DVDs, zip drives and USB memory pens. You will need to show why you have used one medium rather than another. This could be because of the availability of your system, but should also take into account the size of the files and the capacity of the medium. You may use different media to that used to archive your files when you wish to provide a copy of the data to another user.

Identify the best way to transfer files to different types of storage media

There are a number of ways of transferring files from one place to another. You may want to place a copy on another storage device, or you may want to permanently move the files.

- The copy and paste commands let you make an exact copy of one or more files.

- The cut and paste commands move the files to another storage space.

- You can also use the send command to send the files to another storage space, or to send as an e-mail attachment to another user.

Right-click on the file and select the **Send To** option – then select **Storage Device**.

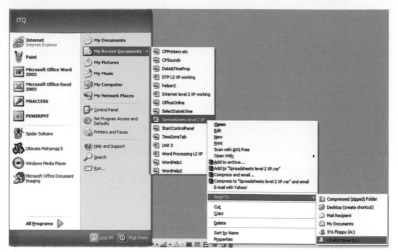

Figure 3.29 Storage Device

Right-click on the file and select the **Send To** option – then select **Mail Recipient**.

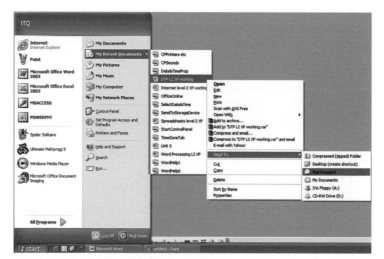

Figure 3.30 Mail Recipient

Level 2 practical task

- Copy and paste one of your files from your hard disk to a floppy disk.
- Using cut and paste, move a file into a new storage area.
- Send a copy of one your files to a USB memory pen.

Keep a note of how you did the task and include screenshots where possible.

Archiving data to make the most of storage space available

Archived files are not held for the same purpose as backups. Backup copies are held as security copies in case something happens to the originals. Archive files are copies of files that are no longer needed in the main working environment but where a copy needs to be stored for reference or possible use in the future. It is quite common to keep electronic copies of old correspondence 'offline' – many accounting records need to be kept for seven years.

As these files are not going to be used regularly it does not make sense for them to be in the active working environment. They would need to be maintained and backed up if they were kept there and would occupy expensive, online storage space.

If you have carried out activities that you need for your 'evidence' but which are no longer needed for your work, it is best to archive them so that you still have them in electronic form but so that they do not occupy valuable 'online' storage space.

There are a number of different systems for storing archive copies of files. In its simplest form they are copies that are held on some form of removable storage system. This could be floppy disks, tape cartridge, micro-fiche, CD-R or DVD.

Level 2 practical task

Chris has now learned how to carry out housekeeping and wishes to 'tidy up' the hard disk. All the files that have a number of less than 20 in them are from previous years' work and do not need to be kept 'online'. As 'hard copies' of all letters are in the paper files, it is not necessary to keep the out-of-date electronic files at all. However, the reports and spreadsheets need to be kept for at least five years.

Look back to Figure 3.28 and make lists of:

- all the files to be deleted; and
- the files to be archived on to floppy disk(s).

Discuss your decisions with your tutor.

Check it yourself – Level 2

What procedures do you or your organisation carry out for archiving of data? Write a brief description of these procedures and place it in your evidence portfolio.

Tools and functions

What you need to know and understand

- What tools and functions of software applications can be used for
- How to select and use appropriate tools and functions for complex tasks

What tools and functions of software applications can be used for

There are two types of software – applications and systems.

Common applications software

The software that is used to carry out the different tasks that you do is called applications software.

Word processing

Personnel Manager
Crink, Totam & Partners
Lancaster Road
Hull
LM3 4TQ

12th June 2000

Dear Ms Foulger

Office Administrator

I am writing in response to the advertisement for the above post in the local newspaper last Friday. Enclosed is my CV which includes the details of two references who you may contact to confirm my suitability for the post.

I am currently completing a part time course at the local college, in the use of a wide range of IT office applications including word processing, spreadsheets, databases and the use of electronic communication systems. The course finishes at the beginning of July and I will have gained an NVQ Level 2 in Using Information Technology. I am keen to return to full time work as soon as the course is complete.

I have recently been doing voluntary work for a national charity, working in their offices in the centre of town. During this time I have gained considerable experience in the application of the skills acquired in my studies. I am an extremely conscientious and enthusiastic person and like to work with others as part of a team.

I have also enclosed a stamped, addressed envelope for your reply.

Looking forward to hearing from you.

Yours sincerely

Word-processing software enables you to create, save, edit and print text documents such as letters and reports.

Modern word-processing facilities include not only sophisticated text manipulation and presentation functions but also the facility for integration of data from other packages and the inclusion of graphical images.

Spreadsheet

A spreadsheet is like a very large piece of paper that is divided into columns and rows, known as cells. What you can see on the screen at any one time is just a small part of the complete spreadsheet available to you. Calculations, using formulae, can be entered into cells and when the value in a cell is changed, all the formulae in the spreadsheet are automatically recalculated to give new results.

Database

A database gives you the capability to create an organised, structured collection of related data that can then be re-organised (sorted), selected and printed.

Queries can be made on the data to select the information before presenting it in a structured report.

Drawing

Drawing software enables you to create pictures and other images, often with facilities to use a wide range of colours and effects. There are packages available for different types of drawing, for example painting, line drawing and computer-aided design (CAD).

Desktop publishing

Desktop-publishing (DTP) software can be used to create documents for publishing by manipulating text and images. Many word-processing packages include basic DTP features, while 'top-of-the-range' DTP will produce copy ready for final printing.

E-mail

Electronic mail, usually known as e-mail, is a communications system that enables you to send and receive messages and files with the certainty that it has been placed in the recipient's mailbox. E-mail is a way of carrying out rapid, text-based communications both in and outside an organisation. In many organisations, the use of e-mail has replaced the memo, and sometimes even letters. To be able to use e-mail you need to have your computer connected to a network and have the appropriate e-mail software. Some mobile phones are now capable of sending and receiving e-mail.

Web pages

The World Wide Web (the Internet) has become an integral part of lives. The Web has significantly changed the way we access information – whether it is for work, education or entertainment.

There are a number of software packages that help you to create your own website and therefore make almost any information available to millions. Your website can easily contain both links and images to make it interesting and fun to use.

Table 3.3 Common applications software

Systems software – operating system

This is the set of instructions and rules which make the computer work. The operating system enables the computer to interpret each key you press, display the character it represents on the screen and make sense of it. It is necessary for the computer to be able to start up, to carry out your instructions and those of the software that you buy, to save the work you do, and to communicate with any attachments to your system such as disk drives, printers, plotters or devices used to communicate with other computers.

When you buy a new computer, it may be necessary to install (set up) these parts of the operating system. It is a simple and straightforward procedure which is mainly carried out by following instructions on the screen and responding to prompts for information. It is important to know which operating system you are using and which version number.

Check it yourself

Which operating system do you have on the computer you normally work on? You need to find out the name of the company who supply it and which it is called. Which version number are you using at the moment? Enter this information in section 1 of the Software checklist on page 77.

Which software applications are available on the system you normally use? For each package, find out the name of the manufacturer, the name of the package and the version number. Enter these details in section 2 of the Software checklist. The three most common applications have already been included on the checklist; you will need to add any others that you use.

How to select and use appropriate tools and functions for complex tasks

Every software application has a number of tools and functions to enable it to be used effectively. There are number of basic tools that you need to use, and others which you may never need to use.

Skills Tools and techniques

What you need to do

- Use basic tools and techniques, such as open, close, save and print files, in folders
- **Level 2** Use common tools and techniques appropriately such as page setup, shortcuts and print preview

Use basic tools and techniques, such as open, close, save and print files, in folders

You will be able to use the basic tools of any application software, either by using the menu system or through icons in a tool bar. You may also be able to use a combination of keys, known as a keyboard shortcut. The main commands you will need to be familiar with are:

- **Open** – This command is used to access the contents of the file. It will open the document and display it on the screen ready for you to work on.
- **Close** – When you have finished using a file it is extremely important to make sure that you close it. This will ensure that it is safely stored on the disk – most software will give you a message to save any changes, if you try to close a file without first saving it.
- **Save** – You will need to use this to save a file with the current filename. If you wish to keep the original file but save a new version with a different filename, or save it in a different storage space, you will need to use the **Save As** command.
- **Print** – You will use this command to get a hard copy (printout) of the document. When using the print command you will be able to select the exact page or pages that you want to print, the number of copies that you want, and the printer that you wish to use.

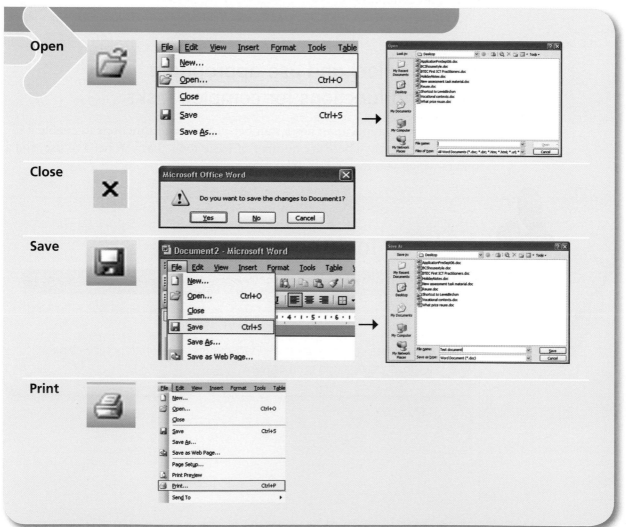

Table 3.4 Basic tools

You will demonstrate these skills as you use the software applications for other units.

Practical task

Using one of the applications that you frequently use:

1 Open an existing file.

2 Save a copy into a different storage space (another folder or a different device such as a floppy disk or USB memory stick).

3 Print the second page *only* of the document.

4 Close the file.

Keep a note of how you did the task and include screenshots where possible.

Use common tools and techniques appropriately, such as page setup, shortcuts and print preview

The main commands you will need to be familiar with are:

Page setup

Whatever kind of document you are producing, a whole range of layout and presentation decisions need to be made. Although there will be slightly different ways of achieving these layout effects, most modern word-processing, database, spreadsheet and desktop-publishing packages will enable you to control the presentation of your documents.

Depending on your printer and its ability to handle different sizes of paper, you will be able to select the following:

- **Paper size** – If you are using a laser printer or inkjet printer it will usually be A4 (8.27 x 11.69 inches or 21 x 29.7 cm) but may also be Legal (8.5 x 14 inches or 21.59 x 35.56 cm) or Letter (8.5 x 11 inches or 21.59 x 27.94 cm). You may also be able to print on a range of different sizes of envelopes and other specialist stationery.

- **Paper orientation** – Most printers are able to handle printing on the paper in either portrait or landscape (see Figure 3.31).

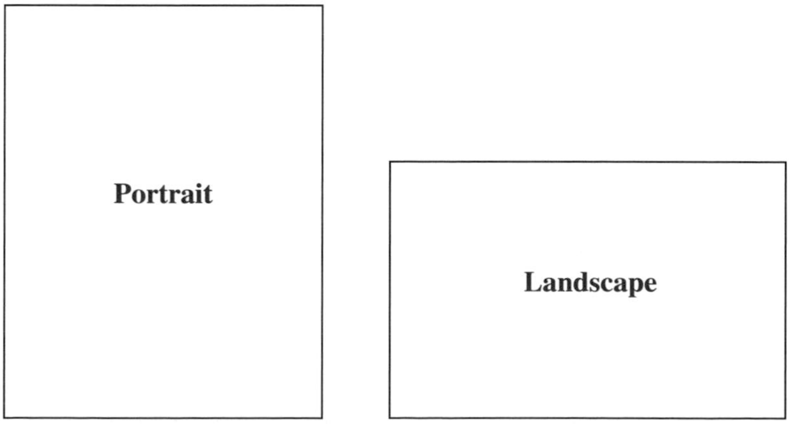

Portrait

Landscape

Figure 3.31 Paper orientation

- **Margins** – The usable area of the page on which you can place the main part of your document is controlled by setting the size of the four margins – top, bottom, left and right (see Figure 3.32).

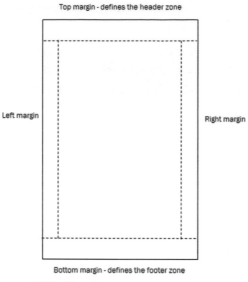

Top margin - defines the header zone

Left margin

Right margin

Bottom margin - defines the footer zone

Figure 3.32 Margins

Depending on what type of software you are using, there may be additional page setup features that you will need to be familiar with.

To access the Page Setup dialogue box, select **File** and **Page Setup**.

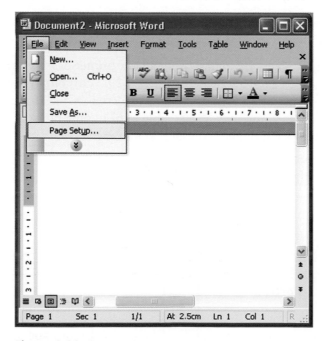

Figure 3.33 Page setup

On the **Paper** tab you can set the paper size and source.

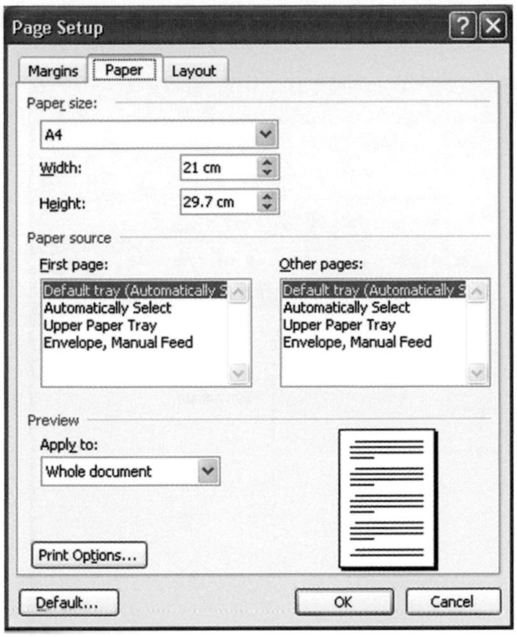

Figure 3.34 Setting paper size and source

Use the **Margins** tab to set Top, Bottom, Left and Right margins and the orientation of the page.

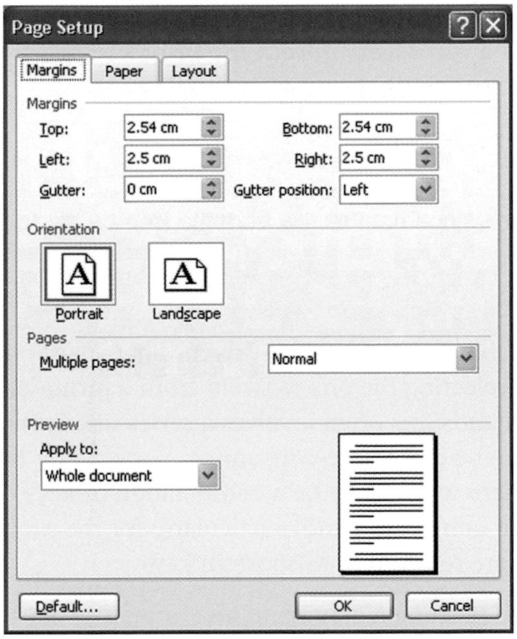

Figure 3.35 Setting margins and orientation

Print preview

This tool is essential to make sure that you check how your document will look on paper *before* you actually print it. It is important that you use this to make sure that the presentation is correct and that you do not waste lots of paper.

To access the Print Preview dialogue box, select **File** and **Print Preview**.

Figure 3.36 Accessing Print Preview from the Menu

Alternatively you can access it from the Print Preview button on the toolbar.

Figure 3.37 Accessing Print Preview from the icon on the toolbar

Shortcuts

Most software that we use is menu-driven. That is, we choose options and commands by selecting the one we want from a group on a list. For more complex commands this often involves a series of selections to refine our choice. This can be quite time-consuming, particularly for frequently used commands. There will usually be a combination of keys on the keyboard to carry out the same command, particularly for the more frequently used actions. These are referred to as shortcut keys.

This method of running a command also applies to starting up a piece of software. These shortcuts are set up as icons that when clicked open the required application. The software that we use most frequently can be set up on the desktop as a shortcut using a simple utility (see Figure 3.38).

From the Start menu select **All Programs**.

Right-click on the program you want on the desktop.

Select **Send To**.

Select **Desktop (Create Shortcut)**.

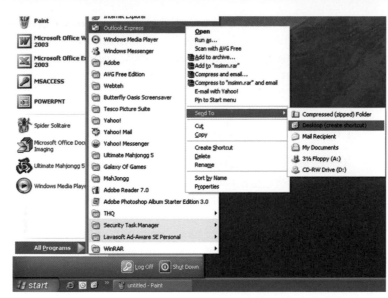

Figure 3.38 Set up shortcut for software application for Windows XP

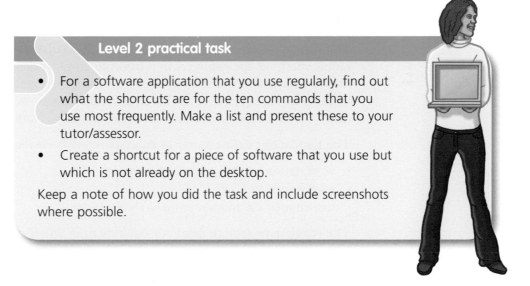

Level 2 practical task

- For a software application that you use regularly, find out what the shortcuts are for the ten commands that you use most frequently. Make a list and present these to your tutor/assessor.

- Create a shortcut for a piece of software that you use but which is not already on the desktop.

Keep a note of how you did the task and include screenshots where possible.

Health and safety issues

What you need to know and understand

- Health and safety laws and guidelines
- Health and safety risks to self in using IT
- **Level 2** Ways to keep risks to people to a minimum
- Health and safety risks to others from common hardware
- **Level 2** Ways to keep risks to hardware to a minimum

You need to demonstrate that your actions do not create any health and safety risks and that you do not ignore significant risks in your workplace. You will also need to demonstrate that you take appropriate and sensible actions to put things right.

Health and safety laws and guidelines

There are still uncertainties about many aspects of a modern, technology-based working environment. Even now, not a great deal of information is available about the long-term effects of working in this kind of environment. Many people are understandably anxious about the possible effects and, in the past few years, there has been a tightening up of the regulations and legal obligations of employers. The main legislation that relates to an employer's obligations is primarily concerned with the use of display screen equipment – VDUs (visual display unit).

Health and Safety (Display Screen Equipment) Regulations 1992

The display screen equipment directives and regulations contain very specific requirements of the employer in relation to employees working with display screen equipment. You should be aware that these regulations apply *only* to employees. However, they are based upon good, safe working practice and ideally should exist in *all* computer areas: at home, work or college.

The regulations define a user as an employee who is required to work at a:

- workstation on the employer's premises
- workstation at home
- workstation on another employer's premises.

The regulations require that your equipment is safe for you to work with.

The regulations require employers to carry out a risk analysis of the workstation to ensure that it is appropriately laid out, with suitable lighting that does not cause glare and reflections on the screen. The employer is required to organise the activities of users so that their daily work using display screen equipment is regularly interrupted by breaks or changes of activity to reduce their continuous workload at that equipment.

If you are a regular, substantial user of display screen equipment, or about to become one, you are entitled to ask for eye and eyesight tests. They must be carried out as soon as is possible by a qualified person and usually before you become a user. After this regular checkups can be requested.

If you are found to need special spectacles the cost of these has to be paid for by the employer. It does not cover people who need normal eyesight correction, but only where a special type is required to deal specifically with a problem in using VDUs.

General health and safety

The main piece of legislation that relates to this is the Health and Safety at Work Act 1974. This legislation makes both the employer and the employee responsible for ensuring that the workplace is a safe and suitable place to work.

The employer must:

- ensure that your workplace is safe and without risks to your health
- ensure that the workplace is clean and control the levels of dust, fumes and noise
- ensure that both plant and machinery are safe to work with and that safe work practices are set and followed
- provide you with all necessary information, instruction, training and supervision for your health and safety
- put in place and implement a health and safety policy
- provide any protective clothing and equipment that is specifically required by health and safety legislation
- report injuries, diseases and dangerous incidents to the appropriate enforcing authority
- provide adequate first-aid facilities and training
- take adequate precautions to prevent fire and provide appropriate means of fire fighting
- provide adequate means of escape
- maintain a workroom temperature of at least 16°C after the first hour of work where employees do most of their work sitting down
- provide, maintain and keep clean washing and toilet facilities
- ensure that employees do not have to lift, carry or move any load so heavy that it is likely to injure them
- ensure that objects and substances are stored and used safely.

As an employee, you are required to be responsible for the health and safety of yourself and others and must co-operate with your employer and:

- follow the organisation's routine health and safety procedures and practices
- take appropriate action if a hazardous or potentially hazardous situation arises
- ensure that your own work area is tidy and free from hazards.

Health and safety risks to self in using IT

Using computers has become part of most people's daily lives and there are a few basic health and safety considerations that all users should be aware of.

You and your workstation

Figure 3.39 shows the correct posture when seated at your workstation and the positioning of the equipment in relation to you.

Figure 3.39 Correct posture for sitting at a workstation

RSI (repetitive strain injury)

This is a condition from which quite a number of people suffer. It is an extremely painful and sometimes quite debilitating injury. It is most likely to occur in people who are carrying out small, rapid movements of the hands, fingers and wrists. It would appear to be something that can be brought about by incorrect posture at the keyboard or excessive use of hands and fingers without rest. Typists on old typewriters were less likely to get it because the range of movement required to operate a manual keyboard was much greater. Using a mouse, particularly for long periods of time without a break, can also be a cause.

The best thing for you to do, particularly if you use a keyboard or mouse for long periods at a time, is to make sure that:

- you have set the keyboard so that it is most comfortable for you
- you position your hands correctly over the keys
- you take suitable breaks.

Fatigue and stress

Computers have increased the speed with which many tasks are carried out and the amount of information that we have available to work with. While this brings many advantages to all aspects of our lives, it can also increase our levels of stress. It is important that we manage the way we work to reduce this. You should make sure that you vary the type of activities you carry out – a change can be as good as a rest – and that you do take appropriate breaks from constant use of the computer.

> **Think about it**
>
> Do you sit for hours at your computer at home surfing the Internet, or in a chat room with friends? Or do you play computer games with your friends? When you are using your computer for leisure activities you can often lose track of time. Health and safety when working with computers is not just about when you are at work. What can you do to make sure that you follow safe practices? Did you know that you can 'pause' most computer games so that you can take a break?

Ways to keep risks to people to a minimum

Good practice when working with VDUs

There are many examples of good practice which can reduce risks to your health. Many of these you can introduce yourself, while others will require the co-operation and support of your employer or colleagues.

One of the most important aspects of your workstation is that it should be adjustable to fit you or whoever is working there. When you get into the driving seat of a car you adjust the seating position for comfort and safe access to the controls. You should do the same when you sit down at your workstation.

Always check the following:

- **The height of your chair**

  - You should have sufficient space below the desk top to be able to move your legs freely.
  - You may need a foot rest so that the back of your legs and knees do not have excess pressure on them.
  - Your arms should be horizontal and your eyes should be on a level with the top of the VDU.

- **The support of your chair**

  - Your back should be supported but without undue pressure.

- **Mobility of your sitting position**

  - You should not sit in the same position for too long.
  - You need to be able to move the position of your chair with ease in relation to the workstation and the different tasks you are likely to carry out.

- **The image on the screen**

  - Adjust the brightness and contrast so that they are comfortable for you – the image should be sharply focused and easy to read.
  - Clean your screen regularly, as dirt and finger marks distort the image.
  - Choose appropriate colour schemes where possible.

- **The layout of the workstation**

  - Move the keyboard, mouse mat, mouse and monitor to meet your work needs.
  - Are you left- or right-handed? You can change your mouse installation to accommodate this.
  - Make sure that you do not need to bend your hands up at the wrists when using the keyboard.
  - Make sure you have sufficient space for papers, disk boxes etc. If you frequently work from paper documents, a document holder may improve the comfort of your workstation. A cluttered workspace will make for reduced productivity as well as fatigue.

- **The lighting conditions in the room**

  - Bright lights should not reflect on the screen – you may need blinds to reduce sunlight at certain times of the day.
  - The location of the workstation needs to take into account both natural and artificial lighting.
  - Do you have sufficient light on the papers you are working from?

Health and safety risks to others from common hardware

Given that computer hardware uses electricity there are a number of potential risks.

Check it yourself

How safe and suitable is your workstation? Complete the health and safety checklist on page 76 to carry out an assessment. Speak to your supervisor about any problems you find and discuss what changes can be made.

Electrical safety

It is important to make sure that you use the equipment carefully. You should make sure that all electrical connections are safe and regularly checked.

Trailing cables

In most computer systems there will be a number of cables connecting the various parts together. It is important to make sure that the cables are secured and out of the way.

Noise

Computers have a number of moving parts, the hard drives and fans, which make a constant noise. This noise, over a period of time, can be quite bad for people, particularly in a work space where there are several computers. This noise can be deadened by the use of suitable carpeting and screens, and quieter fans are now available which considerably reduce this.

Heat

The power supply and monitor in a computer generate quite a lot of heat. It is important to make sure that appropriate ventilation is available for computer users. It is worth noting that the new flat screens produce about a third of the heat that CRT monitors generate.

Figure 3.40 Can you find the five unsafe areas in this work area? How many of these would you be able to correct in your workplace and which ones would you need to report to someone else?

Ways to keep risks to hardware to a minimum

It is very dangerous to have several pieces of equipment plugged into the same power socket, so you should never use a multi-way adapter for the various parts of your computer. Make sure that each is plugged into a separate socket.

The standard power that is available is not smooth, it has 'spikes', power surges, that can damage the equipment. It is therefore a good idea to use a surge protector to reduce the risk of damage to the equipment. An UPS (uninterruptible power supply) is also recommended. This provides a power backup, which takes over when the power supply is interrupted and provides you with time to shut down the computer safely.

Compatibility

What you need to know and understand

- **Level 2** What problems can occur when hardware, software and operating system are not compatible
- **Level 2** Why compatibility standards are needed

You will need to be able to identify any compatibility issues and at least know how to resolve them, even though you may not have privileges to be able to carry out the solution.

What problems can occur when hardware, software and operating system are not compatible?

Printer issues

There may be more than one type of printer on a system; perhaps a laser printer for high-quality, fast printing, and an inkjet colour printer for colour printing. Each of these printers will have their own printer driver, a set of instructions on how to convert the data into the image, and they are very rarely compatible. If you are connected to the wrong printer when you send a document you will usually print a lot of pages with lots of unrecognisable characters.

File storage issues

Floppy disks formatted on an Apple Mac system are differently organised and usually cannot be read on a standard PC.

USB 1.0 ports are not always capable of reading higher-speed USB memory sticks, although high-speed ports should be capable of handling the slower devices. Windows 98 and earlier operating systems will not usually support many USB devices.

Software version issues

Most software will run on a limited number of versions of an operating system. It will usually have been written for the current industry standard and will cease to work fully when this is superseded.

Likewise, files created in an earlier version of an application will not have full functionality, and may not work at all.

Think about it – Level 2

Many documents created in an organisation are standard for a number of years.

The HR department has job descriptions and person specifications for each job role stored. When the organisation upgrades from Windows 2000 to Windows XP there will be a number of upgrades required. What procedures will they need to use to make sure that all their files are still valid. Who might be given the responsibility to check this out?

Why compatibility standards are needed

Although computer manufacturers are in competition, they need to have some standards so that data can easily be shared across systems. Data transfer protocols and file exchange formats that all manufacturers subscribe to are necessary, so that they can compete effectively in the market. Most people will not readily buy equipment that will not work with other equipment.

Think about it – Level 2

The organisation where you work has implemented a new computer system. The operating system and associated software has been upgraded to the latest version.

What are the main checks that will need to be carried out to make sure that all the existing work will be compatible?

What would you do if you found that all your spreadsheet files could not be read by the new application? How could this problem have been avoided?

Data transmission speeds

What you need to know and understand

- **Level 2** What general combinations of hardware and software offer very slow or fast transmission speeds

What general combinations of hardware and software offer very slow or fast transmission speeds

A computer system consists of a number of connected parts. Data needs to be transmitted between these various parts and this will take place at different speeds depending upon the type of equipment and the standards being used.

Internet connection and transmission speeds

The speed with which your Internet connection works will depend on a number of factors, such as how you connect up, where you live etc. The speed is expressed as a number of Kilo, Mega or Giga bits per second (bps).

How you connect up

- With a standard phone and modem, data can be transmitted at speeds up to 56 Kbps.
- ISDN (integrated services digital network) provides digital transmissions over the standard telephone systems and can provide transmission speeds up to 128 Kbps.
- A cable modem is a device that enables you to connect your PC to a local cable TV line and receive data at between 2 and 8 Mbps.
- DSL (digital subscriber line) is also known as broadband. It provides high-bandwith transmission over the telephone line. The current minimum standard is 2 Mbps but is commonly available at up to 8 Mbps. It is expected that this will replace ISDN and cable.
- Mobile phones can now also connect to the Internet and the new UMTS (universal mobile telecommunications services), offering speeds up to 2 Mbps.

Where you live

Not all of these speeds are available to all users. Many are dependent on the national and global telecommunications infrastructures. The availability of these services will depend on whether your local company has made the necessary investment in equipment and line reconditioning, and on how closely you are located to the telephone company.

The type of activity

The speed of your Internet connection becomes most critical when you are downloading and storing very large files from the Internet, or you are looking at websites that have a high level of graphics and animation.

Network speeds

LANs (local area networks) will usually be operating at transmission speeds between 10 Mbps, using twisted pair co-axial cabling, and up to 1 Gbps using fibre optic cables.

Wireless networks are now becoming more frequent. These can operate at speeds up to 54 Mbps and are often used in environments where the workforce needs to be mobile.

Floppy, CD and DVD speeds

Floppy disk drives are the slowest data storage media on your PC, with access speeds at around 500 Kbps. CD drives have a speed indicated on them, for example 8 x CD. The access speed can be calculated at 150 Kbytes per second multiplied by the designated speed, for example 8 x 150 = 1200 Kbytes per second, which is 1.2 Mbytes per second. DVDs operate at 1.32 Mbytes per second multiplied by their designated speed.

USB memory sticks operate at between 1.2 and 24 Mbytes per second.

Check it yourself – Level 2

How long does it take to save a file? Save a file that you are working on in an area on your hard drive, or network area. How quickly did it save? It was probably too quick for you to measure the time or even see any delay. Now try saving the same file onto a floppy disk or other removable storage device such as a USB memory stick. Can you see the time passing as it saves?

Printer connection speeds

Many printers are connected using a parallel port, known as LPT1. However, it is now possible to connect a printer using one of the USB ports, and this will provide much faster transmission speeds. A standard parallel port is capable of 0.115 Mbytes per second, whereas USB can give between 1.5 and 60 Mbytes per second. Although this will not increase the speed at which the printer actually prints the document, it will considerably reduce the time required for the printer to receive the data before it starts printing.

Case study

Sunshine Travel uses computers throughout the organisation. Most staff have access to computers throughout the working day. All the computers and printers are connected to a local area network, which is maintained by the technical support team. Some of the staff have laptops, which they take to customer's premises. The company has a website to promote and market its goods and services. Staff have access to the company's intranet, where all standard documents and procedures are available.

In the **Marketing Department** they use:

- software to prepare marketing materials

- packages to produce graphics for marketing posters

- word-processing packages to communicate with customers

- e-mail as the main internal communication and more and more for external communication

- the Internet to promote the company.

1   What types of software would you recommend that the Marketing Department use to produce their marketing materials, including the graphics?

2   What types of printers and storage media will they use to produce and save high-quality images?

3   Describe the types of backup procedures that might be used to ensure security of the website content. What storage medium would you recommend for these backup files?

4   What are the main health and safety concerns for the staff using the computers in the Marketing department? What procedures would you recommend introducing for these staff?

Computer hardware checklist

Section 1 – The computer	
	Make
	Model
	Processor
	Processor speed
	RAM
	Keyboard
	Mouse
	VDU
Storage devices:	Hard disk
	CD-ROM
	DVD
	No. of floppy disk drives

Section 2 – Printer	
	Type
	Make
	Model
	Speed
	Quality Colour ☐ Black on white only ☐

Section 3 – Other devices	
	Input devices:
	Digitiser
	Light pen
	Scanner
	Graphics tablet
	Other
Output devices:	Sound card
	Plotter
	Other

Health and safety checklist – Workstation assessment

	Yes	No
Screen		
Is the screen large enough?	☐	☐
Is the image stable and flicker-free?	☐	☐
Can you adjust the image so that it is sharply focused?	☐	☐
Can you adjust the colour scheme to suit your needs?	☐	☐
Can you adjust the angle of the screen?	☐	☐
Keyboard		
Is the keyboard of an appropriate size?	☐	☐
Can you feel or hear the keys when pressed?	☐	☐
Is there sufficient space to arrange it to suit your needs?	☐	☐
Workstation		
Is your chair comfortable?	☐	☐
Is the seat height and tilt adjustable?	☐	☐
Is the height of the back-rest adjustable?	☐	☐
Is the back-rest adjustable to fit your back?	☐	☐
Does the chair swivel?	☐	☐
Is the chair mobile?	☐	☐
Have you been given information on adjusting your chair?	☐	☐
Do you have sufficient leg room?	☐	☐
Can you adjust the height of the desktop?	☐	☐
Do you need a footrest?	☐	☐
Is a footrest provided?	☐	☐
Is a document holder available?	☐	☐
Do you have sufficient work space?	☐	☐
Working environment		
Is there excessive glare in the work area?	☐	☐
Are there reflections on your screen from the window?	☐	☐
Are blinds fitted in the room?	☐	☐
Are the lights too bright?	☐	☐
Do you need more directed lighting?	☐	☐
Is the desktop too shiny?	☐	☐

Software checklist

Section 1 – Operating system

Name	
Version number	
Environment	
Version number	
Network software	
Version number	

Section 2 – Application software

Type of application	Word processing
Manufacturer	
Name	
Version number	
Type of application	Database
Manufacturer	
Name	
Version number	
Type of application	Spreadsheet
Manufacturer	
Name	
Version number	
Type of application	
Manufacturer	
Name	
Version number	
Type of application	
Manufacturer	
Name	
Version number	
Type of application	
Manufacturer	
Name	
Version number	
Type of application	
Manufacturer	
Name	
Version number	
Type of application	
Manufacturer	
Name	
Version number	

Section 3 – Network software

Manufacturer	
Name	
Version number	

4 IT troubleshooting for users

Introduction

When your computer goes wrong, it is likely you can call on a technical support person to sort out the problem for you. However, there are many straightforward problems that you may be able to resolve yourself, or at least assist in the diagnosis of the fault.

In an organisation you will not be expected to fix your computer whenever it goes wrong. However, you will be expected to recognise common types of faults that are very straightforward to put right. Certain problems will be beyond your area of responsibility or skills; however you should be able to describe the problem, explain what basic solutions you have already tried, and then seek assistance from the most appropriate person.

The knowledge, understanding, skills and techniques that you will need to demonstrate in this unit can relate to your use of computers both in the workplace and at home.

Hardware and software errors

Some of the errors that occur when using your computer will be simple enough for you to resolve, but there will be others for which you will need to seek advice or assistance.

What you need to know and understand

- Common hardware and software errors and how to sort them out
- Information about errors necessary to help expert give advice

Common hardware and software errors and how to sort them out

When something does not work on your computer, you first need to identify whether it is the hardware or the software that is causing the problem. There are often a few initial checks you can make to diagnose a fault and provide a solution.

Hardware

The following are common computer hardware errors that occur and what you can do to fix them.

Computer startup

The computer does not start up:
- Check that the computer is switched on. Check that the rocker switch at the back of the computer and the socket switch are both on.
- Check that the monitor power cable is connected to the computer power socket and that there is a power cable from the computer to the wall socket.

Keyboard error message at startup:
- Check that the keyboard is attached to the correct connector on the computer (see page 41). In many PCs, the mouse and keyboard connectors are of the same type, known as 5-pin mini-DIN. If you get them mixed up, your mouse and keyboard will not work, and may cause this error, which may be why you receive the error message.
- Check if a key on the keyboard is stuck down, or if there is dirt in between the keys etc.
- Try a different keyboard that you know works. If this one works then you know that the original is faulty.

Disk boot failure, or a non-system disk error message:
- Check that you have not left a floppy disk or CD in a drive.
- Turn the computer off completely, and then try again.

Keyboard

The keyboard produces slightly incorrect characters for some keys:

- Check that your computer has been set to UK settings.

These are the steps to take in setting the computer to UK settings.

Step 1   From the **Control Panel**, double-click on the **Regional Settings and Language Options** icon.

Regional and
Language ...

Step 2   On the **Languages** tab, click on the **Details** button.

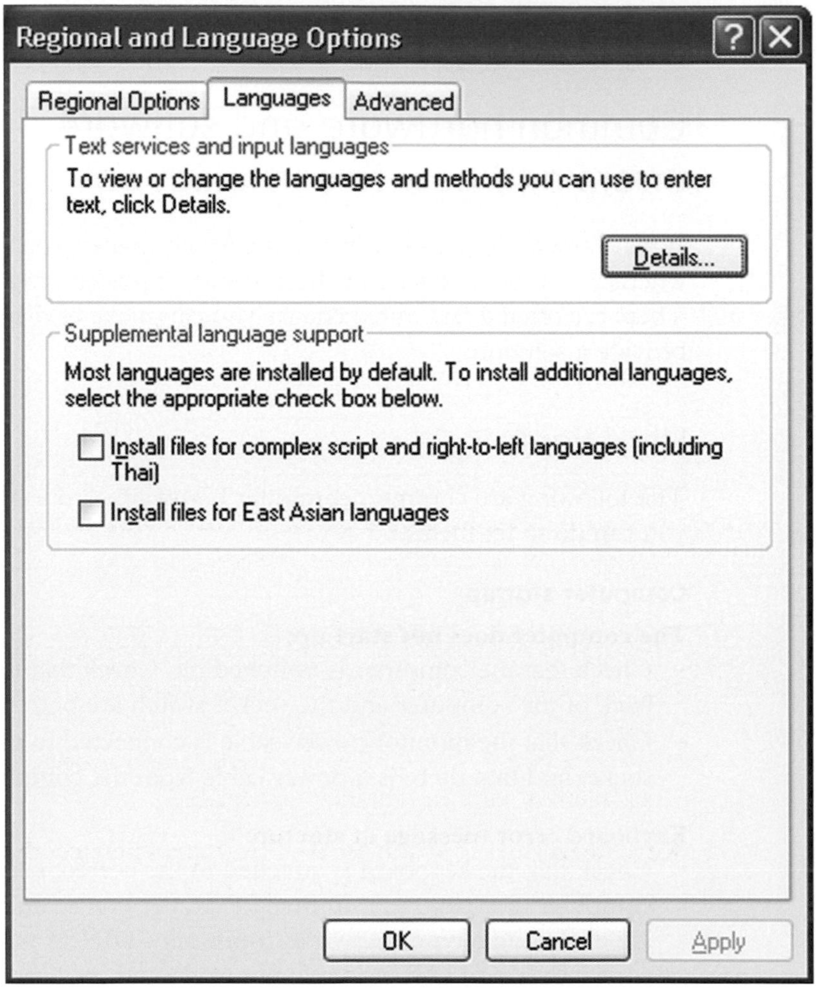

Regional and Language Options

Regional Options | Languages | Advanced

Text services and input languages

To view or change the languages and methods you can use to enter text, click Details.

Details...

Supplemental language support

Most languages are installed by default. To install additional languages, select the appropriate check box below.

☐ Install files for complex script and right-to-left languages (including Thai)

☐ Install files for East Asian languages

OK | Cancel | Apply

Figure 4.1 Select details

Step 3 With the Settings tab selected set the default input language to **English (United Kingdom)**.

Figure 4.2 English (United Kingdom) settings

The keyboard is giving extremely strange codes when you type:

• Check the connection between the keyboard and the computer. This problem may be caused by a loose connection or bent pins on the keyboard cable.
• Try another keyboard that you know works to determine whether the problem is with the original keyboard.

Keys keep getting stuck, or do not depress correctly:

Try cleaning the keyboard. There may be dirt preventing the keys from working properly. You may need to remove the keys and clean underneath. You should use an anti-static cleaner (see page 106 on cleaning a keyboard).

Mouse

The mouse sticks or moves erratically:

Dirt is the most common cause of a mouse working erratically. If this is the case, you need to clean the rollers in the mouse. Open the bottom, take out the ball, and clean the rollers inside.

The pointer does not move on the screen when you move the mouse:

Unplug the mouse and then re-connect it. This sometimes solves the problem. You may have to re-start the computer for this to work.

Printer

The paper jams in the printer:

Turn off the printer. Pull out the paper drawer and carefully remove the jammed paper. Do not pull too suddenly or you may tear the paper leaving part of it still jammed inside the printer, but now much harder to remove. Once you have cleared the paper jam, shut the printer drawer. Restart the printer and run it again to check that the jam is cleared.

The printer keeps jamming or does not feed the paper:

- Check that you are using the correct type of paper for the printer. Some printers will not operate if the paper is too heavy or too wide, for example.
- Check if there is anything caught in the rollers or mechanisms inside the printer. Turn off the printer. Open it and check if there is any obstruction. If there is an obstruction, remove it.
- Check whether the problem is loss of traction caused by dirty rollers. If this is the problem, clean the rollers, using an anti-static cleaner (see cleaning materials on page 104). Remember to turn off the printer first.
- Check all the other parts of the printer; for example the paper guide may be out of place.

The printer keeps asking for a different paper type:

Check that right paper type has been set as the default in your software. In the page setup in Windows software, or in a similar part of other software, you will be able to change the type of paper the printer is expecting to use.

Step 1   Select **Page Setup** from the File menu.

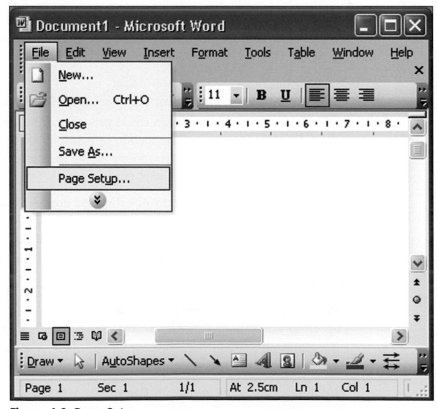

Figure 4.3 Page Setup

Step 2   Move to the **Paper** tab.

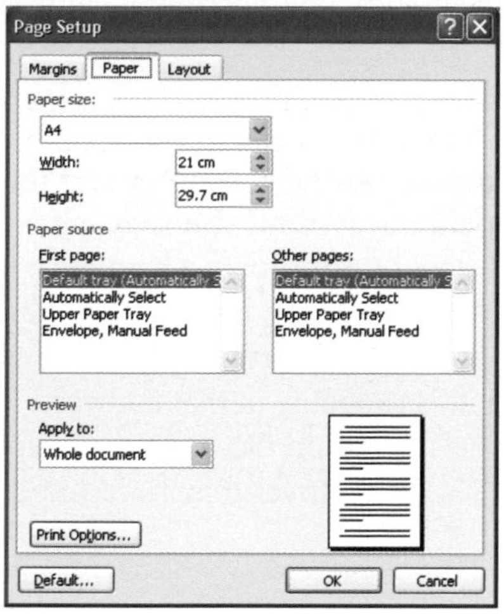

Figure 4.4 Paper tab

Step 3   Select the right paper size from the drop-down list.

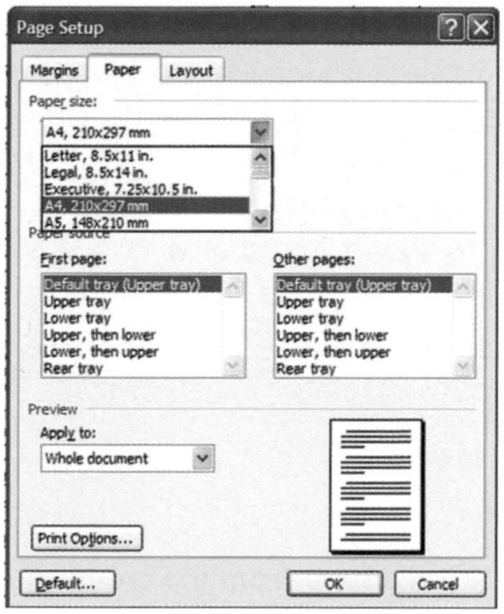

Figure 4.5 Paper size

The printer indicates it needs toner, ink or paper when it doesn't:

- Check that the toner or ink is correctly installed. It is possible to insert ink or toner cartridges incorrectly. Check in your printer manual for details on how to correctly insert the cartridges.
- Check that there is enough paper in the printer. Some printers are a little fussy and don't like to use the last few sheets.

Monitor

Power light is on or flashing, but monitor is still blank:

- Check that the brightness controls are not set too low. The brightness and contrast controls are most likely to be at the bottom of the screen. In a digital monitor, these controls will be buttons. Use these to change the level of brightness and contrast, until you either see a picture, or you are convinced this is not the problem.
- Check the data cable of the monitor and try a different one if possible; in some monitors the cable cannot be detached.

Monitor display is not correctly positioned, and may be distorted:
Adjust the display using the vertical and horizontal controls on the monitor.

Operating system

The system crashes or freezes:

- You may just need to switch off the computer and then start it up again. Depending on your operating system, you may get a message telling you to make sure you shut down in the correct sequence in the future and the system will run a check to make sure that nothing has been damaged.
- Check that the fault is not with the software. If it only occurs with one application, then the fault is probably in that software. If it occurs in several programs, then it may be a common file, such as a display driver, that is causing the problem. This faulty driver may need to be re-installed or a later version used.

> **Check it yourself**
>
> You may have experienced some of these problems when you have been working with your system. What you need to know is which faults you are permitted to put right and which ones you must seek technical assistance for. Make a checklist of all the types of faults that you could encounter and identify which ones you have fixed, which ones you would be allowed to fix if they arose and, for those that you cannot fix, identify who you would have to ask to do this. You should include any other faults that have occurred and how you dealt with them.

Hardware and storage media

Faulty cable connections:

Cables can be accidentally pulled out from the connections in the computer. Check that the cables are securely connected at both ends – some connections have metal clips or screws to help keep them in place. If the cables are connected correctly, try replacing the fuse in the mains plug or try a different power cable that you know works.

The system does not recognise your storage media:

- Check that the medium is not damaged. Removable storage media, such as CDs, floppy disks etc., are prone to damage, as they are frequently inserted in and rejected or removed from the drives, and are carried in bags or left on desks; that is, they are generally poorly looked after.
- Check that the device itself is clean. To maintain it, regularly clean your device with the correct materials.
- Check that the drivers are the correct and most up-to-date versions. If they have been corrupted you can simply reinstall them.

The drive letter for the device does not appear:

Check that the drivers are installed and that they are the correct and most up-to-date version. If they have been corrupted you can simply reinstall them.

If the problem is caused by not having the most recent version, you will have to install that.

You cannot access files on the hard drive:

- If possible, try to back up the affected files and then use Scandisk, or a similar utility provided with your operating system. Although you cannot access the files in the usual way, some of them can be recovered by using the backup tool. The disk utility will then attempt to isolate the damaged parts of the disk.
- If this fails, you may have to format your drive. However, you may not have the authority to do this and therefore should seek further assistance before taking such a drastic step.

Check it yourself – Level 2

You may have experienced some of these problems when you have been working with your system. What you need to know is which faults you are permitted to put right and which ones you must seek technical assistance for. Make a checklist of all the types of faults that you could encounter and identify which ones you have fixed, which ones you would be allowed to fix if they arose, and for those that you cannot fix, identify who you would have to ask to do this. You should include any other faults that have occurred and how you dealt with them.

Software

Sometimes you will try to do something in the software application you are using and it will not work correctly. This will usually be because you do not know the correct way to use this particular facility or tool. The common types of faults and how to resolve them can be found in the specific software option unit information.

There are other errors that you may encounter that are related to the storage of the software and the handling of files you have created.

You cannot see the program you need to use:

Look for the files using the search facilities of your system. Remember to check all your drives. If the software cannot be found then it will need to be reinstalled.

These are the step to follow in searching for a file.

Step 1 From the **Start** menu, select **Search**.

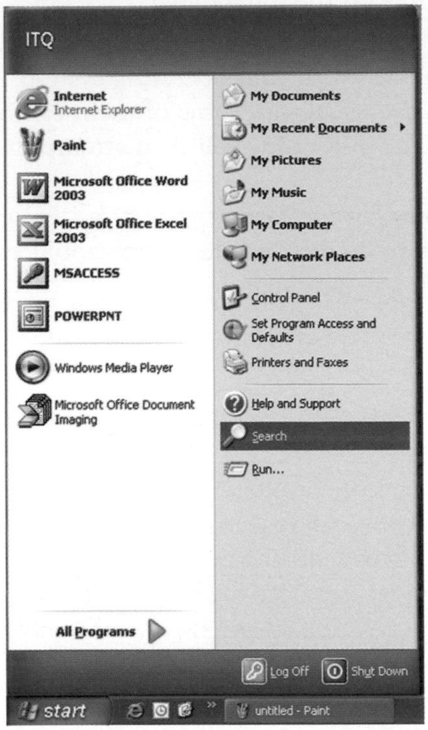

Figure 4.6 Search

Step 2 Enter the name of the file to search for.

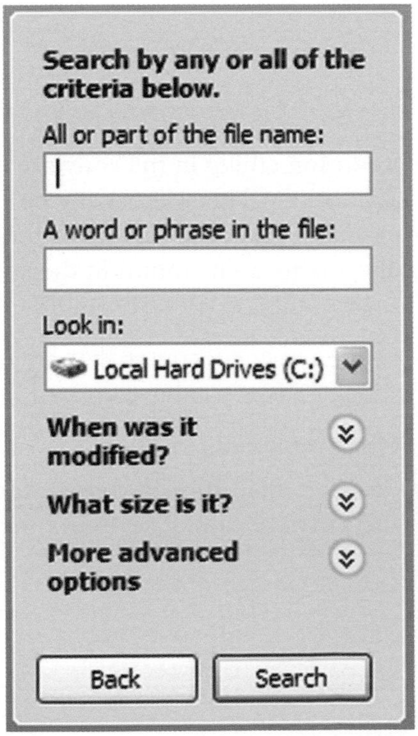

Figure 4.7 Search for file

Some software files or drivers are missing:

• Check that the driver or software is the most up-to-date version. You can usually find the latest drivers on the Internet, or you can request updated drivers from the manufacturers. A fault is often fixed simply by installing a newer device driver.

• Reinstall the software. A full reinstallation of the software often reinstalls the missing files. To do this, you need to completely uninstall the program first; this forces the program to reinstall from scratch, thus ensuring that all the files are copied.

The software is not responding or is running very slowly:

Close it down and start it up again. This can clear the temporary storage areas and improve the performance of the program.

Insufficient disk space:

Check the storage space available on your drive. You may need to delete or archive some of the files if you need more space. If working on a large file, the software may be using some of the disk storage space for temporary storage, also known as caching, and you may run out of disk space. You can avoid this by not having too many large files open.

To check how much storage space you have:

Step 1 Open **My Computer**.

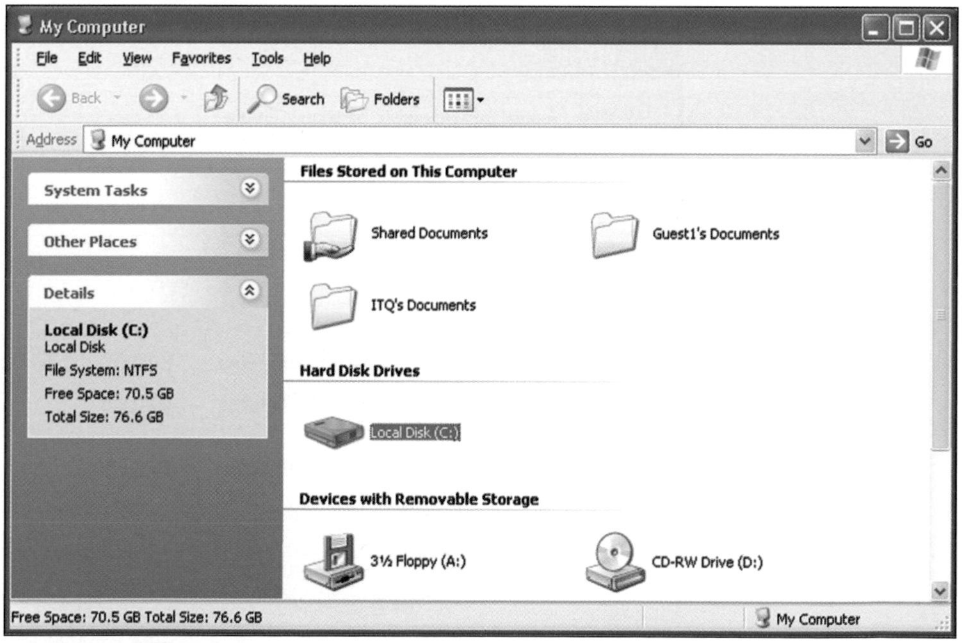

Figure 4.8 My Computer

Step 2   Right-click on the drive and select **Properties**.

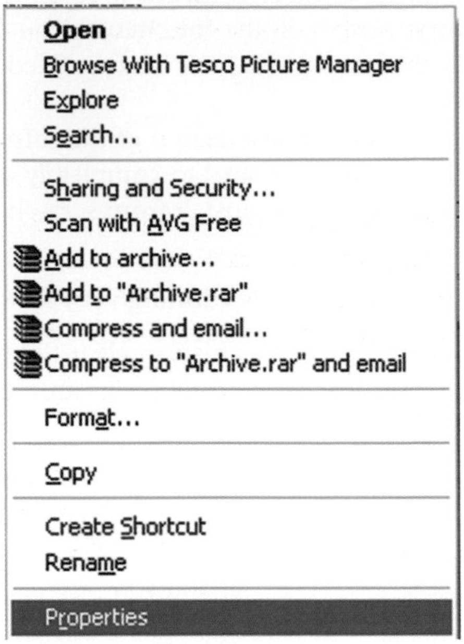

Open
Browse With Tesco Picture Manager
Explore
Search...

Sharing and Security...
Scan with AVG Free
Add to archive...
Add to "Archive.rar"
Compress and email...
Compress to "Archive.rar" and email

Format...

Copy

Create Shortcut
Rename

Properties

Figure 4.9 Properties

Step 3   **Used space** and **Free space** is displayed.

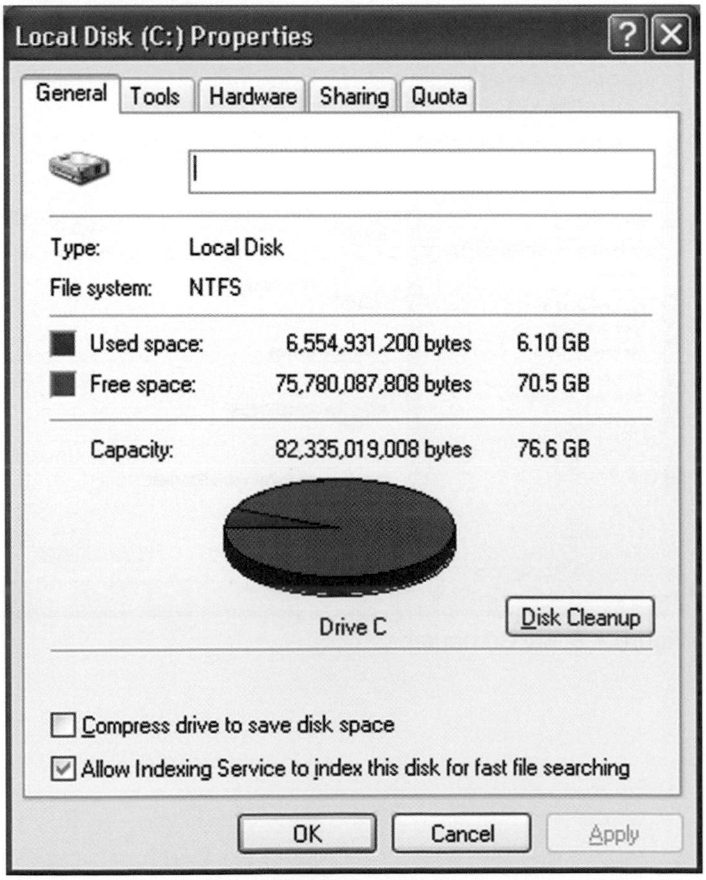

Local Disk (C:) Properties

General | Tools | Hardware | Sharing | Quota

| Type: | Local Disk |
| File system: | NTFS |

	Used space:	6,554,931,200 bytes	6.10 GB
	Free space:	75,780,087,808 bytes	70.5 GB
	Capacity:	82,335,019,008 bytes	76.6 GB

Drive C   Disk Cleanup

☐ Compress drive to save disk space
☑ Allow Indexing Service to index this disk for fast file searching

OK | Cancel | Apply

Figure 4.10 Storage displayed

Read-only file:

- Check that the storage medium is not write-protected.
- Check whether the file is already open in another window, or with another user.

> ### Check it yourself
>
> You may have experienced some of these problems when you have been working with your software. What you need to know is which faults you are permitted to put right and which ones you must seek technical assistance for. For one of the software applications that you are using, make a checklist of all the types of faults that you could encounter and identify which ones you have fixed, which ones you would be allowed to fix if they arose, and for those that you cannot fix, identify who you would have to ask to do this. You should include any other faults that have occurred and how you dealt with them.

Combination of hardware and software

The most difficult errors to deal with are those that are caused by more than one problem, particularly in the case of problems involving both hardware and software.

Document does not print:

- Check that the printer is switched on and ready to print.
- Check that you have the correct printer drivers installed.
- Check the size of the file, particularly with a document containing large images, and that you have sufficient memory allocated to the printer.

Program stops responding:

Check whether it has ceased to respond by using the task manager. You can close the program down, **End Task**, without interrupting other software using this utility.

Step 1 Press **Ctrl**, **Alt** and **Delete** at the same time.

Step 2 Select **Task Manager**.

Step 3 Click on the program that isn't responding and select **End Task** (Figure 4.11).

Figure 4.11 End Task

Check it yourself – Level 2

Faults that are caused by a combination of hardware and software can be the most difficult to identify and resolve. For one example that you have found, list the symptoms of the fault and then write a brief guide for another user on how to resolve it. Ask a colleague or an IT support specialist for an example if you have not come across one yourself.

Data

Problems with file formats:

- If you open a spreadsheet file using word-processing software, an unusual set of characters will appear on the screen. Check that the data is in the correct file format.
- You may have a compatibility problem caused by the data having been created in an earlier version of the software that is not compatible with the

present software that you are using. Many software packages will let you select what version to use. For example, you might be working in Word 2003 but as you know that the person you are going to give the file to only has Word 2000, you can choose to save it in this earlier version format.

Lost or damaged data:

Use the file recovery software to find or repair the data. There is utility software that can undelete deleted files, restore files that have been attacked by a virus, and repair data damaged by formatting.

Check it yourself – Level 2

You may have experienced some of these problems when you have been working with your system. What you need to know is which faults you are permitted to put right and which ones you must seek technical assistance for. Make a checklist of all the types of faults that you could encounter and identify which ones you have fixed, which ones you would be allowed to fix if they arose, and for those that you cannot fix, identify who you would have to ask to do this. You should include any other faults that have occurred and how you dealt with them.

Viruses

See Unit 6: IT security for users, page 131.

Anti-virus measures:

- Back up all your software, including the operating systems, and make sure you can recognise a virus and know what to do about it.
- Prevent viruses getting into the system. You and other users need to be aware of the danger. You also need to operate a system of good hygiene, using disk authorisation software, or providing isolated 'quarantine' computers for use.

Managing viruses:

- Use anti-virus software to detect and, where possible, disinfect or destroy viruses.
- Make sure that infected items are isolated. Use tools to recover corrupted data wherever possible.

Skills Restarting

Restarting the computer can often resolve a problem.

Restart common hardware and software

There are two ways of restarting your computer, also known as rebooting. You can carry out a hard and a soft reboot. A hard start is when you turn the computer off, and then turn it back on again. A soft reboot is when you turn it off using the software by holding down the **Ctrl**, **Alt** and **Delete** keys at the same time, or by pressing the reset button on the computer case. A soft boot is quicker, will reset most of the settings to the startup defaults, but will not clear down systems-level software conflicts. It is usually worth trying a soft reboot first and then use a hard boot only where necessary.

Problems that occur on a network system may be resolved by logging off and logging in again without having to completely shut down the computer.

Restart hardware and software using tools supplied by the manufacturer

The system will have tools to help you shut down the tasks running on the computer. You can use **Task Manager** to help you shut down a piece of software and keep the rest of the system running, or to safely close down the whole system when it has stopped responding. See page 89.

Practical task

- So that you can practise shutting down your computer, closes all the open applications, and remove any storage media safely. Now switch off the computer and then start it up again – a hard boot. Watch the process and note down any messages you get.
- Now repeat this process but try the soft boot. How much quicker was it?
- Now open up an application and then use the task manager to close down the system.

Keep a note of how you did the task and include screenshots where possible.

Information about errors necessary to help expert give advice

When you have a computer problem that you need help with, there are certain things that you need to do. Make a very accurate (sometimes step-by-step) record of what exactly happened. If you receive an error message, copy it down exactly. Whenever, possible take a screenshot of the error as this can be really helpful to an expert when they are trying to work out what has gone wrong. You can do this by pressing Shift and the **Print Screen** key; this captures an image of the screen and places it on the clipboard. You can then paste this image into a suitable application (e.g. Word) and print it out.

You need to be able to give the expert as much information as possible about the hardware or software to assist in the diagnosis and solution of the problem. You can get much of this information from the help facilities of your computer system. For example in Microsoft Word:

Step 1   Select **Help** from the menu bar and click on **About Microsoft Office Word**.

Figure 4.12 Select About from the Help menu

Step 2   The information about the software is displayed.

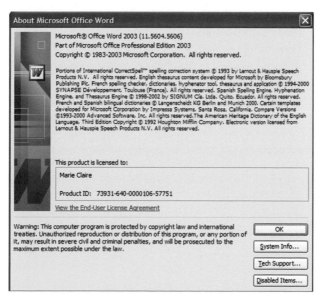

Figure 4.13 Software information

Step 3 You can also display information about the system. Click on **Systems Info…**

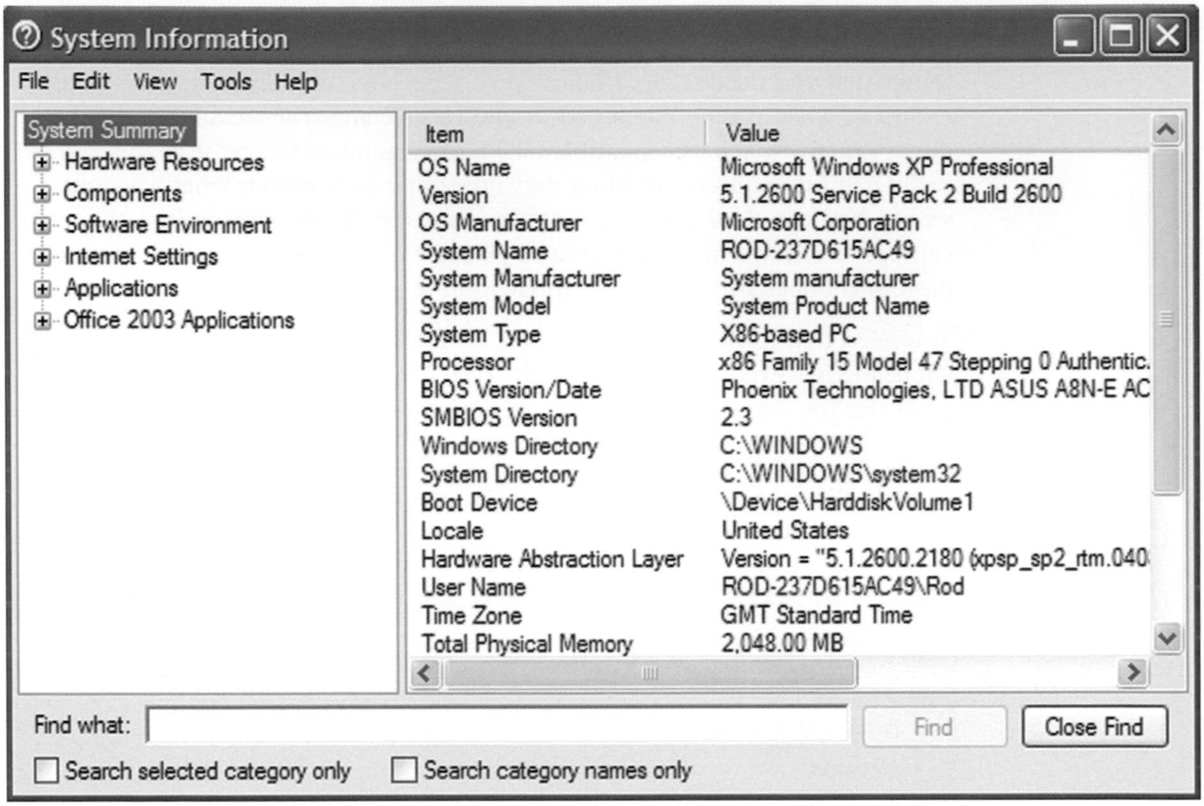

System Information	

Item	Value
OS Name	Microsoft Windows XP Professional
Version	5.1.2600 Service Pack 2 Build 2600
OS Manufacturer	Microsoft Corporation
System Name	ROD-237D615AC49
System Manufacturer	System manufacturer
System Model	System Product Name
System Type	X86-based PC
Processor	x86 Family 15 Model 47 Stepping 0 Authentic.
BIOS Version/Date	Phoenix Technologies, LTD ASUS A8N-E AC
SMBIOS Version	2.3
Windows Directory	C:\WINDOWS
System Directory	C:\WINDOWS\system32
Boot Device	\Device\HarddiskVolume1
Locale	United States
Hardware Abstraction Layer	Version = "5.1.2600.2180 (xpsp_sp2_rtm.040
User Name	ROD-237D615AC49\Rod
Time Zone	GMT Standard Time
Total Physical Memory	2,048.00 MB

System Summary
- Hardware Resources
- Components
- Software Environment
- Internet Settings
- Applications
- Office 2003 Applications

Find what:

Find   Close Find

☐ Search selected category only   ☐ Search category names only

Figure 4.14 System information

What advice is available

What you need to know and understand

- Recognising there is a problem
- How to contact an IT help desk or service
- How to follow verbal instructions from an IT expert
- Recognising the limits of own understanding of skills
- **Level 2** Where and how to find advice on common errors with most hardware and software

Recognising there is a problem

When something appears to go wrong with your computer, you need to be certain that there really is a fault that you need help with. Faults are sometimes reported that could be solved by simple checks.

- Make sure that the power on the printer is switched on before reporting that it is not printing.
- Check the settings of the keyboard – some commands or responses from the keyboard are case sensitive, which means that it should or should not be in capital letters. Check to make sure that the Caps Lock is not on, and then try again.
- Have you accidentally held down the Ctrl key rather than the Shift key?
- Are you using the correct command in the application software – check by using the help files before reporting an error.

How to contact an IT help desk or service

Many organisations have an IT help desk that provides support to users of computers within the organisation. Some have sophisticated systems of recording and managing faults, and many will suggest possible solutions. The process of diagnosing and resolving a fault will be speeded up by a clear description of the fault. Some organisations will have an online fault-reporting system that is constantly monitored so that faults are dealt with as they arrive.

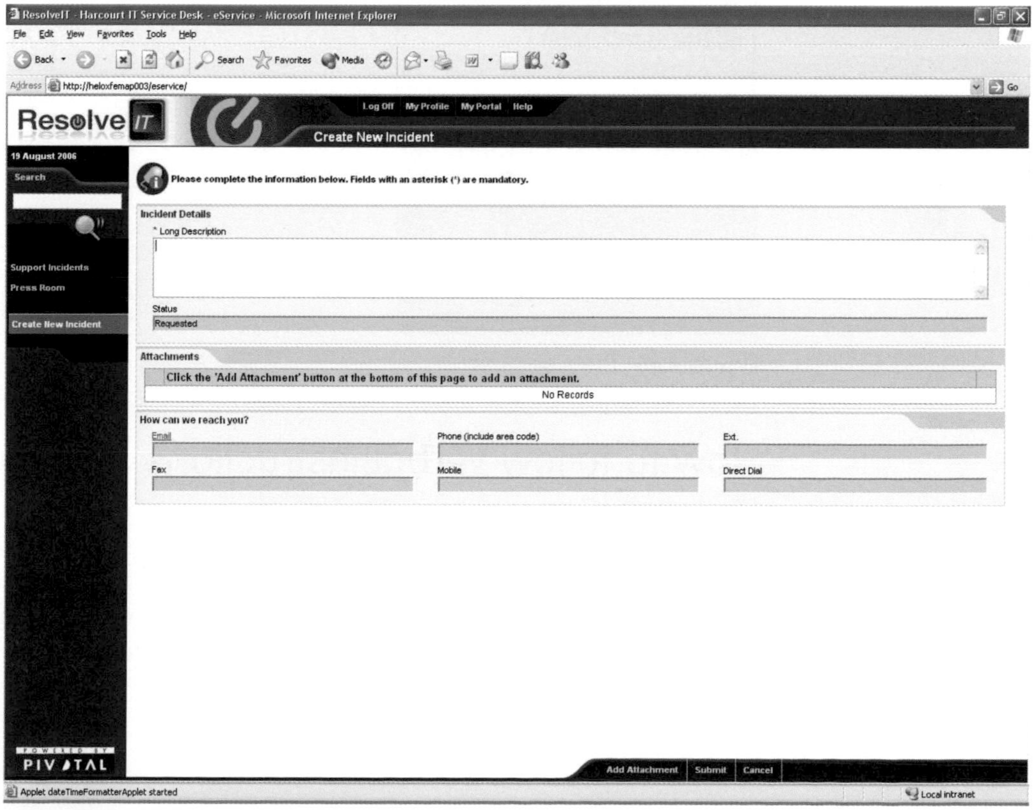

Figure 4.15 A fault report screen

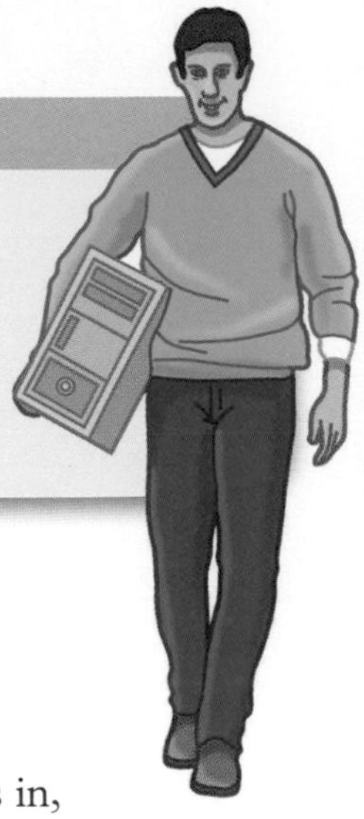

Check it yourself

Do you have a help desk where you work or study? Arrange a time when you can spend a few hours shadowing the work that is carried out on a help desk. What sorts of faults do people contact them about? How are they recorded? Do they think that the help desk is a good way of providing support?

Online helper

The online helper is a useful feature of many help facilities. It provides information based on the keywords that the user types in, or in response to a question, such as 'How do I print envelopes?' It may offer information on how to create and print envelopes, troubleshoot printing envelopes, customise envelope size, etc. The online helper can be used as you carry out a task, and will suggest the kind of help you might need if you have a problem. The 'assistant' is usually an animated cartoon character that offers a friendly helping hand.

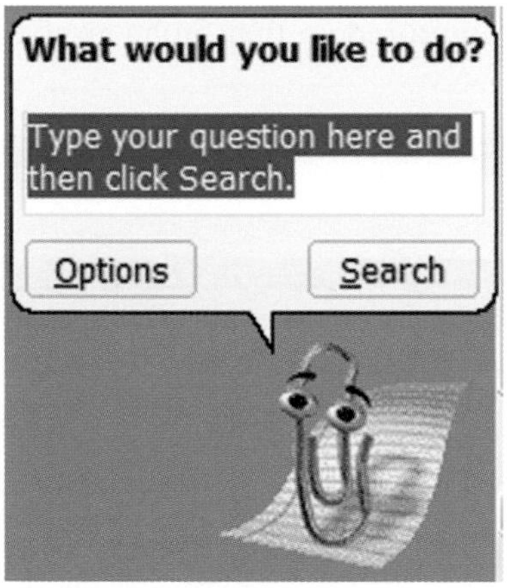

Figure 4.16 The Assistant

How to follow verbal instructions from an IT expert

If an IT expert is giving you instructions on how to fix a problem, you must follow those instructions exactly, step by step. If the expert is instructing you by phone, give them feedback as you progress, so that they can take account of this information, as it may help them with the diagnosis and finding a solution.

Recognising the limits of own understanding of skills

Never be afraid to admit that you do not know what is wrong or you do not know how to deal with a problem. If you attempt to deal with a problem without knowing what you are doing, you could make it worse.

Where and how to find advice on common errors with most hardware and software

Online help

Many software suppliers now supply the online help facility as the main source of information for the user. This enables you to call it up on to your screen as and when you need it. However, not all these help systems are very helpful and many do not cover all you need to know about the software. You may also be able to get help from the Internet help resources provided with the software.

You can find help with creating headers in a Microsoft Word document in the following ways:

The Table of Contents (under the help function) is organised into a number of sections, usually presented in a sequence that a new user or relatively novice user may wish to access help.

You would need to look in the section headed Creating Documents, and click on the book symbol to show all the sub-headings – in this instance **Headers and Footers** will provide some help.

Using the contents can be very useful if you do not know exactly what you are looking for, or just for browsing when you want to learn something new.

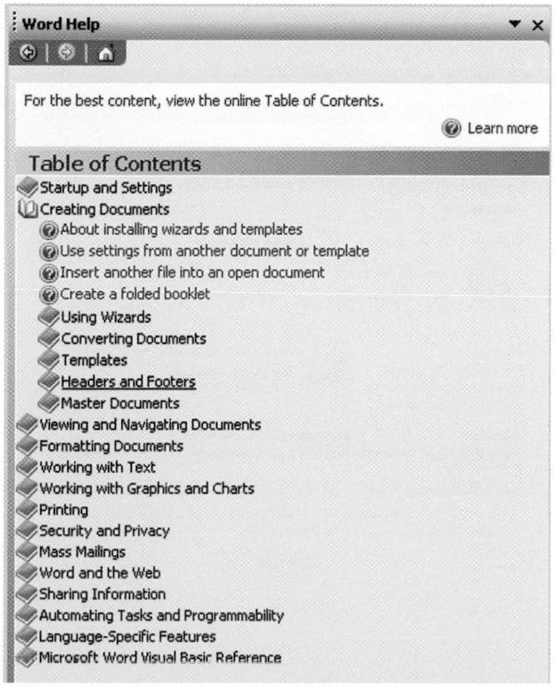

Figure 4.17 Table of Contents

The **answer wizard** can be used to help you search the online help.

You type in a question, for example 'How do I create a header?', and the helper will offer you a list of possible sections that may give you the assistance you need.

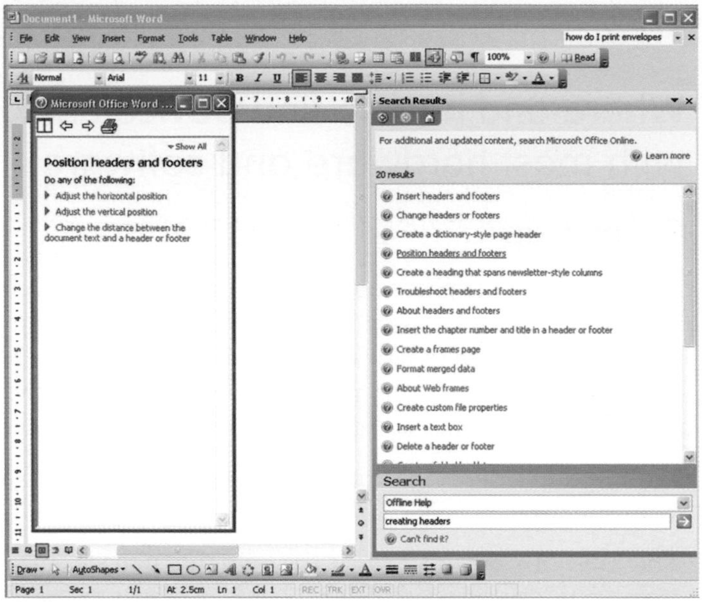

Figure 4.18 Answer wizard

You may also be able to get additional help by connecting to the website for the software product (Figure 4.19). This will give you access to the latest information about the software and hints and tips.

This provides an interactive, alphabetical listing of all the help available.

You can type a topic title, for example 'header' and the available sections are displayed.

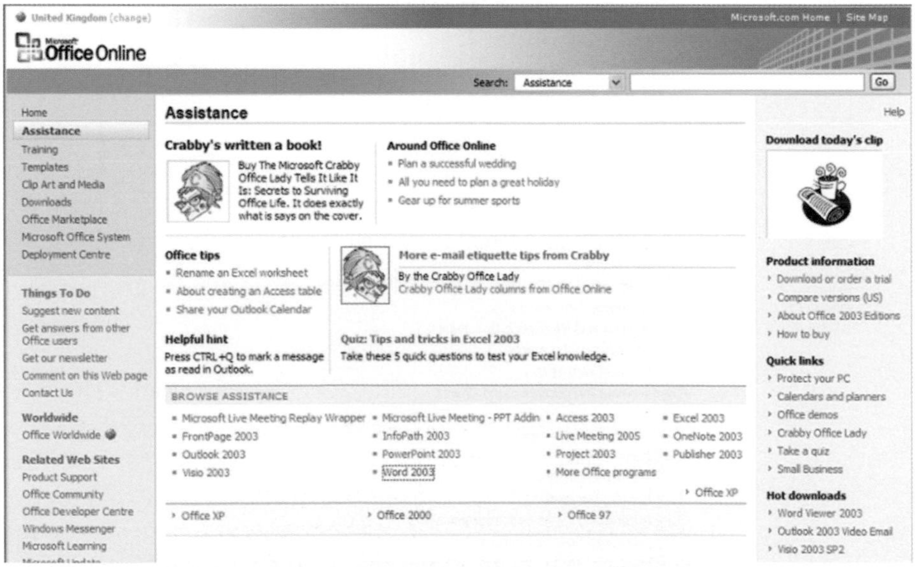

Figure 4.19 Microsoft Office Online

Working with one of the pieces of software that you know fairly well, you are going to use the online help facility. Using the index, find the information on how to carry out two or three features that you *do* know how to use. Read these and compare this with your own understanding of these features.

Now select something that you *do not* know about. You could do this by reference to the contents or the index. Read through it and then try it out on the computer. Think of a particular use that you might have for this new feature. How 'user-friendly' is the online help?

Internet-based help

Many software online help facilities provide a direct link to the supplier's website. From here you may get useful tips and techniques to help with problems you may have, and that many of their customers have already asked about. There is usually a FAQ (frequently asked questions) section which may have the answer that you need. There is also the opportunity to get up-to-date information about new features and to download updates and other files such as additional ClipArt.

Figure 4.20 Microsoft FAQs

Other help

Many organisations produce simple information sheets for frequently used features of software. These are usually written by users rather than by computer experts and will often be more 'user friendly' and useful. A wide range of books and quick reference guides for the more commonly used software packages are also available. These are very useful for those who know how to use the software but need something to refer to, particularly for commands that they do not use very often.

Skills Correcting errors and problems

What you need to do

- Identify the cause of common errors
- Use resources to correct errors
- **Level 2** Choose and use methods that have worked in the past to correct different types of error
- **Level 2** Check that errors have been corrected

Identify the cause of common errors

There are a number of questions to help identify the cause of an error:

- What task were you carrying out when the problem occurred and what exactly had you just done?
- Have you ever come across this problem before?
- Have you carried out this particular activity successfully before?
- And have you changed anything since then, either hardware or software?

Use resources to correct errors

You will need to show that you have used a number of resources to assist you to correct your problems. This should include using the help menus provided with the software. You should also use guidelines from the manufacturers; you will fined the latest versions on their website.

Practical task

What resources are available for your software? Look at the help menu for each piece of software that you use. Is there information about extra help on the web? Go to the website and look at the FAQs.

Keep a note on how you did the task and include screenshots where possible.

Choose and use methods that have worked in the past to correct different types of errors

Finding and fixing a fault frequently involves recognising a problem that you have dealt with before and using that experience to put things right. You can also use the experience of others, rather than struggle to find a solution by yourself. As you gain this experience, keep detailed notes on the problem and how it was solved, so that you can refer to them when the problem arises in the future.

Check that errors have been corrected

When a repair is completed, you need to run a full test of the aspect of the system that was not working to make sure the problem is solved. For example, if the problem occurred as you were saving a file, open up that file and try to save it again.

Practical task

Set up a log to record the faults you come across and how you fixed them. This log should include details of the fault, the symptoms that you identified, the resources that you used to help you fix it, how you checked to make sure that the problem was fixed, and which errors were beyond your capability or responsibility and how you dealt with them.

Keep a note on how you did the task and include screenshots where possible.

Compatibility issues

What you need to know and understand

- **Level 2** What problems can occur when hardware, software and operating system are not compatible
- **Level 2** Why compatibility standards are needed

See Unit 3: Operate a computer, page 70.

You will need to be able to identify any compatibility issues and at least know how to resolve them, even though you may not have privileges that allow you carry out the solution.

Case study

Sunshine Travel uses computers throughout the organisation. Most staff have access to computers throughout the working day. All the computers and printers are connected to a local area network which is maintained by the technical support team. Some staff have laptops which they take to customers' premises. The company has a website to promote and market its goods and services. Staff have access to the company's intranet, where all standard documents and procedures are available.

In the **Sales Department** they use:

- specialist credit-control software to manage customers' accounts

- a sales order and invoice package, which is part of the company's financial control system

- word-processing software to communicate with customers

- e-mail as the main internal communication, and more and more for external communication

- presentation software to demonstrate products and services to customers.

When a member of the sales team goes to visit a customer they link up to the Internet to show the company's website. They also show presentations using a laptop.

1 What should they do before going out so that they can be certain everything will work OK when they are on the customer's premises?

2 Where should they store the presentation so that they could still show it even if the laptop was not working?

5 IT maintenance for users

What you need to know and understand

- Routine and non-routine maintenance
- Health and safety issues
- **Level 2** Upgrading hardware and software

Introduction

Computers need to be maintained to make sure that they are working correctly and safely, and that the information stored in them is protected. There are a number of basic tasks that every user should carry out regularly and for which you will need knowledge, understanding, skills and techniques; there are others for which you need the assistance of an experienced ICT systems support person.

In this unit, maintenance means the basic housekeeping tasks that you as a user need to do to keep your part of the system clean and working efficiently. It doesn't mean opening up the computer, or repairing parts of the system. You will probably have very limited permission to do maintenance, but there will be certain routine, simple jobs that it would be normal for you to do.

Routine and non-routine maintenance

What you need to know and understand

- Routine maintenance
- Why routine maintenance is important
- What problems may occur if maintenance is not carried out
- **Level 2** Non-routine maintenance
- **Level 2** What maintenance to leave to the professionals

Routine maintenance

Routine maintenance is the tasks that a computer user carries out as part of normal working practices. It includes looking after the equipment, cleaning the main parts, replacing materials in the printer, and maintaining the computer files.

Skills Cleaning the hardware

What you need to do

- Select suitable cleaning methods and materials
- Clean hardware so that it works efficiently, for example keyboard, mouse roller ball
- Clean hardware to keep it looking good

All the computer equipment and the complete workstation need to be kept clean and free of dust. Some of this may be done by technical support staff, however the basic cleaning can be done by the user. Any cleaning that you do must be done safely. Make sure that you take all the necessary safety precautions. For example, equipment should be turned off at the power and a laser printer should be allowed to cool before starting work on it. Always check what to do if you are not sure.

Select suitable cleaning methods and materials

Make sure that any cleaning materials you use are safe to handle. Read any instructions or warnings on the product or its packaging before you use it; for example, to wear gloves to handle the product or to take care not to inhale fumes from cleaning fluids. Also make sure that the product is appropriate for cleaning the equipment; more harm than good can be done if you use the wrong cleaning substances. Always check in the manual, or with technical support staff, to find out any specific 'do's and don'ts'. Keep up to date with any new products by reading office equipment and computer magazines. Always make sure you switch off the equipment before you clean it!

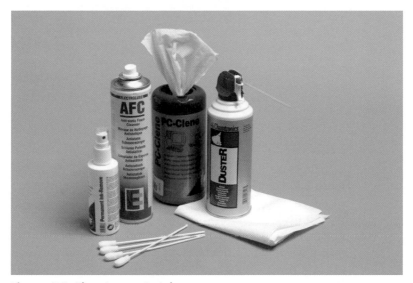

Figure 5.1 Cleaning materials

Clean hardware so that it works efficiently, for example keyboard, mouse roller ball

You may be expected to take responsibility for the cleaning of the following.

Disk drives

This is similar to cleaning a music or video cassette. Floppy-disk and CD cleaners are available for running inside the drive, to clean the read/write heads and prolong the life of the drives, thereby reducing the risk of damage to your disks.

Mouse

A mouse is very prone to dirt, particularly the rollers that run on the ball. (Figure 5.2). These can be cleaned using a cotton bud moistened with water. Make sure you use a mouse mat to reduce the level of dirt and to improve the performance of the mouse.

To clean the mouse:

Step 1   Disconnect the mouse.

Step 2   Turn it over and remove the cover.

Step 3   Remove the mouse ball.

Step 4   Clean the ball with a lint-free cloth.

Step 5   Clean the rollers using a cotton bud moistened with water.

Step 6   Blow out loose dust and dirt using compressed air (in a canister).

Step 7   Replace the ball and cover, and reconnect.

Optical mice are becoming more common. These have the great advantage of not having a mouse ball and therefore need far less regular cleaning. You can wipe all the surfaces of this type of mouse with a damp lint-free cloth when necessary.

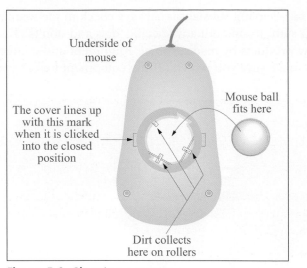

Figure 5.2 Cleaning a mouse

Mouse mat
This is only useful if it is kept very clean and free from dust; a quick wipe once a week with a damp cloth can make all the difference.

Keyboard
A wipe over with a damp cloth on a regular basis will remove most dirt left by sticky fingers.

Do you know how much damage the spilling of a fizzy drink or cup of tea can do to a keyboard? The acid in a fizzy drink can completely destroy the electrical contacts in the keyboard; the milk or sugar in your tea are particularly sticky when dry and will stop the keys from working properly. If something gets spilled on a keyboard you should:

Step 1 Turn off the equipment immediately.

Step 2 Place the keyboard upside down.

Step 3 Notify technical support so that they can clean and check it.

Base unit
Keep this clean and free from dust; there can be a build up of dust in the vents from the fan.

Printer
Keep the outside of the printer clean, wiping the casing using a damp cloth.

Inkjet printers will usually have a software utility that you can run to clean the inkjet nozzles if required. You should not clean the inside of an inkjet printer except where specified in the manual.

Cleaning inside a laser printer should be done with great care. Make sure that you do not come into contact with the toner. You may need to wipe out toner dust from the inside using a dry, lint-free cloth, but be careful as toner particles can cause an irritation when breathed in, so you may need to wear a mask.

Scanner
Keep the outside of the scanner clean, wiping the casing using a damp cloth.

To clean the glass:

Step 1   Turn off and unplug the scanner.

Step 2   Wipe the glass using a mild, non-streak glass cleaner and a lint-free cloth.

Step 3   Dry the glass immediately before closing the lid.

Clean hardware to keep it looking good

You can keep these facilities clean in the following ways:

- **Screen**   Anti-static screen wipes are quick and can make a great difference to the quality of the display. This will also ensure that you are able to work more effectively.
- **Cases**   A wipe over with a damp cloth on a regular basis will keep them clean.
- **Desktop**   Keep your desktop tidy, free from clutter and clean it regularly to ensure that it is dust free. You should make sure that all cables and leads are arranged neatly and secured so that they do not present a safety hazard (see Health and Safety).

Practical task

You need to have evidence that you have routinely cleaned hardware. Create a log sheet where you can record the date, hardware type and activity carried out, such as 'Used CD cleaner'. Include a column where your supervisor can initial the entries to confirm that you completed the task correctly. It would also be helpful to have a record of any problems that arose and how you dealt with them.

Keep a note on how you did the task.

Skills Maintaining hardware and software

What you need to do

- Replace materials used in printers
- **Level 2** Carry out routine maintenance to printers, following manufacturers' instructions for users
- **Level 2** Identify any non-routine maintenance needed to hardware and carry it out, following manufacturers' guidelines

Replace materials used in printers

You will need to know how to replace the main materials used in your printer. This will include loading paper and, depending on the type of printer, the toner or ink cartridge.

Change a toner or ink cartridge safely

You may need to do this at the same time as general maintenance and cleaning. You need to know details about the printer to make sure that you use the correct cartridge; the wrong one could cause serious damage. Before starting, switch off the printer and make sure your hair or any scarves or ties, clothing or items of jewellery, are not likely to get entangled in the equipment.

Changing a laser printer cartridge will vary from make and model. Here is a simple guide to the steps that you will need to take.

Step 1 Turn off the printer.

Step 2 Open the cover or front.

Step 3 Remove the old cartridge by pulling the handle. Lift it out gently and place on a scrap piece of paper.

Step 4 Remove the new cartridge from its plastic bag – you may need scissors to open the bag.

Step 5 Gently shake the cartridge from side to side.

Step 6 Place the new cartridge in the printer. You may need to push it gently but you should not need to force it.

Step 7 Close the printer cover.

Step 8 Print a test page – this may need to be repeated if there are smears.

Note: You will need to check the precise procedures in the manual for your machine.

To change the ink cartridges in an inkjet printer will also vary from make and model. Here is a simple guide to the steps you will need to take.

Step 1 Turn on the printer.

Step 2 Press the button to change or check ink cartridge and wait for the cartridge carrier to slide out.

Step 3 Remove the cartridge – it will often need to be lifted up to release it.

Step 4 Carefully remove the tape from the new ink cartridge.

Step 5 Locate the new cartridge in the carrier making sure it is properly seated – it will often 'click' into place.

Step 6 Press the change button again and the cartridge will return to its original position.

Step 7 Print a test page – you may need to run an alignment utility to ensure perfect printing.

Note: With some printers the process is run through the printer software.

Make sure that you know how to clean up any spillage of toner and how to dispose of the old cartridges in an environmentally considerate way. Look at the instructions in the box of your new laser or inkjet cartridge to find out how to recycle your old one. Many companies will provide instructions, packaging materials and free postage if you wish to recycle your old cartridge, which is then refilled and used again.

Load the paper tray or feed for continuous stationery

Paper for laser and inkjet printers must be loaded the right way up (there should be an arrow on the paper's packaging to indicate this). Continuous paper should be properly clipped on to the sprockets.

> **Practical task**
>
> You need to have evidence that you have routinely replaced materials in your printers. Create a log sheet where you can record the date, printer type and activity carried out, such as 'Change printer cartridge'. Include a column where your supervisor can initial the entries to confirm that you completed the task correctly. It would also be helpful to have a record of any problems that arose and how you dealt with them.
>
> Keep a note on how you did the task and include screenshots where possible.

Carry out routine maintenance of printers, following manufacturers' instructions for users

As one of the organisation's 'computer experts' you need to make sure that you know where plain and letter-headed paper and labels are kept and how to use them. Others in the organisation may come to you for assistance with problems such as loading different types of paper, unjamming the printer, and generally dealing with minor printer problems. These are the things you should be able to do:

- **Check the computer-to-printer cable** It should not be in a tangle, have any kinks, cuts or any signs of damage through crushing. It should be securely connected at both the computer port and at the socket in the printer.

- **Clear a paper jam safely** Make sure the printer is switched off first and that you do not let your hair or any scarves/ties, clothing or items of jewellery get entangled in the equipment. (**Note:** You need to know the correct procedures and have the authority to open up the printer. If you don't, ask the technician or your supervisor to show you what to do so that you can do it under supervision next time.)

- **Install a new printer driver** You will need to find out if you have authority to access the disk area where these are stored. Make sure that you inform other users of the changes you have made and how to use them. For example, a different printer driver may change the layout of a document by altering the page breaks or margin settings, and may also alter the fonts and special effects on a document.

Most new printers will be detected by your system when you connect them; these are known as 'plug and play'. Just connect the printer and the system will carry out the setup.

If a printer has an installation CD, simply insert the CD into the drive and the installation will start automatically. Just follow the instructions, usually accepting the options offered. If more than one printer is installed, you will need to designate one of them as the default printer.

These are the steps to follow in designating a default printer.

Step 1   From the **Control Panel,** double-click on **Printers and Faxes.**

Printers and Faxes

Figure 5.3 Printers and Faxes icon

Step 2   Single-click on the printer you wish to set as the default.

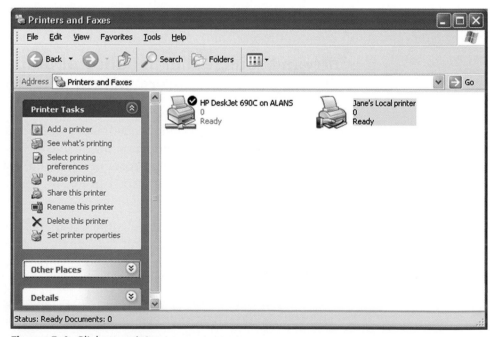

Figure 5.4 Click on printer

Step 3   From the **File** menu, select **Set as Default Printer.**

Figure 5.5 Set the default printer

Step 4   The default printer is set – ✓ shows setting.

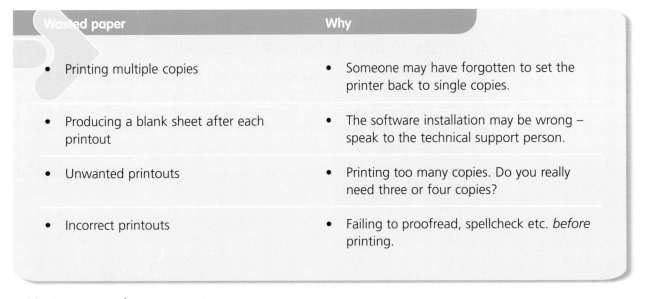

Figure 5.6 Default setting icon

It is important to keep the area around the printer tidy and clean. For example, waste paper lying around the desk and floor is a potential health and safety hazard. One of the problems of printing is paper wastage. There are various reasons why this might occur (see Table 5.1).

Wasted paper	Why
• Printing multiple copies	• Someone may have forgotten to set the printer back to single copies.
• Producing a blank sheet after each printout	• The software installation may be wrong – speak to the technical support person.
• Unwanted printouts	• Printing too many copies. Do you really need three or four copies?
• Incorrect printouts	• Failing to proofread, spellcheck etc. *before* printing.

Table 5.1 Reasons for paper wastage

Identify any non-routine maintenance needed to hardware and carry it out, following manufacturers' guidelines

Skills Managing files appropriately to maintain performance

What you need to do

- Name and organise files and folders so that it is easy to find documents needed
- Back up personal data to suitable storage media at appropriate intervals, such as to server or floppy disk
- Delete unwanted personal files regularly to maintain performance
- **Level 2** Change default settings for saving data

The process of looking after your disk storage systems is known as housekeeping.

The main functions you will need to be familiar with in order to do this are those for:

- creating directories (folders)
- copying
- deleting
- making backups.

Name and organise files and folders so that it is easy to find documents needed

The work you keep on your computer is stored in a file. Every file needs to have a name, which needs to be meaningful and helpful so that you can find it easily. Many organisations have guidelines as to what names to use. This may include information to show who owns the file, when it was created and when it was last updated.

You will need to organise your files into folders just as you would organise paper files. For the different folders of work you should use appropriate and helpful names.

For further information, see Unit 3: Operate a computer, page 47.

This is how to organise your files into folders.

Step 1 From the **Control Panel,** select the disk drive and then right-click.

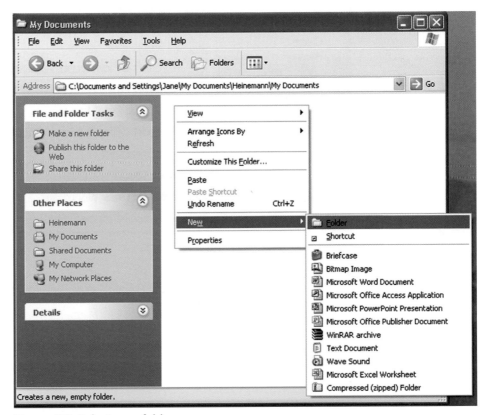

Figure 5.7 Select new folder

From the menu select **New** and then **Folder.**

Step 2 A new folder will be placed on the disk, called New Folder. Click inside the name and change it to something meaningful.

Figure 5.8 New folder

You can also create folders from **My documents.** The process is very similar:

Step 1 From **My documents** click on the **File** menu, select **New** and **Folder.**

My Documents

| File | Edit | View | Favorites | Tools | Help |

New ▶ | Folder

Create Shortcut | Shortcut
Delete
Rename | Briefcase
Properties | Bitmap Image

Close | Microsoft Word Document
| 3D Studio MAX Scene
Publish this fol | Microsoft Office Access Application
Web | Microsoft PowerPoint Presentation
Share this fold | Paint Shop Pro 6 Image
| Microsoft Office Publisher Document
Other Places | Text Document
| Wave Sound
Desktop | Microsoft Excel Worksheet
Shared Docum | Compressed (zipped) Folder

Figure 5.9 Select from My Documents

Step 2 A new folder will be placed in **My documents** called **New Folder**.

New Folder

Figure 5.10 New folder

Click inside the name and change it to something meaningful.

You can also create a new folder to store your work from inside the application. When you choose to save your document:

Step 1   Click on **File** and select **Save As** from the menu.

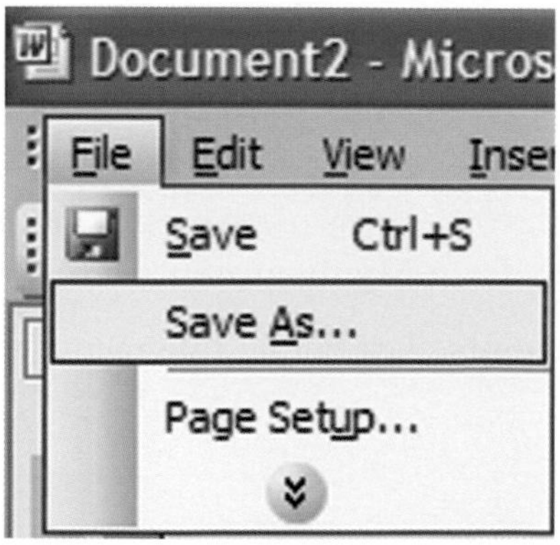

Document2 - Micros

| File | Edit | View | Inse

Save   Ctrl+S

Save As...

Page Setup...

⌄

Figure 5.11 Save as

Step 2 Click on the **Create New Folder** icon.

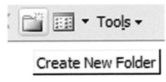

Create New Folder

Figure 5.12 Create new folder icon

Step 3 Enter name of new folder.

Figure 5.13 Enter folder name

Practical task

Demonstrate your skills by organising the files that you use for your ITQ qualification so that you can find them easily.

- Create a main folder called ITQ.
- Create a sub-folder for each unit that you are doing.
- Tidy up your storage media by moving files into the right folders. Print a copy of this to use as part of your evidence.

Keep a note on how you did the task and include screenshots where possible.

Back up personal data to suitable storage media at appropriate intervals, such as to server or floppy disk

In every computer environment, at work or at home, you should make backup copies of both the software on the system and of your work. Backup copies are kept for security reasons. The data stored on the main computer system will usually be 'live' data – that is, currently in use. It will include things like budgets that are being amended and/or monitored against, on-going correspondence which still needs to be referred to, minutes of meetings etc.; in other words, the day-to-day work of the office. If this was 'lost' it would create extra work and could cause considerable disruption to the smooth running of the department or section of the organisation.

There are many reasons why you might lose your data:

- If power is lost while the read heads are in contact with the hard disk you may experience what is known as a 'disk crash'; the whole disk may be completely destroyed.
- Viruses can destroy or corrupt your data.
- Files may be deleted by accident; it may be very difficult to recover them.
- Unauthorised users may access files and accidentally or maliciously tamper with the data.

You can use the *copy* command to make an exact copy of one or more files. However, this has limited use, particularly when the files to be copied are larger than the space available on a removable storage disk, as you cannot split a file between two or more disks. However, there are a pair of commands specifically designed to assist you with this procedure: one makes the backup copies and the other restores the data should the original files become damaged or lost.

The *backup* command copies the files on to a numbered set of disks, prompting for the next disk as required. It does not, however, create readable or directly usable copies of the files. A backup command usually works by creating on each disk two files, one containing the data from the files and the other – often called a control file – identifying the names, sizes and creation dates of the files, and also details of the sequence of the disk in the backup procedure.

The second command enables you to *restore* some or all of the data from these disks. It uses the information in the control file to find the data and to prompt you through the process as it restores the data from each disk.

These commands will usually allow you to carry out the back up procedure in a number of different ways. You can back up or restore:

- all the files in the folder
- all the files in the folder and any subfolders of that folder
- only those files that have been updated or created on or after a specified date/time
- only those files updated or created since the last backup.

These are the steps to follow in backing up files.

Step 1 From the **Start** menu select **All Programs**, go to **Accessories**, **System Tools** and select **Backup**.

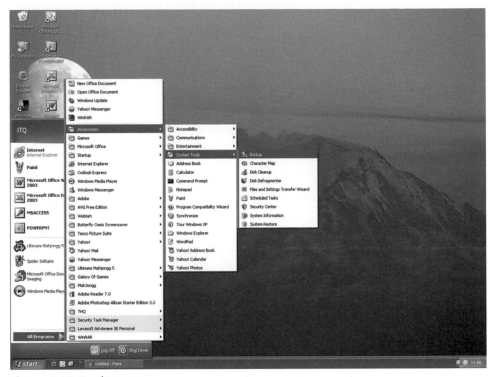

Figure 5.14 Backing up

Step 2 This takes you to a wizard to help you through the process. Click on **Next.**

Figure 5.15 Backup or Restore Wizard

Step 3   Select **Backup files and settings.**

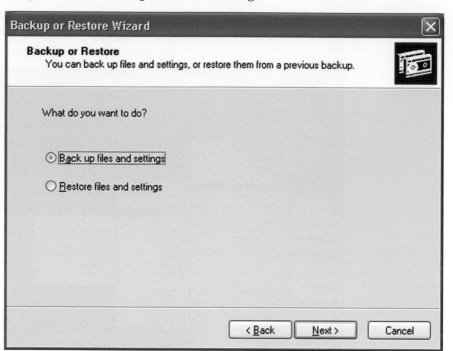

Figure 5.16 Backup files and settings

Step 4   Select **My Documents and settings.**

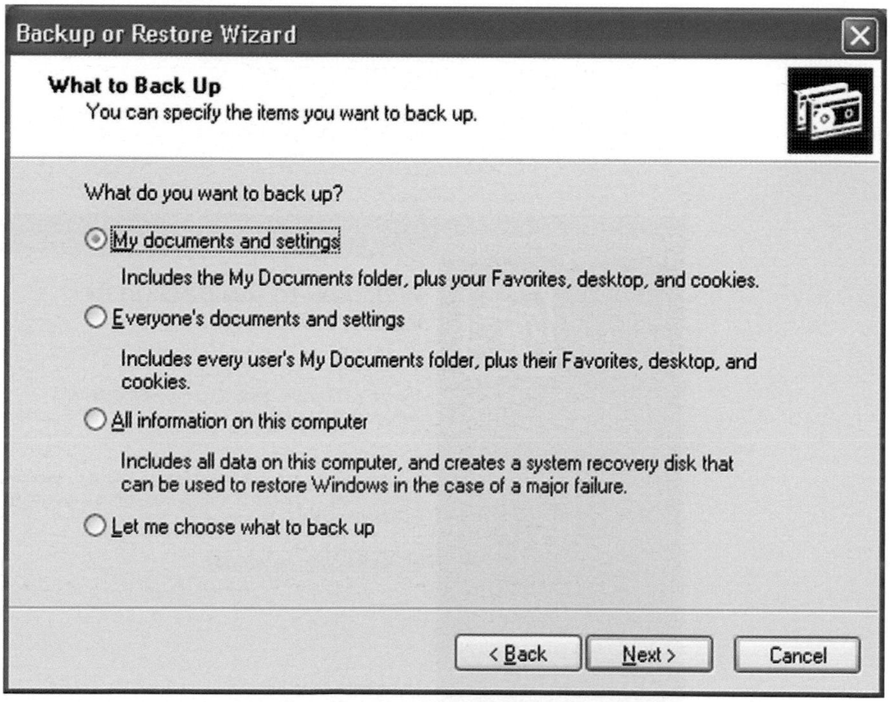

Figure 5.17 What to back up

Step 5   Choose where to save the backup and give the backup a name.

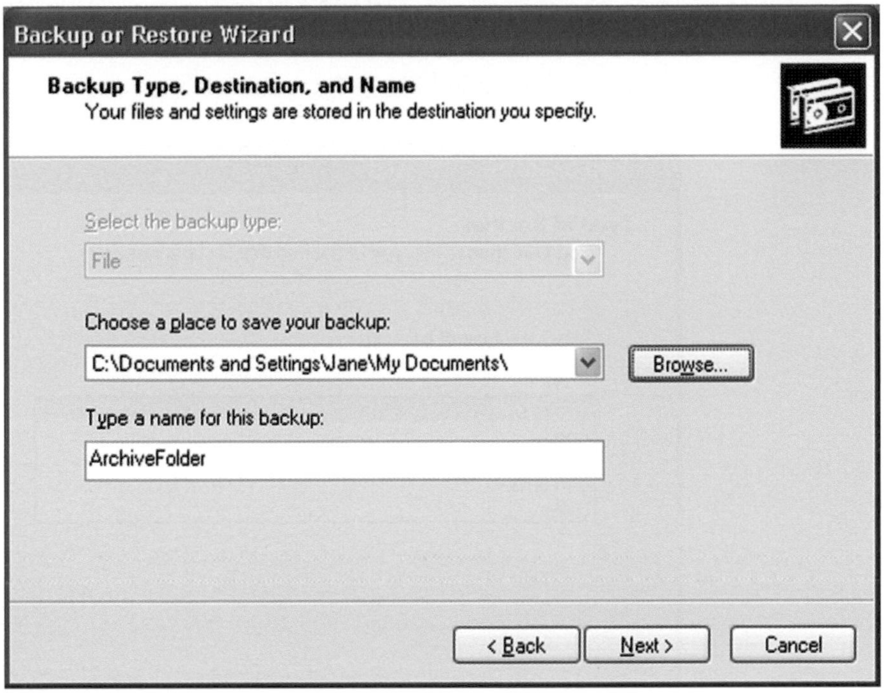

Figure 5.18 Where to save the backup

Step 6   Click on **Finish** to start the backup.

Figure 5.19 Completing the backup

If you click on the Advanced option before starting the backup you can select which type of backup you want to run.

- Back up all the files – Normal; or
- Back up modified files – Incremental.

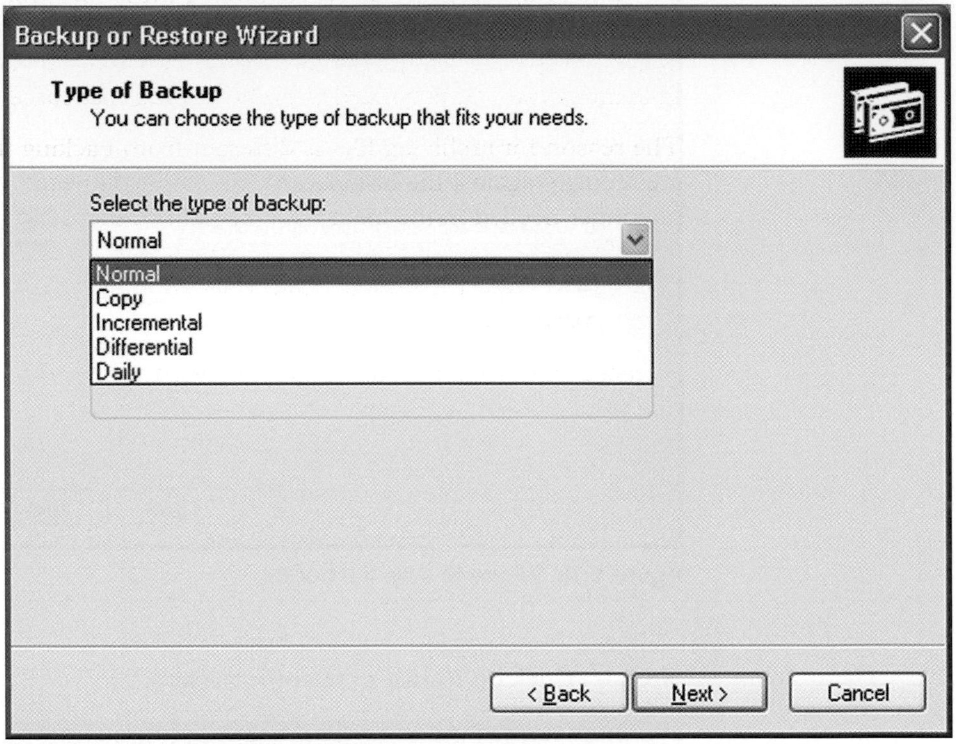

Backup or Restore Wizard

Type of Backup
You can choose the type of backup that fits your needs.

Select the type of backup:

Normal

| Normal |
| Copy |
| Incremental |
| Differential |
| Daily |

< Back   Next >   Cancel

Figure 5.20 Advanced option

In many organisations, particularly when working in a network environment, some of these procedures will be carried out centrally, although most users will have responsibility for their own personal files.

Practical task

The files that you create for your qualification are important and need to be looked after.

- Make a backup copy of your files on to a suitable removable device.
- You then need to keep this backup copy up to date. Each week, back up all the new or updated files.

Keep a note on how you did the task and include screenshots where possible.

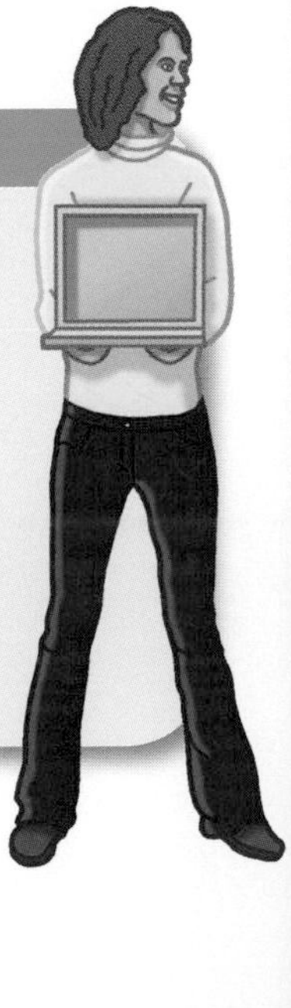

Delete unwanted personal files regularly to maintain performance

It is necessary for your computer files to be maintained on a regular basis. Large numbers of unnecessary files stored on disks occupy considerable amounts of disk storage space. Removing these files will increase that space, however make sure that a file is no longer required before you delete it. Some workplaces will have guidelines on how long to keep certain types of documents, so you may need to archive some files rather than delete them.

The reason for archiving files is different from backing up files. Backup copies are security against the originals being lost or damaged. Archive copies are files no longer needed in the main working environment but which may be needed for reference or use in the future. Electronic copies of old correspondence may be kept 'offline' – for example, many accounting records need to be kept for seven years.

As these files are not used regularly, they do not need to be in the active working environment. If they were, they would need to be maintained and backed up, which would occupy expensive online storage space.

Archive copies of files can be stored in various ways. Most are simply held on some form of removable storage system, which could be a floppy disk, tape cartridge, micro-fiche or even CD-R or DVD. For a standalone computer system this could be floppy disks, CD-R or DVD; in a large network system, where a considerable amount of data needs to be backed up, this will usually be using data tapes with capacities in excess of 500 GB, or DVD-R for lower volumes. Removable hard drives are now also being used, although they are far less transportable and therefore not suitable for secure offsite storage.

Practical task

You need to maintain your own storage media regularly.

- Delete any files that are no longer required.
- Remove old files that you do not need immediately, but might need to keep – that is, create an archive copy.

Keep a note on how you did the task and include screenshots where possible.

Change default settings for saving data

Data storage systems can quickly become untidy. For example, if you are creating a new piece of work, get interrupted, you save it in a hurry, but forget to put it in the right folder. You can prevent this by setting up your own system so that files are automatically saved in a specified folder. These default settings can save you a lot of time searching for files and then moving them to the correct folders.

Step 1 Select **Options** from the **Tools** menu.

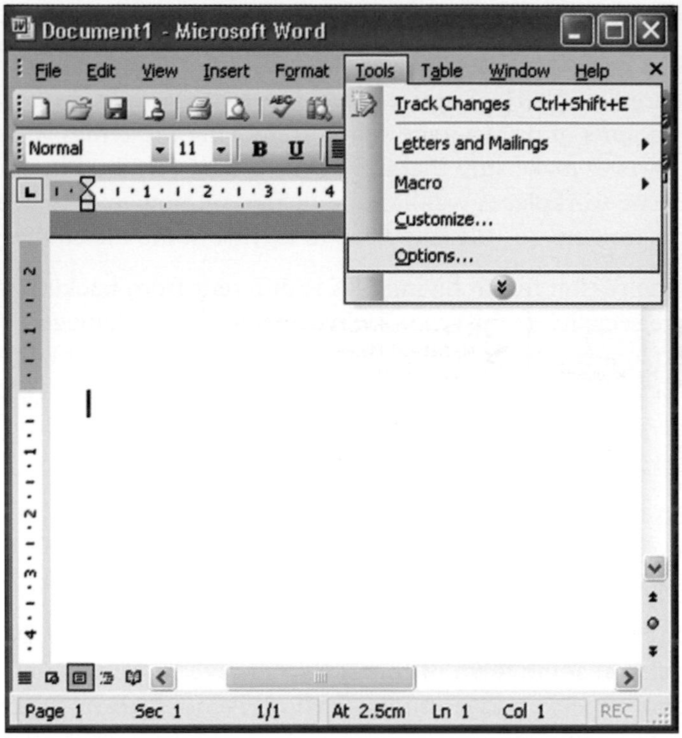

Figure 5.21 Options

Step 2 Select the **File Locations** tab.

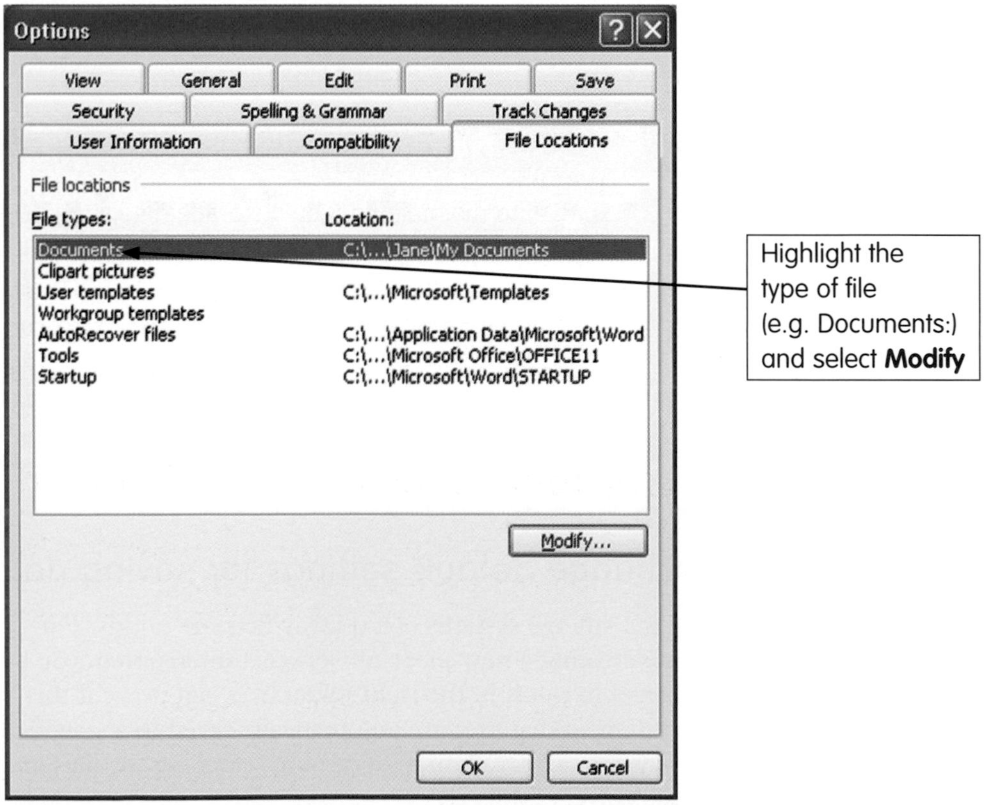

Highlight the type of file (e.g. Documents:) and select **Modify**

Figure 5.22 File locations

Step 3 Select the drive and folder where the files are to be saved.

Modify Location

Look in: ITQ's Documents

Desktop
  My Computer
    Guest1's Documents
    ITQ's Documents
    Shared Documents
    3½ Floppy (A:)
    Local Disk (C:)
    CD-RW Drive (D:)
    DVD Drive (E:)
    c$ on 'Mesh PC (alans)' (T:)
  My Network Places
  My Documents
  Zero2Hero
FTP Locations
  Add/Modify FTP Locations

My Recent Documents
Desktop
My Documents
My Computer
My Network Places

Folder name:

OK
Cancel

Figure 5.23 Save files to folder

You can also set auto-save timings within applications. You can specify how frequently you want this to take place, which will reduce the loss of data by automatically saving your work after the specified time.

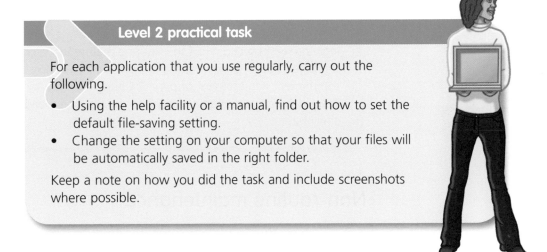

Level 2 practical task

For each application that you use regularly, carry out the following.

- Using the help facility or a manual, find out how to set the default file-saving setting.
- Change the setting on your computer so that your files will be automatically saved in the right folder.

Keep a note on how you did the task and include screenshots where possible.

Why routine maintenance is important

Routine maintenance can help identify potential problems before they become a fault. This reduces the risk of disruption to your work because of a fault in your system. If you alert the technical staff in good time, they can prevent the fault occurring.

An example is checking that there is sufficient paper in your printer every day, so that you reduce the risk of running out of paper, particularly when you are doing an urgent task. It also helps you to record how much paper you use, so that you can budget effectively.

Having a well-organised disk-filing system enables you to work more efficiently; you will be able to more readily locate your files – even those you created some time ago.

Having a clean and tidy working environment is safer and more healthy, and much more pleasant to work in.

What problems may occur if maintenance is not carried out

Routine maintenance, particularly of your storage areas, can significantly reduce the chance of losing work you have been doing on the computer. Even when you do lose work, the disaster will be minimised if you have maintained good backup procedures.

If you do not check all the basic parts of your system regularly and keep them in good condition, you may experience interruptions caused by faults that could have been avoided with regular maintenance.

Computers that are not regularly maintained will often run more slowly. This will increase the time it takes to do a job and lead to frustration.

Check it yourself

What routine maintenance do you carry out on your computer, and how frequently? What cleaning tasks have you carried out recently? And what cleaning materials do you use? Enter this information in section 1 of the Routine maintenance checklist on page 129. What routine maintenance do you carry out on the printer? Replacement of paper? Changing a printer cartridge? Enter this information in section 2 of the Routine maintenance checklist.

Non-routine maintenance

You may be authorised to carry out a number of non-routine maintenance tasks. These tasks are not pre-planned, rather they are ones that need to be carried out over and above everyday maintenance.

There is a range of file-management tools in your operating system to help you maintain and, if necessary, repair your files and data-storage areas.

- As files are saved, deleted, re-saved and updated, a disk can develop bad sectors – that is, areas where data cannot be read from, or saved to, correctly. The error-checking tool helps to manage these so that you avoid data loss.

- Files saved and then updated may not be saved in one area of the disk, and so become fragmented. This can slow down the access time for a file, particularly a very large one, as each part of the file has to be located.

- Temporary files are used by the system to save data as you are working, and when you access the Internet temporary files will be saved on your hard disk. Periodically, you will need to run a disk clean-up to delete most of these unwanted files.

To run a disk clean-up:

Step 1 From the **Start** menu, select **Accessories**, **System Tools**, **Disk Cleanup**.

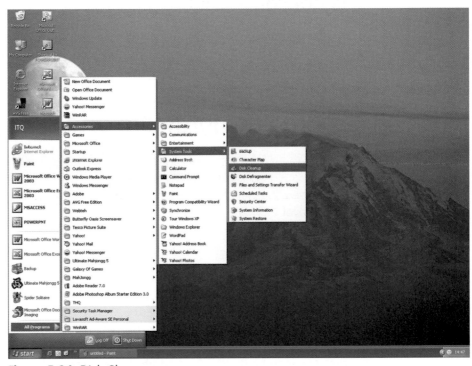

Figure 5.24 Disk Cleanup

Step 2 Check the options in the Disk Cleanup for ... dialogue box. Once you are happy, click **OK**.

Step 3 Click on **Yes**.

What maintenance to leave to the professionals

If you not have permission to maintain a piece of equipment then seek assistance. Permission is usually given only if you have received training by an expert. If a fault occurs that is beyond your authority to correct, you must make a note of any error messages or warnings that are displayed. A clear account of what took place prior to the problem can often assist the ICT maintenance expert in diagnosing the fault.

You may find it useful to keep a maintenance log.

Health and safety issues

What you need to know and understand

- Health and safety laws and guidelines
- Health and safety risks to self in using IT
- Health and safety risks to others from common hardware
- **Level 2** Ways to keep risks to people to a minimum
- **Level 2** Ways to keep risks to hardware to a minimum

See Unit 3: Operate a computer, page 63.

Upgrading hardware and software

What you need to know and understand

- **Level 2** What the benefits of upgrading may be
- **Level 2** What the drawbacks of not upgrading may be
- **Level 2** The need to check compatibility of software and hardware upgrades with other parts of a system

The hardware or software that you use will sometimes need to be changed or improved. You are unlikely to carry this out, however you need to understand what needs to be done, why it might be required, what effect it may have on the way you work, and the problems that can be caused by an upgrade.

What the benefits of upgrading may be

There are several reasons why hardware or software may need to be upgraded:

- The need to improve the performance of equipment. If the number of users accessing the system increases, you may need a computer with faster processing capability, so that you can work more effectively.
- The need to carry out additional activities. New tasks may be added to your job, or new software is available which would enable you to carry out an activity using the computer rather than doing it manually.
- The decision by an organisation to upgrade its hardware or software across the organisation.
- The equipment is not capable of running a particular piece of software that you need to use.

Think about it – Level 2

How long have you had the computer and software that you are using? What tasks run slowly on your computer? Are you using the latest version of the software? Are there tasks that you can't do on your computer because it has not been upgraded recently? What upgrade would make the biggest difference to the way you work on your computer?

What the drawbacks of not upgrading may be

- If you have not upgraded the hardware or software you use for several years and the manufacturer stops producing it, in time the manufacturer may no longer provide support for it. So, if something goes wrong, you will not be able to fix it. This could mean that you cannot do your work.

- If you do not upgrade your system it is likely that you will not always be able to carry out tasks in the best possible way. Upgrades usually provide you with improved or new processing capability.

Think about it – Level 2

You are working in a busy architect's office and one of your main duties is to distribute building designs and plans both within the organisation and to clients all around the world. The standard operating system used in the company is Windows 2000 and you use AutoCAD 2003 to produce the designs. The latest version of AutoCAD cannot be installed as it won't run to its full capability with the operating system you are using.

Many of the organisation's competitors have upgraded their software already. What will happen to the business where you work if they don't upgrade their operating system soon?

The need to check compatibility of software and hardware upgrades with other parts of a system

- You sometimes need to use a new piece of software. You may not be able use it, or may not have full functionality, if your hardware, or operating system, is quite old.

- You may have a new piece of hardware but the software you are using, particularly the operating system, may be too old to run, or not have full functionality.

Case study

Sunshine Travel uses computers throughout the organisation. Most staff have access to computers throughout the working day. All the computers and printers are connected to a local area network which is maintained by the technical support team. Some staff have laptops, which they take to customers' premises. The company has a website to promote and market its goods and services. Staff have access to the company's intranet, where all standard documents and procedures are available.

In the **Finance Department** staff use:

* specialist software to keep the organisation's accounts

* spreadsheets to produce budgets and management information – these are not stored centrally

* word-processing software to send letters etc.

* e-mail as the main internal communication, and more and more for external communication

* the intranet to access company documents.

The technical support team provides network and PC support, maintaining all software services and the e-mail system. It is responsible for daily backups of all central data and software and there is a bespoke fault-reporting system to log and track faults.

1 How might you organise the Finance Department's files so that they are easy to find?

2 What type of maintenance tasks would you expect staff in the Finance Department to carry out?

3 Why might the organisation need to upgrade the hardware if the specialist accounts software was upgraded?

4 What non-routine maintenance might be carried out by the IT experts in the Finance Department?

Routine maintenance checklist

Section 1 – Cleaning	Frequency	Materials
Floppy-disk drive		
CD drive		
DVD drive		
Mouse		
Mouse mat		
Screen		
Cases		
Printer		
Desktop		
Section 2 – Printer materials		
Paper		
Ink toner/cartridge		

IT security for users

Introduction

Every user of an ICT system needs to be aware of the security risks to their equipment and their data, and what they must do to make sure that the system is safe and secure. Provided you are using your computer correctly and following all the required procedures and guidelines of the organisation, you should be able to achieve the evidence (of knowledge, understanding, skills and techniques) for this unit through your daily use of the computer as you produce evidence for some of the other units.

Day-to-day security risks

What you need to know and understand

- Risks to data from people
- Risks to data from hardware or software not working properly
- Risks of receiving and opening attachments from e-mail
- **Level 2** Risks of downloading software from the Internet

Risks to data from people

Theft

Most computer systems hold large amounts of data so it is important to work in a way that ensures that the data cannot be stolen. Identity theft is a rapidly growing crime – an individual's personal information is stolen and then used to gain access to systems such as credit cards; many people do not know this is taking place until a noticeable amount of money has been stolen. Business data is also vulnerable. Sensitive and valuable data, such as customer lists, financial information, and research-and-development data, is often the target of theft. Portable devices, such as laptops and PDAs (personal digital assistant), are also very vulnerable as they are so easy to steal that you need to make sure not to leave them lying around.

Think about it

The widespread use of IT makes it much easier for employees to steal important information from their employers.

According to research, almost 70 per cent of people have stolen key information from their workplace. The information most at risk is customer contact details, in the form of e-mail address books, and customer databases. Most of the stolen information is e-mailed to personal accounts; other information is burned to CD.

How vulnerable is the data where you work? Does your workplace remind employees of their obligations and responsibilities with regard to keeping data secure?

Viruses

A computer virus is a program which attacks your computer (usually without you knowing it) and can cause the computer to stop working properly. Some viruses affects software and others damage the data: however, not all viruses are harmful. Some viruses have an immediate effect while others can remain undetected until triggered into action by an event.

If your computer suddenly doesn't work as effectively as it usually does, for example it operates more slowly, or you lose data from files, it is possible that your system has become infected by a virus.

Viruses are written anonymously by programmers, usually with malicious intent, and are usually introduced through floppy disks, CDs and through network connections.

Think about it

Virus writers target topics or events that interest lots of people. They have targeted the 2006 World Cup, for example; worms and Trojans have been introduced, aimed especially at football fans from all over the world.

Businesses need to make sure that employees are vigilant about virus threats at all times, even when the e-mail and attachment appear to be harmless. Companies are known to send e-mails disguised as viruses to their staff in order to monitor their responses and identify those more easily enticed to open such messages or attachments.

Unauthorised access

All computer systems – that is, the software and the data stored on them – are at risk of being accessed by people who are not authorised to have access. These people are known as 'hackers'. The 1990 Computer Misuse Act defines three categories of crime that computer hackers may be involved in:

- The unauthorised access to computer material, which includes unauthorised use of a user ID and password, and trapping a computer user to reveal their password.
- The unauthorised access to a computer system with the intention of committing a further crime, which includes hacking into a system in order to fraudulently acquire money.
- The unauthorised modification of computer material, which involves corrupting and deleting programs and data, including infecting the computer with a virus.

Think about it

In the last few years there have been several cases in which a hacker has gained access to US military records and other government systems. When it occurs there is often a considerable amount of media coverage, but very little about what happens to those responsible afterwards. Are they prosecuted? And what sort of sentences do they get if they are found guilty? Does the legislation as it stands really protect the systems and the data?

Did you know that there are web groups where these hackers exchange tips and experiences?

This Act is now more than 15 years old, so new legislation is being introduced to take into account the considerable changes in computer systems during this time, and in particular the wide use of the Internet.

Risks to data from hardware or software not working properly

Faults

Computer data and software can be damaged if the equipment develops a fault. There are steps you can take to limit the effect of this:

- To reduce the impact of data-storage devices developing faults, make sure you frequently backup your data and your system setup. The technical staff within an organisation may be responsible for systems information.
- You should save your work regularly. Saving it every 10 minutes is thought to be reasonable.

Errors

Errors do occur when inputting data, so it is important to make sure that the validity and accuracy (integrity) of the data meets the standards required. Most software packages have a range of built-in checking facilities such as spelling checkers, however there is still considerable scope for making mistakes.

Integrity of data is the correctness of the data throughout its life in the system. To ensure this, there needs to be adequate checks for validity and accuracy at the point of data entry. The following are some of the checks:

- **Verification of data**   This involves checks to make sure that the data is entered accurately. For example, the data is entered into the computer twice by different people, the two versions are compared by the computer and any data with differences is rejected for checking and re-input.
- **Capture of appropriate data**   You should collect and store the data in the best way so that it will not need processing just to keep it current. For example, date of birth rather than age, as the latter changes and becomes inaccurate as time goes by.
- **Batch totals**   These are particularly important when handling numeric, mainly financial, data. For example, the total value of a set of invoices is calculated at the start of the input process. As each invoice is input the computer keeps a running total of all of the invoices. When the complete set (batch) has been input the computer compares the input total with the calculated total and will only accept the batch if the totals match.

- **Validation of data** This is needed to make sure that the data is an allowed value or response. For example, the payroll system may be set up to accept only a range of values if no one has a salary above or below a limit or, to make sure that only the correct names of an organisation's departments can be entered, they are selected from a 'pick list'.
- **Check digits** These are extra digits, usually in an account number, which are based on the numbers in the account number and their sequence. If any number is entered incorrectly, or the numbers are entered in the wrong order, then the check digit will indicate that this is not a valid account number. For example, your electricity or telephone account number has an additional digit which ensures that if any one digit of the code is entered incorrectly then it should be identified as an error *before* you get the bill! This doesn't mean that the bill is correct but it does mean that the bill is sent to the right person.
- **Onscreen checking** This is visual checking (proofreading). For example, when your account number is entered, your name is displayed on the screen for the operator to check before continuing with the rest of the input.

It is essential that there are adequate controls throughout processing to ensure that the data is not accidentally altered or destroyed during processing.

- **Control totals** These are produced by the system at various stages of a process, which should be checked manually as well as by the system to identify any errors or corruption of data. For example, in a cheque-printing system, during the first stage of the process, which involves identifying those suppliers for whom cheques are to be printed, the total value of all cheques will be calculated together with the total number of cheques. This control information will be printed and passed on to the next stage of the process. As the cheques are printed, a running total will be made of the values together with a count of how many cheques. These second process control totals will be compared by the computer at the end of the process but should also be printed for a manual check.

Loss

It is extremely important that you look after your data. As we become more and more dependent upon electronic data storage, both at work and in our personal lives, so it becomes more important to make sure that this data is not lost or destroyed.

To protect your data from being lost you will need to:

- make sure that only authorised people can access the data – see 'Control of access to hardware and software' below
- carry out regular backups – see Unit 5: IT maintenance for users, page 116.

Risks of receiving and opening attachments from e-mail

Viruses can be introduced into any computer which communicates externally with another electronic source. The most common ways for viruses to get into your computer are from files attached to e-mails, from files downloaded from the Internet, or from files being copied from an external storage device such as a floppy disk.

Take care with any e-mails from an unknown source. Many organisations will have guidelines about handling e-mails with attachments from an unknown source, particularly where there is no subject information.

Think about it

Did you know that more than 1000 e-mail messages are sent every second in the UK? However, nine out of ten of these are unwanted messages, spam, being sent out by companies and virus writers. The finance industry is responsible for more of these unsolicited e-mails than any other.

Risks of downloading software from the Internet

Anyone can put anything on the Internet, which raises risks in downloading software from the Internet, even though it may be an invaluable source of information. You need to be cautious. In many organisations, only a member of the computer support team is allowed to download software for staff. This reduces the risk of software infected with a virus being introduced into the system; it also makes sure that only software with a valid licence is used. (See Unit 5: IT maintenance for users, page 126.)

Control of access to hardware and software

What you need to know and understand

- Recognise the importance of controlling access
- Ways to control access to common hardware
- **Level 2** Ways to control access to common storage media
- **Level 2** Ways to control other people from editing data
- **Level 2** Ways to control access to common software

Recognise the importance of controlling access

The first line of defence against many of the risks above is to restrict access to the computer systems so that only authorised users can use them.

Ways to control access to common hardware

There are several ways to control access to hardware. There are physical controls:

- Locking doors to an area where sensitive data is held. Although a very simple and basic access control, it is still a valid means of limiting access.
- Ensuring that visitors to areas are not able to view the data that appears on computer screens: for example, taking care in positioning equipment, particularly in areas where access is not restricted; users following procedures about exiting from software, particularly to avoid leaving sensitive data visible onscreen.

There are also a number of logical controls:

- **Passwords**   Most computers in the workplace are set up so that they can only be used if you have a valid user name and password.
- **Changing passwords**   Regularly changing user passwords reduces the risk of unauthorised use. For example, in most organisations the system will automatically prompt you after a set number of days to change your password.
- **Communications controls**   These ensure that only authorised people can connect to the computer from an external link. For example, a system known as 'dial-back' is used by many organisations. When a user – for example, a home worker or someone based at another site – connects to the computer, the system knows from the user's login and password who they are and will have details of the authorised user's phone number. The link is immediately disconnected and the computer 'dials-back' to the external system from which they will be connecting.

At work your computer systems will almost certainly be protected by a firewall. You should make sure that you also have one on your own computer. A firewall is a piece of software which blocks unwanted traffic from entering your computer. The anti-virus software works in conjunction with the firewall and scans the files that are allowed in to make sure that they are safe.

Check it yourself

How is access to your computer system controlled? What physical controls are in place? Can anyone access any computer? Do you have to use a password to use your computer? How frequently do you have to change it? Are there requirements on passwords such as the minimum number of characters, or the need for a mixture of numbers and letters?

Ways to control access to common storage media

Some removable storage media can be set to restrict access to the data:

- Floppy disks have a tab which can be opened so that the data can only be read but not overwritten.
- Non-rewritable CDs are used to provide data and software which cannot be altered or over-written.

Think about it

Passwords are the weakest link in the security of a system. A 'strong' password will be more difficult for anyone to guess, and this has become more important as 'password-guessing' software has become so sophisticated.

For your password to be strong it should be at least 7 characters long and should not be similar to your name or your user name. It should consist of a combination of letters, and this should include both upper and lower case letters, some numbers and at least one symbol.

How 'strong' are the passwords that you use?

Ways to control other people from editing data

One of the biggest problems with freely available access to documents in electronic form is that it is then very easy and straightforward to copy this information, or to edit it. Potentially, this can give rise to forgery and fraud.

Access to data can be restricted in a number of ways:

- You can set individual files with password protection so that they can only be read and not edited without the password (Figure 6.1).
- User profiles can be set up to provide access to data on a *need-to-know* basis. This means that access is denied to anyone unless they are positively identified as needing access to that system or data. For example, an organisation may require that all password levels have to be requested in writing by the user with a description of why he or she needs the data. This then has to be counter-signed by the line manager.
- There is software, such as Adobe Acrobat, that can be used to create documents in a protected dataformat (pdf). The software to read these files is freely available and can be downloaded from the Internet.

Figure 6.1 Password requested to open the file

Ways to control access to common software

Where software is shared in an organisation, user names and passwords will often be set up with different levels of access, so that only certain people in the organisation can access the software.

- **Permissions** This is a system which particularly operates on a network. For example, if you use a computer at work, your password will probably give access to the main set of programs such as the word-processing and spreadsheet packages, but if you do not work in the finance department you will not have access the accounts system.

Skills Protecting hardware, software and data

What you need to do

- Use a login identity (ID) and password to access computer systems
- Store personal data and software safely
- Back up data following guidelines
- Use anti-virus software to protect applications
- **Level 2** Set password levels on software and data
- **Level 2** Make backups of operating systems data
- **Level 2** Download software patches to fix any security flaws
- **Level 2** Take appropriate action to keep risks to a minimum

There is a wide range of tools and techniques that can be used to reduce or prevent these risks to your computer system. Remember, prevention is always better than the cure.

Use a login identity (ID) and password to access computer systems

Your login ID and password should never be disclosed to anyone else, nor should it be written down so that someone can find it or see it. You will need to show that you have used a system that required you to login.

Store personal data and software safely

It is very unlikely that you will be responsible for the protection of the software on your system; this is usually the responsibility of someone in the technical team. However, you need to be aware of the importance of keeping software disks secure to ensure that they are not used illegally, and also so that they do not get damaged.

Personal data relates to data about individuals, and the protection of it is covered by the Data Protection Act (see page 144). You will therefore need to show that you store this data safely and in line with your organisation's procedures to ensure that you comply with the legislation and that the data is safe.

Back up data following guidelines

See Unit 5: IT maintenance for users, page 116.

Use anti-virus software to protect applications

Anti-virus software helps detect a virus and often makes the infection harmless, either through destroying it or at least placing it in quarantine so that it is isolated from the rest of the system. You need to have anti-virus software running all the time on your system and it is essential that this is kept up to date as new viruses are being written and introduced all the time.

There are many anti-virus software programs available such as Norton Anti-virus, McAfee VirusScan, Sophos Anti-virus, and many others. All of these products will protect your computer system and can be set to alert you when new viruses are released; they also enable you to download the updates to your software.

You need to show that you are aware of the dangers of viruses to your system, the software and the data. You need to actively demonstrate that any disks you introduce are virus checked, and that files downloaded from the Internet or attached to an e-mail are free from any viruses.

Practical task

When did you last check your computer for viruses? How up to date is your anti-virus software?

Virus-check your computer system. Use the anti-virus software to check the files on a remote storage device such as a floppy disk.

Keep a note on how you did the task and include screenshots where possible.

Computer systems are particularly vulnerable to attack from viruses when you receive attachments to e-mails. Most anti-virus software can be set up to automatically scan attachments as they arrive in the system so that you can be sure that they are safe to open.

The steps below show how to set up an automatic scan using AVG Anti-virus, other packages will follow similar steps.

Step 1   You can configure your anti-virus software to perform automatic scans.

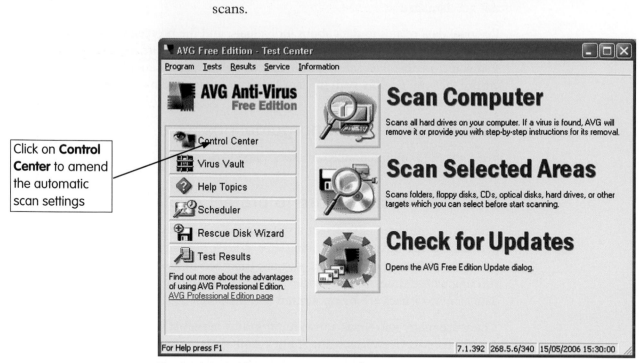

Click on **Control Center** to amend the automatic scan settings

Figure 6.2   Configuring anti-virus software

Step 2   Select the scanning option you wish to set (e.g. E-mail Scanner) and click on **Properties**.

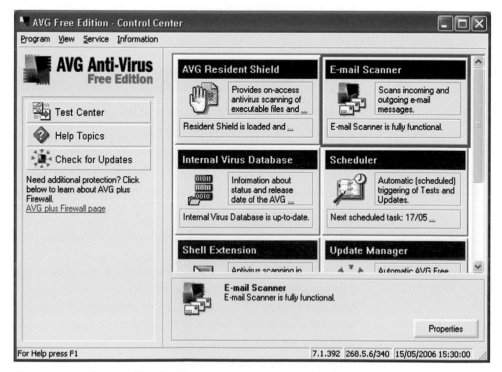

Figure 6.3   Advanced Settings

Step 3 Customise the scan settings, e.g. scan inbound e-mails, scan outbound e-mails etc.

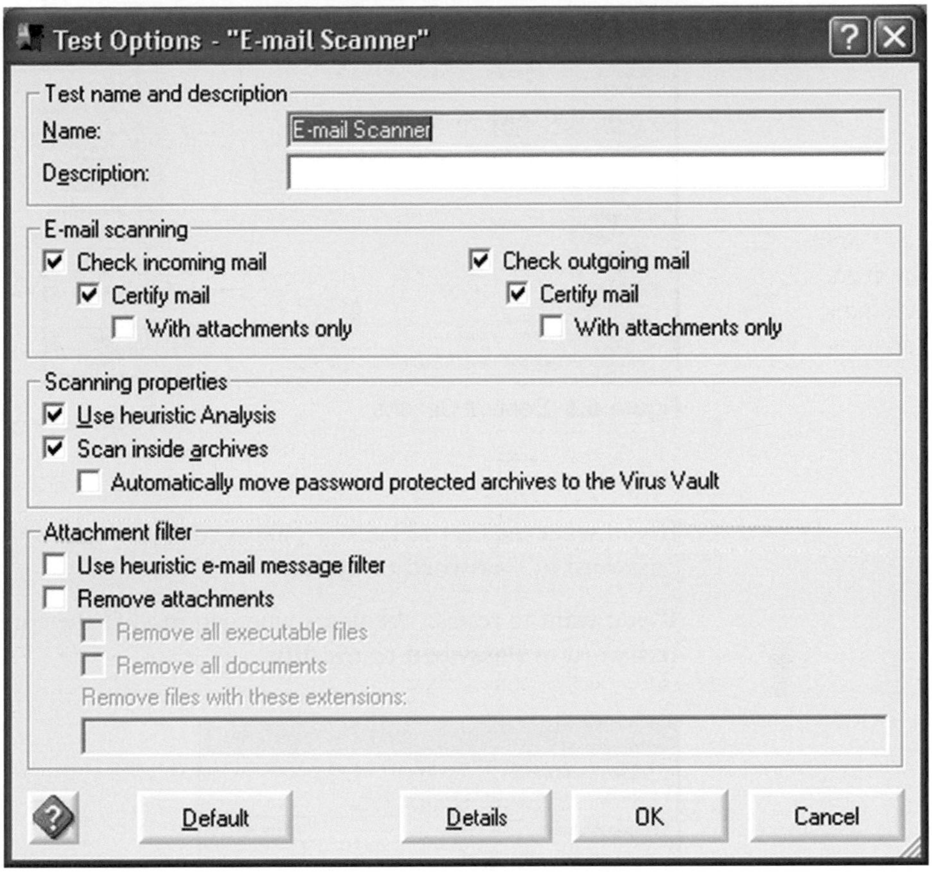

Figure 6.4 Advanced features

Set password levels on software and data

You are unlikely to have the authority to set up password levels for access to software, as this is not usually given to a user. However, you need to understand how to do it. You will need to have the opportunity to see how this is done.

Most general software applications have a tool that lets you password-protect a file. Some, such as spreadsheets, will let you protect areas of the worksheet to prevent unauthorised access. You will need to find out how to password-protect data in all the software applications that you use. To set passwords in Microsoft Excel:

Step 1 In the **File** menu, select **Save As**.

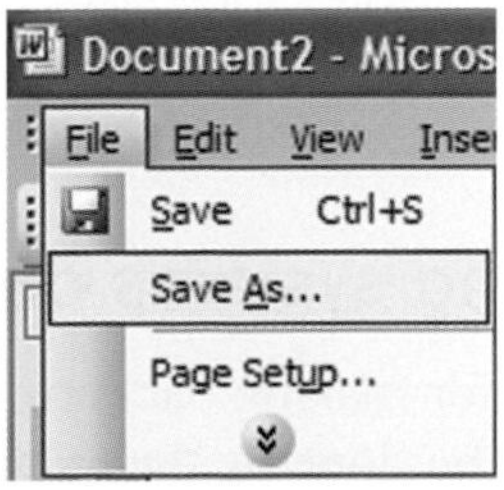

Figure 6.5 Save As

Step 2 In **Tools**, select **General Options**.

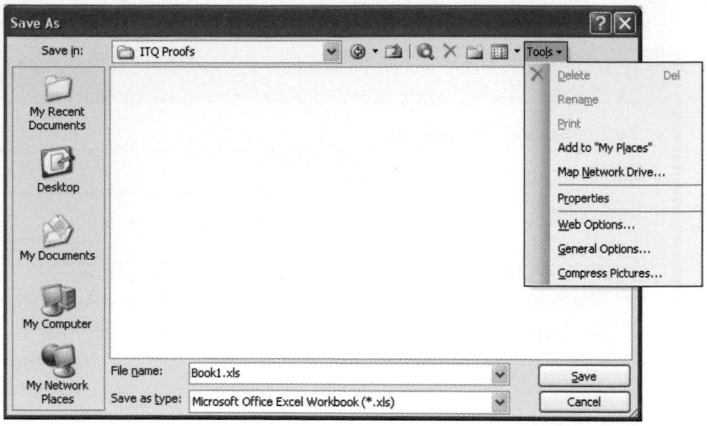

Figure 6.6 General Options

Step 3

If you want the user to know a password to view the spreadsheet, enter a password in **Password to open**.

If you want to restrict the users who can modify the spreadsheet, enter a password in **Password to modify**.

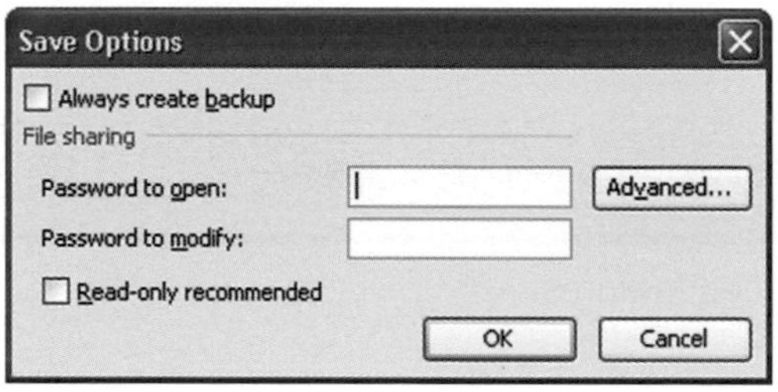

Figure 6.7 Viewing and restricting passwords

Step 4 Click on **OK**.

Level 2 practical task

For one document that you have created:

• Set a password to open the file (make sure you remember the password).

• Set a different password to allow a user to modify the file.

Keep a note on how you did the task and include screenshots where possible.

Make backups of operating systems data

It is unlikely you will be responsible for making backups of the operating system, as this will usually be done by the technical team. However, you need to know how to do it.

Download software patches to fix any security flaws

It is very rare for a piece of software to be completely error-free. Also, as new hardware and software is released, it is necessary for the software writers to add small sections of code to enable the software to work with these new products. These sections of program code are called patches.

It is extremely unlikely that you will have the authority to download these software patches and install them on your computer in the workplace, but you will need to find out how to carry out this process.

Take appropriate action to keep risks to a minimum

You will need to show that you take appropriate care and follow your organisation's guidelines when opening e-mails with attachments. Although you are unlikely to be able to download software to your computer in the workplace, you need to know how it is done and what actions are taken to ensure that this software will not damage the system.

Level 2 practical task

- Find out who is responsible for making backups of the operating system software in your organisation.
- Contact them and arrange a time when they can show you how it is done. Make notes, and keep this as evidence for your qualification.

Keep a note on how you did the task and include screenshots where possible.

What laws and guidelines affect use of IT

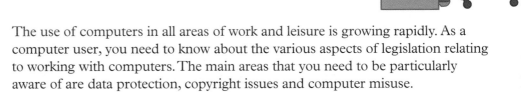

What you need to know and understand

- What laws and guidelines affect day-to-day use of IT
- **Level 2** How different IT activities are affected by laws and guidelines

The use of computers in all areas of work and leisure is growing rapidly. As a computer user, you need to know about the various aspects of legislation relating to working with computers. The main areas that you need to be particularly aware of are data protection, copyright issues and computer misuse.

What laws and guidelines affect day-to-day use of IT

Data protection

What is meant by data protection and why is it necessary?

- More and more information about people is being stored on computers and more and more people have easier access to it.
- Worldwide communication systems are becoming more powerful by the day. It is now possible to access data held almost anywhere in the world.
- The speed and processing power of computers means that data about individuals is more likely to be analysed and brought together.
- The increased use of computers in both business and the home means that almost anyone has access to this technology. The costs of online access is reducing rapidly, so this expansion will continue.

There are many advantages to such widespread computerised data access, however it requires individuals and organisations to handle it responsibly to ensure that personal data, and the individuals concerned, are protected. How many organisations do you think hold data about you in an electronic form?

Table 6.1 lists the likely computerised record holders for most people in the UK today. The list is by no means complete, but is intended to highlight the extent of electronic collection and storage of personal data. We seldom realise that the personal information we give to such organisations is going to be held as a permanent record, and we rarely think twice about supplying the details. Data users are required to advise you that this information will be held and to give you the opportunity to request that it is not made available elsewhere; however these conditions are often part of the small print so that you don't notice them.

While most users record this data for legitimate reasons, there are many organisations who 'sell on' mailing lists of personal information which frequently results in people receiving junk mail and unsolicited sales approaches.

Check it yourself

Go through the list in Table 6.1 and identify how many of these data users probably have data about you. Are there any others that you can think of? Add them to the list.

What is the legislation?

The legislation for data protection covers that which relates specifically to this country and is usually made by the passing of an Act of Parliament, and that which relates to the requirements of the European Union, which is usually set down as directives with which all member countries must then conform. The current British legislation is contained within the **1998 Data Protection Act**, which replaces the 1984 Act. The 1984 Act was concerned with 'Personal Data', that is, information about living, identifiable individuals which is 'automatically processed'. The 1998 Act sets rules for processing personal information and applies to organised paper records as well as those held on computer.

It is based upon eight guiding principles:

- Data must be processed lawfully and fairly – this includes the requirement that this data has also been obtained fairly and lawfully and that the data subject has been notified of the intention to process this data.
- Data must be held only for specified purposes – these have to be identified at registration.
- Data must be adequate, relevant and not excessive – the amount of data held should be the minimum necessary to meet the specified purposes.
- Data must be accurate and kept up to date.
- Data must not be held for longer than is necessary.

- Data subjects should be able to access their data and, where appropriate, have it corrected or deleted.
- Security systems must exist to ensure that unauthorised users cannot access, process, alter, destroy or disclose data.
- Data must not be transferred to a country outside the European Economic Area, unless that country has a similar level of protection for the rights of data subjects.

Organisation	Type of data	Tick the ones that apply to you
• Health Authority	• Personal details including name of doctor	☐
• Doctor	• Medical history	☐
• Local Authority	• Residential and possibly employment and benefit details	☐
• Bank	• Credit rating and history, some employment details	☐
• Employer	• Employment history, some medical records	☐
• DVLC Swansea	• Car and driving licence details	☐
• PNC	• Car details	☐
• Inland Revenue	• Tax and employment history	☐
• Education Authority	• Education and some family details	☐
• Insurance companies	• Motor – motoring offences, driving details and history	☐
	• Life – health, employment, family details	☐
	• Home – home security, value of possessions	☐
• Credit card and hire purchase companies	• credit rating, income, expenditure, life style	☐
• Societies and organisations e.g. AA, RAC, Reader's Digest etc.	• Limited but tend to have lifestyle details	☐
• Large retail outlets where you have used a credit card	• Basic personal details plus details of purchasing history	☐

Table 6.1 Organisations and data they hold

How does it work?

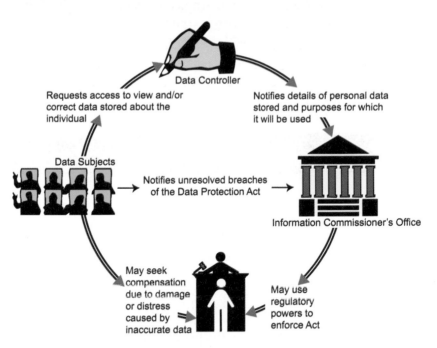

Data Controller

Requests access to view and/or correct data stored about the individual

Notifies details of personal data stored and purposes for which it will be used

Data Subjects

Notifies unresolved breaches of the Data Protection Act

Information Commissioner's Office

May seek compensation due to damage or distress caused by inaccurate data

May use regulatory powers to enforce Act

The **Information Commissioner's Office** has specific responsibilities for promoting and enforcing the Data Protection Act 1998. The organisation storing the data will have a **data controller**. This is the person who determines how and why data is to be processed in that organisation. The individuals whose data is stored are known as **data subjects**.

The main operational aspects of the 1998 Act are the requirements on all data controllers (those within an organisation who determine how and why data is to be processed) to:

- notify the Information Commissioner's Office of the details of the types of data they hold and for what purposes
- ensure that their systems have adequate controls to maintain the integrity of the data
- ensure that they have adequate security on their systems to safeguard against unauthorised access
- set up procedures to enable the data subject to access their data and to have corrected any inaccuracies, unnecessary records or misuse.

There is no requirement to notify manual records covered by the Data Protection Act, although they can be notified voluntarily.

The process of notifying the Information Commissioner's Office can be carried out either using the Internet, completing an online form or by telephone when a draft notification form is completed based on the information provided during the conversation and is then sent for confirmation.

The Data Protection Register, which contains the details supplied by the data controllers, is a public document maintained by the Information Commissioner's Office. A copy should be available in major public libraries and you can carry out a search on the website: *www.ico.gov.uk*.

Having identified and registered details of the personal data that is to be held, the data controller then needs to make sure that systems are set up to ensure the quality, accuracy and integrity of the data.

The legislation is designed to stop the storage of 'unnecessary' personal data. No data controller should be holding personal data without good reason, nor should data be kept for longer than is necessary. When data controllers register, they are required to specify the purpose for which they are holding the data. As a data subject you may challenge this and have the data deleted if you can demonstrate that there is no legitimate reason for keeping it, but first you need to be able to see exactly what is held.

The data subjects – the people that the data relates to – can request access to most data to check that the information is accurate and held for legitimate purposes. All registered data controllers are required to have a procedure for data subjects to gain access to their data.

Breaches of the data protection legislation

If you become aware of a breach in the legislation in your organisation, what should you do? First, you need to make sure you are familiar with the procedures within your organisation for dealing with this situation. If you are fully aware of the requirements of the law, but your colleagues or your supervisor are not, as the 'expert', and a responsible employee, you should advise them of the situation. This should be done as tactfully as possible, drawing their attention to the organisation's procedures for ensuring compliance with the legislation and dealing with any breaches.

Privacy and Electronic Communications (EC Directive) Regulations 2003

New regulations also came into effect from December 2003 relating specifically to sending e-mails for marketing purposes. There are two new rules that apply.

- **Rule 1** applies to all marketing messages sent by electronic mail, regardless of who the recipient is, and requires that the sender:
  - must not conceal their identity, and
  - must provide a valid address for opt-out requests.
- **Rule 2** only applies to unsolicited marketing messages sent by electronic mail to individual subscribers, and states that the sender:
  - cannot send such messages unless they have the recipient's prior consent to do so.

Disability

The Disability Discrimination Act 1995, which was updated in 2005, requires that employers make reasonable adjustments so that they do not discriminate against employees and customers with a disability. This may involve an organisation making adjustments in its working facilities to accommodate an employee with a disability. Specialist or adapted equipment will enable the employee to access the technology.

Many software applications have accessibility facilities to make the software easier to use. For example, it is possible to magnify part of a screen to make it easier for someone with a sight disability to use, and for those with a hearing disability there are screen readers that use a synthetic voice to read to the user as the cursor moves around the screen. There are many alternative devices that can be used for entering data into the computer, including joysticks, concept keyboards and other pointing devices. Voice recognition software has greatly improved and adaptive text software, similar to that used in mobile phones, can greatly improve text input.

Most websites are designed so that people with a disability can access them. There is guidance available as to what colours and layouts are most appropriate and that work effectively with screen readers. If you are using web-page-development software, you will need to clearly demonstrate that your pages are accessible.

Practical task

Select one of the sites that you use regularly and assess how accessible it is. Is there any information about accessibility on the site? Is there a magnifier available? What could make the site easier to use?

Keep a note on how you did the task and include screenshots where possible.

Health and safety

See Unit 3: Operate a computer, page 63.

Copyright

Copyright concerns the ownership of rights in printed and recorded materials and software. The current legislation in the UK is the Copyright, Designs and Patents Act of 1988. It restricts what you are allowed to copy, how many times and for what purposes. The contents of this book are covered by copyright law. The author and publisher had to make sure that the words and images did not 'belong' to anyone else. The copyright of the text in this book belongs to the author. If you wish to use something that belongs to someone else, you must seek permission, acknowledge their copyright and, usually, pay to be allowed to use it. If you don't, it is the same as stealing.

There are two different areas of concern regarding copyright and IT. One relates to software and the conditions under which you are permitted to use it and the other is about the use of data, images and text which are held in digital form.

Software

Software is very costly to produce and very easy to copy. When you acquire a piece of software you do not usually own it – what you have purchased is a licence to use it. There are many different types of software licences and it is always important to read the small print to make sure you are aware of what you can and cannot do with the software. The licence could be any one of the following:

- **Single-user licence** You may use this software on one computer only – the licence is usually for the user, who may transfer the software from one machine to another as long as it is used on only one machine at any time.
- **Multi-user licence** You may have an agreed number of users with access to this software – this may be by installation on a set number of computers, or it could be for specified numbers with network access.
- **Site licence** You may be licensed to use the software for all the users on a site – some software providers consider a site to mean a physical location, while others interpret it more loosely, so that it could mean a whole organisation.
- **Machine licence** Sometimes the software licence is attached to a particular computer rather than the user – in this instance you cannot transfer the software to a different computer without the permission of the copyright holder.
- **Server licence** On a network, the licence may be restricted, like a machine licence, to a particular network server.
- **Network licence** In a network environment you may have a licence for software to be used across the whole network – again there are a number of different ways the term network is interpreted. Most network systems software will be licensed under a network licence.

It is illegal to copy and use software in a way that has not been licensed. It is extremely unlikely that anyone working in an IT department would ask you to do this. However, someone who doesn't understand copyright could, unknowingly, ask you to use it illegally; for example, someone who has software on a computer at home and would like to use it at work. If this happens, you should politely explain the law and consult your supervisor.

There is software that is available on a different basis, such as shareware and freeware. This is software that may not have been developed by a commercial organisation and so there is not the same concern about loss of income through unauthorised copying.

- **Shareware** is usually freely distributed in an unsupported form. It will usually come with details of how you can pay a nominal charge which will entitle you to patches (corrections), add-ons (enhanced features) and updates.

- **Freeware** is software for which there is no charge, and can be freely distributed and used. This sort of software is not usually a full-feature application but often consists of a number of utilities and useful routines. This may be distributed through CD-ROMs attached to magazines etc., or it could be available on the Internet.

Own organisation's guidelines

Many organisations are reluctant to report or publicise the extent to which some of these illegal activities take place because of the damage it could do to their credibility. Most organisations will have some level of security for access to the buildings, the staff work areas (particularly if it is a place that is open to the general public), and the computer systems (mainly through passwords, location of equipment, etc.). However, much of this crime is brought about through failure to follow procedures. How easy is it to 'talk your way in' to the building where you work or study, or walk in unchallenged? How secure are your passwords? What procedures exist for handling confidential information? What should you do if you become aware of breaches of security or misuse?

Check it yourself

Produce a brief, word-processed report on the security systems in your organisation (this could be where you work, or at college). This will include information about getting into the building as an employee/student, arrangements for visitors, and areas open to the general public.

- Describe the procedures for access to the computer systems, both physical security and passwords. If possible, include an example of a breach of security and how it was dealt with.

How different IT activities are affected by laws and guidelines

In recent years the development of technologies that enable data, images and text to be readily captured and held in digital form has considerably increased concern about copyright. All the aspects of copyright in the print world now also apply in the digital world, but are more complex and potentially more difficult to control.

Scanners and software, which not only capture images and store them electronically but also have the capability to convert scanned text pages into text characters that can then be manipulated through word processors etc., are now very cheaply and readily available. Access to the Internet, and the ability to freely download information in any form, provides a major potential source of information. This means that large quantities of words can be rapidly stored, altered and transmitted across networks. It also means that in the course of your everyday work, it would be easy to reproduce text and images belonging to someone else, without considering whether you are breaching copyright regulations.

Storing personal data (e.g. names and addresses)

All users of computer systems must make sure that they comply with the requirements of the Data Protection Act when they are working with personal data. You will need to be able to demonstrate the procedures that you follow to ensure that this data is safe and used correctly. You will need to know what procedures are in place to ensure that this data cannot be accessed by unauthorised users. Remember – you also need to make sure that this data is kept secure when it comes out of the computer; make sure that printouts of personal data are also securely stored or disposed of.

Think about it – Level 2

How often do you enter your personal details, such as name, address and telephone number, on to a form? Most of the time this information is stored in a system covered by the Data Protection Act.

Do you check to make sure that there is a statement about what will be done with this data? There will usually be a check box that you can tick to restrict the use of the information other than for the original reason for which you are supplying it.

Downloading images from Internet

The Internet is a rich and varied resource for images. However, you will need to make sure that you follow appropriate procedures to ensure that you do not put your computer system at risk when you download images and other data from the Internet. You will need to make sure that you do not download files with viruses, by using appropriate anti-virus software. You will also need to demonstrate that you have checked the copyright status of these files to make sure that you can use them.

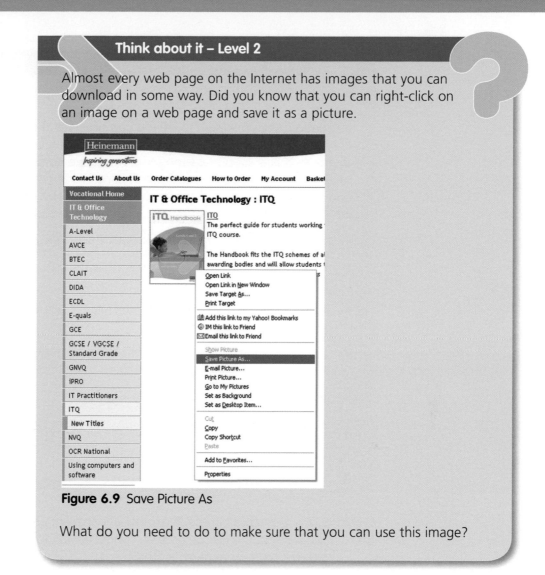

Think about it – Level 2

Almost every web page on the Internet has images that you can download in some way. Did you know that you can right-click on an image on a web page and save it as a picture.

Figure 6.9 Save Picture As

What do you need to do to make sure that you can use this image?

Inappropriate e-mails

The ease with which most individuals can access e-mail systems raises issues of security. High-risk or confidential information can very easily be distributed across such a system. All users need to be aware of this and, in particular, the immediacy of e-mail. If a piece of paper is put in an envelope for the post, there are many stages along the way when it could possibly be intercepted, but with e-mail once the send button is pressed there is little that can be done. In addition to this, one of the main sources of computer viruses nowadays is from external e-mail systems. Great care should be taken when reading unsolicited mail from an unknown source, and particularly when opening attachments.

A number of legal cases recently have helped to give e-mail the same legal status as paper-based documentation. E-mails are subject to the same libel, privacy and obscenity laws as paper-based communications. The Regulation of Investigatory Powers (IRIP) Act puts e-mail on the same standing as telephone calls and letters, allowing the interception of e-mail by government. Corporations can monitor employees' e-mail as long as they have stated their plans to do so.

Case study

Sunshine Travel uses computers throughout the organisation. Most staff have access to computers throughout the working day. All the computers and printers are connected to a local area network, which is maintained by the technical support team. Some staff have laptops which they take to customers' premises. The company has a website to promote and market its goods and services. Staff have access to the company's intranet where all standard documents and procedures are available.

In the **Personnel Department (Human Resources)** they use:

- word-processing software to communicate with staff and applicants

- an HR software package to keep records of sickness, qualifications and other personal data

- e-mail as the main internal communication, and more and more for external communication

- the Internet and intranet to advertise jobs.

1 What information will the Personnel Department be using that is covered by the Data Protection Act?

2 What sort of security should they have to make sure that this data is kept safe?

3 Many files stored in the Personnel department are confidential. What controls could be used to restrict access to the files and to prevent them from being edited?

4 What aspects of the copyright legislation relates particularly to the IT systems in this department?

Specialist or bespoke software

- What the purposes for using IT are
- What tools and functions can be used

Introduction

This unit is about being able to select and use a suitable specialist or bespoke software application to carry out your work. The unit is particularly for people in work who are using software that has been written for a special application and where the functions cannot be directly related to one of the more general applications units, for example an accounts package, music-composition and editing software, logistics-planning application etc. Some organisations will have had a software application specifically written for them so that particular tasks can be carried out; this is known as a bespoke application, for example stock control, credit management, engineering diagnostic etc.

The type of evidence that you produce for this unit will depend entirely upon the specialist or bespoke software used. You will need to be able to show that the tasks you have done can demonstrate your knowledge, understanding, skills and techniques to the required level.

What the purposes for using IT are

What you need to know and understand

- Why the software that was used was appropriate for the task
- Why and how using the software was an appropriate way of carrying out the task

Why the software that was used was appropriate for the task

You will need to show that you have thought about what you have done, what software you have used, and why. Would another piece of software have been as good? You will need to show that you have thought about whether the particular task would be done better using a different piece of software. Could a database package have produced the information needed, and as easily? You will need to show that you have an understanding as to what makes this software different and why.

Case study

Sunshine Travel uses computers throughout the organisation. Most staff have access to computers throughout the working day. All the computers and printers are connected to a local area network which is maintained by the technical support team. Some staff have laptops which they take to customers' premises. The company has a website to promote and market its goods and services. Staff have access to the company's intranet where all standard documents and procedures are available.

In the **Payroll Section** they use:

- a payroll package to manage the staff pay system
- spreadsheets to produce budgets and management information
- word-processing software to send letters etc.
- e-mail as the main internal communication, and more and more for external communication

Case study continued

The company uses the payroll software to calculate the wages for both weekly and monthly paid staff. The tax and National Insurance contributions are deducted and the software produces the information to pay staff directly into their bank accounts. Staff in the section regularly edit the details to ensure that staff are paid the correct amount and reports can be produced to analyse the company's pay costs.

1   Could other software applications be used to calculate the pay? Which ones might be used? Find out why they would not be as appropriate.
2   Carry out some research to find out about payroll software. What other features might it include?
3   What information that is used by the Payroll system will be required by other departments, such as HR? How might the relevant data be made available?

Why and how using the software was an appropriate way of carrying out the task

You need to ask the question 'Are there other ways of doing it?'. You need to be able to justify why using IT systems and the appropriate software will give you what is required. You also need to ask the question 'Is it always best to use a computer?'. There will be times when the answer is 'No' and you need to be able to explain why.

Level 2 case study

In the **Sales Department** of Sunshine Travel they use a CRM (customer relations management) system to keep track of all their customer contacts and sales opportunities.

Every customer has an account for which there may be multiple contact names and numbers. Whenever any form of contact is made (phone call, visit, e-mail, meeting or sale) the details are recorded in the system. All appointments – that is, planned contacts – are also recorded to make sure that the complete picture is always available.

Staff in the sales team always retrieve all activity information about a customer before they make further contact – they will not visit a customer without knowing what has happened previously, and so can be sure that they have the complete picture of the relationship that already exists.

It is also possible to use the system to make direct contact with the customers through e-mail and it can also be used with word-processing software to produce letters to customers.

The system can be used to produce a range of management reports and the data is also exported to other applications packages, such as spreadsheets, to carry out analysis and produce statistical reports.

1   Could this type of information be provided without using CRM software?

2   The use of this type of software has grown enormously in the last ten years. Carry out some research on CRM systems and their use to find out about the range of functions that are available.

3   What types of information might the sales team search for in the CRM system before they contact a customer?

4   What applications might you use to process information exported from the CRM system?

What tools and functions can be used

• What the tools and functions of software applications can be used for
• How to select and use appropriate tools and functions for the tasks

What the tools and functions of software applications can be used for

You will be using a number of the functions available in your specialist software. You will need to agree with your supervisor which functions you should know about and how to use them. You will need to make sure that you know what the purpose is of each of the functions and when they should be used.

Case study

In the **warehouse** of Sunshine Travel they use:

- specialist stock-control software to manage the levels of stock available
- e-mail as main internal communication, and more and more for external communication.

As the goods for a customer's order are taken off the shelves and packed, the staff in the warehouse enter the details into the stock-control system and the stock level for each item is immediately updated.

The warehouse manager has set a minimum stock level for each item held in the warehouse. This is used to help the manager order more stock so that they do not run out of anything.

Orders to suppliers are created every day. These are created using information from the stock-shortages report. This shows all the stock items that are below the minimum stock level.

When goods are received from suppliers, the details are entered into the stock-control system and the stock level for each item is immediately updated.

The warehouse manager receives a report every month which shows how much is in stock for every item. This information is used to carry out a stock check. This is to make sure that the information in the stock-control system matches the actual stock on the shelves.

The stock-control system is also used by staff in the sales team. They use it to check that there is enough in stock when they confirm an order with a customer.

1 Carry out some research to find out about stock-control software.

2 What other features might it include?

3 The stock-control system needs to be accurate. What types of validation would you expect to find as the data is input?

4 What alternative software could be used to record and monitor stock levels? Why is a specialist package more appropriate?

How to select and use appropriate tools and functions for the tasks

It is not sufficient for you to know about the functions and how to use them. You must also be able to decide which function to use to carry out a particular task.

Check it yourself

List each of the functions in your software that you know about in the Functions checklist on page 165. For each function you will need to write a brief description of what the function is used for. You also need to describe a task that you have used it for.

Skills Handling files

What you need to do

- Use file-handling techniques for the software

Use file-handling techniques for the software

Many software packages have very similar commands for handling files. You will usually be able to use the basic tools of any application software either by using the menu system or through icons in a toolbar. You may also be able to use a combination of keys, known as a keyboard shortcut. The main commands you will need to be familiar with are:

- **Open** This command is used to access the contents of a file. It will open a document and display it on the screen ready for you to work on.
- **Close** When you have finished using a file it is extremely important to make sure that you close it. This will ensure that it is safely stored on the disk – most software will give you a message to save any changes if you try to close a file without first saving it.

- **Save**   You will need to use this to save a file with the current filename. If you wish to keep the original file but save a new version with a different filename, or save it in a different storage space, you will need to use the **Save As** command.

- **Print**   You will use this command to get a hard copy (printout) of the document. When using the print command you will be able to select the exact page or pages that you want to print, the number of copies that you want, and the printer that you wish to use.

Practical task

For your software, explore all the standard file-handling techniques of the software that you use and show that you know how to use them all.

Keep a note on how you did the task and include screenshots where possible.

Skills Combining information

What you need to do

- Use basic techniques to combine information
- **Level 2** Add information from one type of software to information produced using different software

Use basic techniques to combine information

The specialist software that you use must have a function to join information together. You will need to find out how to do this and then you will need to use it on at least one occasion. It may involve joining two files together, possibly inserting one inside another. It could include merging of two sets of data to produce the final result.

Add information from one type of software to information produced using different software

At Level 2 you must be able to use information from two application packages. You might need to take the data from your specialist software and put it into a spreadsheet in order to carry out some calculations, or into a database in order to sort or select some information.

Practical task

For the software that you use:

- Carry out a task that needs you to join two sets of data together.
- Create a simple step-by-step set of instructions to describe how to do this.

Keep a note of how you did the task and include screenshots where possible.

Skills Entering, editing and processing information

What you need to do

- Use appropriate techniques for entering, editing and processing information

Use appropriate techniques for entering, editing and processing information

You will need to carry out tasks that will involve entering data and editing it. You also need to carry out some form of processing to turn the data into information. What type of process used will depend upon the specialist software. In a stock-control system this could include producing a list of stock items that are below the minimum stock level, or a stock list for a stock check.

Skills Checking information

What you need to do

- Use appropriate techniques to check information.

Use appropriate techniques to check information

Accuracy is one of the most important aspects of data processing; if the data is not accurate, you will not be able to produce useful information. There may be tools available within the software to check text data, such as a spellchecker. You will also need to use proofreading techniques to visually check your data, both text and numbers.

If you are working with images, you will need to check the quality of the graphics, make sure that the images are of an appropriate size for the task, and that labels are accurate and correctly positioned.

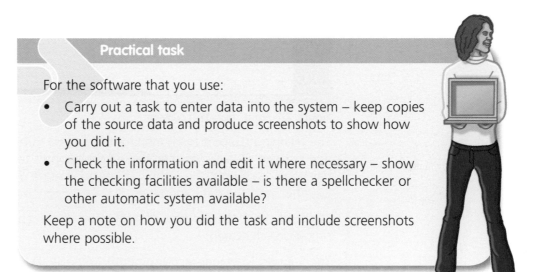

Practical task

For the software that you use:

- Carry out a task to enter data into the system – keep copies of the source data and produce screenshots to show how you did it.
- Check the information and edit it where necessary – show the checking facilities available – is there a spellchecker or other automatic system available?

Keep a note on how you did the task and include screenshots where possible.

Case study

Sunshine Travel's **technical support team** provide network and PC support, maintaining all software services and the e-mail system. They are responsible for daily back ups of all the central data and software. To help carry out this service they use:

- a bespoke fault-reporting system to log and track faults
- e-mail as the main internal and external communication.

Faults and service requests are logged on the fault-reporting system that has been designed to meet their particular requirements. Staff within the organisation can log the faults themselves, or can call to speak to a technical support person on the help desk. All calls to the help desk are logged on to the system by the technician.

Figure 7.1 Fault-reporting system

The technical support team monitor the system throughout the day and jobs are allocated to members of the support team. When a job has been dealt with, the technician records details of the action taken together with the date and time.

Staff can check the progress of a fault they have reported using a simple search screen.

The Support Manager receives monthly reports showing the number of faults that have been reported and dealt with, and an analysis of the types of faults and the time taken to respond. The system can be interrogated to find out about faults that are outstanding at any specific time, and to show those that have not been dealt with in a reasonable time.

1 Search to find a help-desk software package.
2 What other functions does this software offer?
3 What other types of software application could be used to provide the information for the help desk?
4 What sort of information would the technicians combine with the e-mail system, and why?

Functions checklist

Software tools and techniques		
Tool	What used for	Task

Evaluate the impact of IT

- What effect use of IT has on individuals and organisations
- How to improve access to IT
- What security risks there may be
- How IT can improve learning
- Health and safety issues

Introduction

This unit is about how you and others use IT and how it has affected how we live and work. This is largely a theoretical unit. You are expected to think about what you do and how IT affects the way we work. It is also about how you can improve your knowledge, understanding, skills and techniques in the use of IT and therefore the prospect of better job opportunities.

What effect use of IT has on individuals and organisations

Ways that use of IT affects what people do – at home, in work, at school, leisure

IT is a part of our lives; we use it almost without thinking. Our homes are filled with the technology we use on a daily basis. Washing machines, microwave ovens, and many other appliances in the kitchen use IT to automate and control how they work. Digital-television programmes enable us to make choices: we can decide which football match to watch, or which favourite competitor in a game show or football match to vote for, just by using the television remote.

Many jobs have changed because of IT. Businesses can store and access information using the technology, which means that many employees need to have good IT skills to do many of the jobs required. People can use the technology to conduct business around the world without needing to move from their computer.

Computers are used in education. Websites can be accessed to find out information and to revise for exams. Homework can be done on a computer and it can even be sent electronically to the teacher.

IT has become an essential tool for health care. Hospitals, doctors' surgeries and your local chemist all use computer systems to keep records of their patients. A doctor can call up onscreen a complete medical history of a patient and can monitor a patient's illnesses and treatment. Heart monitors, X-ray machines and cameras controlled by robotic arms for carrying out surgery, are examples of the range of technology used in medicine today.

The computer-games leisure industry is huge; millions of households have dedicated games consoles for playing these games. On a visit to the cinema or to a football match, the information you see displayed on huge screens, and the constant updates, is generated by electronic technology. The tickets will be sold using IT, either over the Internet or at the ticket office, as are mailings with the latest news of events.

Think about it

How does IT affect your life – at home, in work or at school, and in your leisure time? For each of these, make a list of where and for what you use technology. Find out how different this is from five years ago.

Benefits of gathering and organising business information using IT

Computers have changed the way information is used in business. Information can be stored and shared among many people, and contacts can be made around the world, almost instantly. The systems for paying for goods and services have become very sophisticated and business-to-business financial activity is almost entirely electronic.

Many people seldom use cash to buy things; they mainly use electronic methods such as debit or credit cards. Supermarket shopping can be paid for with your bank card, and you can also get 'cash back' if you need it.

Many businesses now have a website. This may be a simple site with information about the organisation and how to contact it; however, some businesses have very sophisticated sites and it may be their main way of operating.

A business's information could be at risk from viruses and hackers accessing confidential information; so they need to make sure that their system is secure from viruses and hacking – see Unit 6: IT security for users.

Many organisations gather a large amount of information about their customers; they know what you buy regularly in their shops if you have a loyalty card and can send you details of special offers on the types of products that they know you buy. Businesses that sell goods on the Internet are able to build up a profile of their customers and can then make suggestions as to what they might be interested in the next time that they visit the site.

How online services are changing people's access to information

The Internet has had an enormous impact across the world. The World Wide Web gives almost instant communication to anywhere in the world. We also use the Internet for many daily tasks.

- **Banking** You can access your bank account details without going to the bank. You can check to see how much money you have, you can pay your bills and organise a loan.
- **Shopping** The process of buying goods and services online is much easier than having to physically go to different places to buy what you want. You can buy what you want from a wide range of providers, you can put your purchases in a 'shopping basket', pay for it electronically, and

have it delivered to your door. All large supermarkets offer this service and record what you buy each time, so that you can just amend your last 'shopping list' for the extras that you need next time (Figure 8.1).

View basket		**Checkout**	
⊖ 1 ⊕	Tesco Healthy Eating Semi-Skimmed Milk 1.136ltr/2 Pints	0.53
⊖ 1 ⊕	Flora Vegetable Spread500g	0.98
⊖ 1 ⊕	T Healthy Living Skinless 2chicken Breast Fillets 250-319g	3.01
⊖ 1 ⊕	Finest Sweet Pointed Peppers Twinpack	1.28
⊖ 1 ⊕	Spring Onions Bunch	0.49
⊖ 2 ⊕	Courgettes Loose Class 1	0.80
⊖ 1 ⊕	Tesco Spinach 300g	0.96
⊖ 1 ⊕	A Bag of White Seedless Grapes Class 1 Loose (approx. 500g - 650g per bag)	1.62
⊖ 3 ⊕	Loose Oranges Class 1 Each	0.54
⊖ 6 ⊕	Bananas Loose	0.72
⊖ 1 ⊕	Kingsmill Wholegrain & White Medium 800g	0.88
⊖ 2 ⊕	Schweppes Lemonade 2 Ltr Bottle	1.68
Total guide price		£13.49

Figure 8.1 Shopping online

Many people buy holidays online. They can search for the best deals, or design their own itinerary, and most companies offer discounts to those who buy in this way.

- **Keeping in touch**   E-mail and chatrooms make it easy to keep in touch and to make new friends. For many it is the primary method of contacting friends and family all over the world. You can also attach pictures and photos to your e-mail so that important occasions can be shared, almost instantly. However, you must beware of unwanted e-mail. Make sure you have software to protect you and your systems from unwanted mail, some of which can be offensive, and from viruses that can damage your systems.

- **Public services online**   Central government and local authorities have websites to provide information about the services available. You can go online to find out about local news, how to pay bills, search for planning information, search for jobs, find out about parking, and a lot more (Figure 8.2).

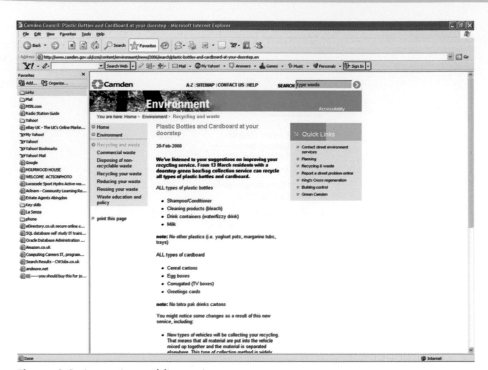

Figure 8.2 Accessing public services

Where and how to find information about changes and developments to hardware and software

New IT software, hardware, and better ways of using the technology are developing all the time. Therefore, it is important to keep up to date with these changes.

The Internet is one of the main sources of information about IT developments. The main computer hardware and software companies' websites are a good starting point for finding out about new products and services. When buying computer equipment and software you will usually have the opportunity to register with the manufacturer as a user. Many of these manufacturers will contact you to let you know about developments – often through an e-mail or other Internet message.

There are also websites that give advice about hardware and software and to help you keep up to date. Use a search engine to help you find these sites. Type in the key words, such as 'Word Processing' or 'CD Drives', that are most likely to direct you to sites of interest.

There are computer newspapers and magazines that give you up-to-date information on developments, such as *PC World, Computer Buyer, Computer Weekly*. Some are quite general and cover a wide range of topics, but others focus on a particular area or type of user. For example, there are magazines for networking, project management, and also for IT in the public sector, or banking.

A local library and college has information about courses and other events that can help to keep you up to date with IT developments; you can also search on the Internet for these.

How to improve access to IT

What you need to know and understand

- How using IT can improve people's access to information
- **Level 2** What difficulties some people have in using IT
- **Level 2** What difficulties some people have in accessing documents that have been produced using IT
- **Level 2** Where to get advice about software and equipment that can help people use IT

How using IT can improve people's access to information

IT can empower people, particularly those with restricted access. It has made a huge difference to people with disabilities. It means not having to leave their home to access information, which they can get on the Internet.

Increasingly, information is being stored on computers and the development of powerful, easy-to-use searchable databases has made this information easy to find. For example, to find out where your ancestors lived, you can access the appropriate census databases, or the electoral roll.

You can also access the information when you want to; it is not time restricted, as much of it is available on the Internet. It is there when you connect up, regardless of the time of day.

What difficulties some people have in using IT

There are a wide range of hardware and software solutions to assist people who have difficulty using IT. For example, there are alternatives to a standard mouse; a small mouse may be needed for making very small finger and hand movements, or a joystick or roller ball may be more suitable for moving the cursor around the screen. There are also different ways to enter text and numbers than by using a standard keyboard. Special overlays can make sure that only one key is pressed at a time, and a variety of special keyboards are available to meet many users' needs, such as keys with raised Braille characters for visually-impaired users.

Computers can recognise the human voice. Voice recognition software can now be used by visually-impaired users to input information with quite a high level of accuracy – the software can even be made to understand a particular voice and accent.

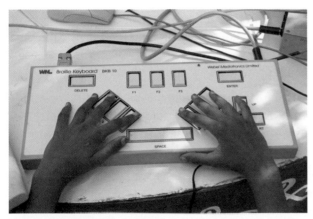

Figure 8.3 A Braille keyboard

There are accessibility guidelines for the development of websites. Certain colours and features are difficult for people with visual impairment; for example, flash animations can be hard to see. People with visual impairment can use screen reader software to tell them what is on the screen as they move a cursor on the screen. Images that do not have alternative text or complex images, such as graphs or charts, are often not well described.

The digital divide

There are also many people who have difficulty accessing IT because of their circumstances.

- **Cost** Although the cost of buying equipment and software has fallen considerably over the years, it is still beyond the means of many people. There are still people who cannot afford a telephone and who definitely cannot afford the cost of Internet access.

- **Location** The level and speed of Internet access is different in different parts of the country; it is usually more limited in rural areas. The public transport is also more restricted in these areas and therefore it is more difficult to get to locations where there are Internet facilities can be accessed. The people in the world's less-developed countries also, generally, have less access to the information on the World Wide Web.

- **Skills** Many people still do not have the skills required to access electronic information. They may lack the IT skills and the opportunities to learn, and may not have the literacy skills to make use of the information they find.

- **Age** Young people are familiar with the IT age: they use computers at school, are familiar with electronic tills in shops, spend much of their leisure time in playing computer games and accessing the Internet. However, many older people, particularly those who have not been in employment in recent years, may not be so familiar with computers and will not be regular users. Even so, there is an ever-increasing number of 'silver surfers' – i.e. retired people who use the Internet on a regular basis.

What difficulties some people have in accessing documents that have been produced using IT

Computer-generated documents are often better presented and can be more easily reproduced. However, for people who are visually impaired the documents will need to be made more readable. This can be achieved by increasing the size of the text font and the line spacing using features of the software.

There is also software for converting text into Braille for people who are not able to see the printed word; this can then be printed by special Braille printers. This makes much of the information on the Internet accessible to those who cannot see the printed word.

Similar software packages can be used to convert text to an audio file which can be recorded on to CD for those who are hearing impaired.

Where to get advice about software and equipment that can help people use IT

There are specialist organisations, such as RNIB, who provide advice about the range of software and equipment that can be used. Find out about these organisations and how to contact them by searching on the Internet. Most have very informative and helpful websites describing what is available.

Figure 8.4 RNIB provides advice on software and equipment

Local and central social services departments also have information on their websites and at their offices. They may also have a scheme to assist people with getting the appropriate software and equipment to help them in their work and home life.

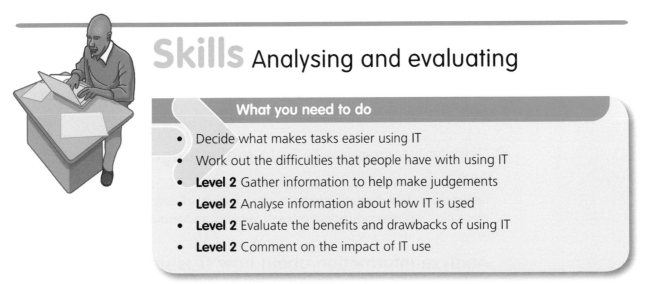

Skills Analysing and evaluating

What you need to do

- Decide what makes tasks easier using IT
- Work out the difficulties that people have with using IT
- **Level 2** Gather information to help make judgements
- **Level 2** Analyse information about how IT is used
- **Level 2** Evaluate the benefits and drawbacks of using IT
- **Level 2** Comment on the impact of IT use

Here you need to carry out a small project. It could relate to your own use of IT, but would be better if you could extend this to include your friends or colleagues.

Practical task

Using the headings below, carry out a small investigation about IT and the benefits of using it. You will need to consider the advantages and drawbacks for both the people using IT and in terms of the finished product.

For example, you may produce publicity material which you distribute to your company's customers each month. This may involve using desktop-publishing software to produce the material, a database with names and addresses of the customers (which could be accessed either through a spreadsheet or a database package), and word-processing software to produce the letter that is sent out with the material.

Present your findings in a report. This report does not have to be a formal written document, you might wish to create it as a presentation or a set of web pages – use it as a way of demonstrating your skills.

Keep a note on how you did the task and include screenshots where possible.

Decide what makes tasks easier using IT

This is where you need to think about the different ways of doing the tasks and why using IT makes it easier. Can you get better information? Is it quicker? Do you need to share it with others? Will it be more accurate and reliable?

Work out the difficulties that people have with using IT

What are the problems that people can have with using IT? Do they have the skills? What if the computer goes wrong?

Gather information to help make judgements

You will need to use more than one example to be able to draw valid conclusions. It is also a good idea to use a variety of different uses of IT as these may well show different types of benefits and issues.

Analyse information about how IT is used

You need to look at all the information you have collected and discuss what it means.

Evaluate the benefits and drawbacks of using IT

You need to compare and contrast. You may wish to present this in a table form which will then help you to compare each aspect.

Comment on the impact of IT use

You need to arrive at a conclusion based on what you have found out. Do the benefits outweigh the drawbacks? You should be able to discuss this in some detail.

What security risks there may be

What you need to know and understand

- Risks to data from people
- Risks to data from hardware or software not working properly
- Risks of receiving and opening attachments from e-mail
- **Level 2** Risks of downloading software from the Internet

See Unit 6: IT security for users, page 131.

How IT can improve learning

What you need to know and understand

- Identify the different types of IT-based learning materials and activities available
- **Level 2** Compare the benefits and drawbacks of e-learning with other methods of learning

IT has become an important resource and tool to support learning. Computers are used in education, from nursery schools to universities. Learning from a distance is much easier by computer.

Identify the different types of IT-based learning materials and activities available

The Internet gives access to a vast store of information on almost any topic. You can search for information by using a search engine. The Internet also has many sites designed to help you learn (Figure 8.5).

IT-based learning materials can be created easily and quickly to offer many different ways of learning. Handouts can be presented very effectively by combining text and images to make the material more interesting. Simple spreadsheets and databases can be used as analysis tools for making a topic easier to understand. For example, the data collected during a scientific experiment can be put into a spreadsheet so that calculations can be carried out and the results then displayed in graphs and charts. Geography students could access a database containing large amounts of demographic data from which they could extract relevant data sets to aid their understanding of the subject.

CD-ROMs are used to provide a wide range of IT-based learning materials. Encyclopaedias and dictionaries, and many other reference materials, are available on CD-ROM. These electronic resources will have search facilities so that you can find your way to the relevant part of the material. This will often include not only text but also diagrams, photographs and video clips.

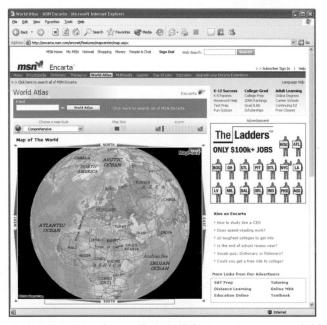

Figure 8.5 Encyclopaedias and dictionaries are available on CD-ROM and online

Interactive whiteboards are used in the classroom to make presentations more lively and interesting. Presentation software has animation features for teachers to create interactive material that gives the learners choice about how to the access the information. These presentation materials can be used by individuals and for whole-class teaching, using the interactive whiteboard.

IT-based learning material can be enlivened by the use of graphics, animation, video and interactive links. Activities can be set up so that students can interact with them. They can decide the order in which to do things and can repeat whatever they do not fully understand.

Much of the learning material has been written using web-development tools. If you are familiar with using the Internet, you should be able to quickly find your way around the web pages. Because these pages have been formatted for the web, they can also be made available on the Internet. These materials use the interactive features of a website and can make learning fun. It is much easier to learn at your own pace, and when and where you choose to learn.

Computer industry tests, such as the Microsoft and CISCO certificates, are done online. Students are usually given multiple-choice questions to answer. These are marked almost immediately and the results are given straight away. More and more tests are being provided in this way. The driving test theory paper is an online test, and you can now do the key skills exams as on-screen tests.

E-mail and discussion boards enable learners to communicate with teachers and trainers. This eases the isolation of e-learning and provides help and support on topics that have not been fully understood. You can share ideas with your fellow students, just as you would in a traditional classroom.

Video-conferencing provides an opportunity for interactivity between students and instructors who are not located in the same place. So, people can participate in an activity even though they are in another part of the country or on the other side of the world. VLEs (virtual learning environment) are now used in many educational institutions. A VLE provides students and teachers with access to IT-based learning materials, facilities to take online assessments, submit coursework electronically and communicate with the whole VLE community.

Compare the benefits and drawbacks of e-learning with other methods of learning

Benefits

E-learning can be flexible. It is possible to learn at almost any time and in almost any place. If you have a busy work schedule, you may be able to fit your learning in after work or at the weekend. You can also manage the pace of your learning and can go back and check anything you don't understand. However, unlike learning from a book, you can get feedback as you go along because of its interactive nature.

IT can be used to make the subject more interesting through the interactive nature of material. Pictures, animated graphics and video clips help in bettering understanding of what you are learning, while providing a greater variety of information.

Students can be highly motivated by this type of learning; it also enables them to control what they do, and when. However, they need to be self-disciplined and not spend their time simply 'clicking' through the material.

Drawbacks

E-learning discriminates against those who do not have access to the technology. If home study requires Internet access, then only those with the facilities to access the Internet can take part. IT skills are also needed to use the resources for this form of learning; and you need to be able to use these skills confidently and effectively. Those with limited IT skills will not gain the sort of benefits that will have a strong enough impact on their learning.

What happens if the technology fails? This is a major drawback of this type of learning. You need to plan for it happening. Make sure that all your current work is correctly saved and that you make regular backup copies. If the equipment fails, you will need an alternative way of accessing the resources.

These problems are likely to be resolved fairly quickly in a college or at work, but at home you may need to use the facilities of a local library or those of a friend, until yours is fixed.

E-learning can be very motivational and exciting, however it is carried out in isolation from others. Face-to-face communication can be an important part of how we learn, particularly when we don't understand something. Although there is no direct personal contact in using e-mail and discussion boards, they can alleviate the problem. Video-conferencing is an option for providing visual and verbal contact from a distance.

Skills Learning

What you need to do

- Get help from an appropriate person or source when needed
- Seek advice from a colleague or expert about the most appropriate learning opportunities to meet any skills gaps identified
- **Level 2** Identify own learning needs in using IT, with help from other people
- **Level 2** Find sources of information about opportunities for learning IT skills
- **Level 2** Use appropriate sources of information to find out about developments in using IT
- **Level 2** Get advice about the most suitable ways of learning

This is an opportunity for you to look at how you can extend your skills. What else do you need to know to do your job better? What do you need to do to get to the next level of expertise? This could be carried out as part of an appraisal within your workplace.

Practical task

Using the headings listed below to help you, carry out a self assessment of your IT skills and how to improve them.

- First you will need to make a list of the IT skills you have, then a list of the ones you think you need to get. You may need to talk to colleagues and your supervisor to find out what other tasks you might need to do in the future.
- You then need to find out about the different ways of acquiring these skills and how to go about this.

Keep a note on how you did the task and include screenshots where possible.

Get help from an appropriate person or source when needed

How do you get assistance when you can't do a task? Is there someone you can get help from or could you find out using the range of help facilities within the system? Is there help on the Internet?

Seek advice from a colleague or expert about the most appropriate learning opportunities to meet any skills gaps identified

Sometimes the additional skills that you have identified will require more than just a simple answer. You may need to go on a course, or use some online learning material.

Identify own learning needs in using IT, with help from other people

Ask your colleagues and supervisor what else you need to know. Look at the software that you are using; there will be parts that you never use. Find out what they are and whether they would be useful to you.

Find sources of information about opportunities for learning IT skills

What training opportunities are available to you? There may be training within the organisation, courses at your local college or community centre, courses on the web, or friends who will be able to share their expertise with you.

Use appropriate sources of information to find out about developments in using IT

IT uses are developing and growing very rapidly. As the hardware and software changes so people are finding more and more ways that the technology can be used for work, education and leisure. There are many ways that you can find out about these developments, probably the main one being through the Internet. Many computer magazines are available both in paper form and on the web, with articles and features about what is happening in the world of computers.

Perhaps your colleagues will also be able to tell you about new developments as well. Make sure you keep in touch with what is happening in the organisation you work or study in, and remember the technical-support staff are a good source of information.

Get advice about the most suitable ways of learning

Find out from your colleagues and supervisor about the different ways of learning and what are the advantages and drawbacks of each of them. Can you learn this by yourself?

Health and safety issues

What you need to know and understand

- Health and safety laws and guidelines
- Health and safety risks to self in using IT
- **Level 2** Ways to keep risks to people to a minimum
- Health and safety risks to others from common hardware
- **Level 2** Ways to keep risks to hardware to a minimum

See Unit 3: Operate a computer, page 63.

Applications units

The practical aspects of the applications units are not covered in detail here. You will find details on how to use the different tools and functions in manuals and books about each of the specific applications. At the end of the section there is a list of Heinemann resources, such as New CLAiT and CLAiT Plus, e-Quals and ECDL. At the end of each unit there is a skills checklist and at the end of the book there are Appendices with quick reference guides as to how to carry out common skills tasks.

For each of these units you will need to produce at least two tasks for assessment. At Level 1 these tasks will be of a straightforward nature, but at Level 2 they will need to be comprehensive activities. They will need to demonstrate understanding of the knowledge and the ability to carry out all the skills requirements. The units are the following:

9   Artwork and imaging software

10   Internet and intranets

11   E-mail

12   Word-processing software

13   Spreadsheet software

14   Database software

15   Website software

16   Presentation software

17   Use IT to exchange information

Artwork and imaging software

What you need to know and understand

- Produce information
- Artwork and images
- File formats
- Laws and guidelines

Produce information

What you need to know and understand

- Know who or what the information is for, where it will be used (e.g. onscreen or hard copy) and when it is needed
- **Level 2** How to produce information that communicates clearly and accurately with the audience, where and when it is needed

Know who or what the information is for, where it will be used (e.g. onscreen or hard copy) and when it is needed

When you produce a piece of work it is important that you know its purpose, that is, you know who is going to use the information and what for. For example, if you are creating a newsletter for teenagers to read you will need to use a different layout, probably with different fonts and colours, from one created for people living in a care home.

Information that is produced as hard copy, that is, printed, will be used in a different way from information displayed on a computer screen. Again, the way you present and lay out the information will need to be different. Screen-based information does not usually have large amounts of close text in small-sized fonts, and colours will not be appropriate for hard copy unless colour printing facilities are going to be used.

Most information is needed by a specified time in the workplace. When you are producing a piece of information you will need to make sure that you are aware of the deadlines, and what the issues are if these deadlines are not met. You will need to be able to organise your time so that you are able to provide the information when it is needed.

How to produce information that communicates clearly and accurately with the audience, where and when it is needed

Every piece of software has a range of tools available to help you produce accurate information.

There will usually be a form of spellchecker to help with input errors. However, not all errors can be identified in this way. Proofreading is an essential step that you should always go through before printing or supplying any information you have produced.

Print preview facilities should always be used to view hard-copy information before it is printed to check the layout, pagination etc.

Artwork and images

What you need to know and understand

- How to produce simple artwork and images that are appropriate
- **Level 2** How to produce more complex artwork and images for a variety of uses

How to produce simple artwork and images that are appropriate

You will need to make sure that you know how to use the features of your graphics software, particularly in terms of controlling the size of an image and the orientation (portrait or landscape). Only simple artwork and images are required at Level 1. This means you will need to have an understanding and the skills to produce simple shapes, and use clipart or a picture from a digital camera.

How to produce more complex artwork and images for a variety of uses

At Level 2 you will need to create more complex artwork and images using a range of features such as using layout grids in DTP software, or filters and effects in image manipulation software. See the Quick Reference Guide on page 253 for using layout grids on DTP software.

File formats

What you need to know and understand

- Know how to save files in different formats
- Which formats take up more or less space than others
- **Level 2** What file formats are suitable for websites
- **Level 2** What file formats are suitable for print publishing

Know how to save files in different formats

There are a large number of different formats used to save pictures and images. These include digital picture formats such as jpeg and psd, bitmaps such as bmp, and vector graphics such as gif. There will be a number of options available in the graphics software that you use. You can choose the format as you save the file (Figure 9.1).

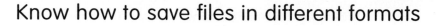

Figure 9.1 Choosing format as you save

Which formats take up more or less space than others

Many graphics files can be very large and, generally speaking, for digital and bitmap images, the higher the quality of the image, the larger the file size.

Bitmap images

These are created in pixels and consist of blocks of colour. Images that have been created through a scanning process will be in this form. Most painting and art packages produce images in this format. Company logos, pictures to be included in leaflets and graphical representations of data will usually have been created in this format. Depending on the quality of the graphics format and the package used, as the images are increased in size, so the smoothness of the lines may be reduced. However, particularly with the greater use of graphics in web pages, file formats have been developed to give good quality without the files being too large. A jpeg (joint photographic experts group) is a compressed-image file format that is good for storing photographs but with some loss of quality.

Vector graphics

These are constructed using lines, and will typically be used for many technical applications, as the resulting images are more precise and better able to be manipulated as objects. These are usually created using digitisers and graphics tablets, but can also be produced using programs to draw lines between Cartesian (x, y) co-ordinates.

There are specialist graphics packages for the drawing office, known as CAD (computer-aided design/draughting). Engineering drawings of all types can readily be produced using these packages. Many can be used directly to control the manufacture of the designed item.

True three-dimensional images that can be rotated must be vector images. Computer games, where you move through a three-dimensional space and need to view objects from all directions, and virtual reality use this type of graphics.

Software that is used to produce an organisation chart, flow diagrams etc. will also produce vector graphics.

What file formats are suitable for websites

When you create images to use on a website you will need to make sure that the image does not take too long to 'build' when your web page is being viewed on a slow connection. For this reason, many graphics for websites are stored in a compressed file format. Jpeg file format is most frequently used for photographic-quality images and gif files are good for small icons and animated images but because they are limited to 256 colours are not so good for photos.

What file formats are suitable for print publishing

Graphic images for print will often be produced using bitmap files, which are high-quality images but are not compressed and therefore result in large files. The psd files are primarily produced using Photoshop but can transfer across a range of platforms. The eps file format is used to produce high-quality images that will print identically on all postscript printers. An rtf (rich text format) is a universal file format that can be imported into any text-processing software but, unlike simple text-processing software, can include style, size and colour.

Laws and guidelines

What you need to know and understand

- What laws and guidelines affect day-to-day use of IT
- **Level 2** What and how IT activities are affected by laws and guidelines

What laws and guidelines affect day-to-day use of IT

You will need to be aware of:

- Data protection – see Unit 6: IT Security for users, page 144.
- Disability – see Unit 6: IT Security for users, page 149.
- Health and safety – see Unit 3: Operate a computer, page 63.
- Copyright – see Unit 6: IT Security for users, page 149.

You also need to take into account the guidelines set by your employer or other organisation you work for.

What and how IT activities are affected by laws and guidelines

The copyright laws are of particular relevance when using artwork and imaging software. You will need to make sure that you have permission to use this material, particularly ClipArt and images downloaded from the Internet.

Check it yourself

You need to demonstrate that you are competent in a range of skills for this unit. Complete the Artwork and imaging software skills checklist on page 187. You will need to make sure that you meet any gaps in your skills before you complete your evidence.

Skills checklist

Handle files	Level 1		Level 2	
	Create files using the software	☐	Organise files	☐
	Open files using the software	☐		
	Save (As) files using the software	☐		
	Print files using the software	☐		

Create drawings, artwork and images	Level 1		Level 2	
	Draw basic shapes – lines, boxes, arrows	☐	Use painting software	☐
	Create artwork combining text pictures and other elements	☐	Use drawing software	☐
	Download digital pictures from a camera	☐	Use DTP software	☐
			Use image-manipulation software	☐
			Take account of page or canvas size	☐
			Take account of colour mode	☐
			Take account of file size and format	☐

Insert, manipulate and edit artwork and images	Level 1		Level 2	
	Insert ClipArt	☐	Group and ungroup	☐
	Insert digital images	☐	Use filters to create special effects	☐
	Align drawing objects	☐	Edit existing templates	☐
	Rotate drawing objects	☐		
	Flip drawing objects	☐		
	Arrange drawing objects	☐		
	Cut drawing objects and pictures	☐		
	Paste drawing objects and pictures	☐		
	Crop drawing objects and pictures	☐		
	Trim drawing objects and pictures	☐		

(Continued)

Skills checklist (Continued)

Insert, manipulate and edit artwork and images	Level 1		Level 2	
	Resize drawing objects and pictures	☐		
	Insert text	☐		
	Change font	☐		
	Change colour	☐		
Check images	**Level 1**		**Level 2**	
	Check size, alignment and orientation of images	☐	Check colour modes	☐
	Check file format is suitable	☐	Check filters	☐
			Image resolution suitable for where and how to be used	☐
Check text	**Level 1**		**Level 2**	
	Use spell check	☐	Proofread to check that text looks professional	☐
	Use grammar check	☐	Check line, paragraph and page breaks	☐
	Use word count	☐	Check headings and subheadings used appropriately	☐

Internet and intranets

What you need to know and understand

- Connection methods
- Browser facilities
- Information and other opportunities
- Internet security risks
- Laws and guidelines

Connection methods

What you need to know and understand

- How to connect to an intranet
- What different types of hardware, software and connections can be used to connect to the Internet
- **Level 2** What own connection will and will not do

How to connect to an intranet

An intranet is a locally provided private service, usually using a web browser to view the information. You need to be connected to your local area network (LAN), which will usually need a cable with an RJ45 connector connected to a LAN socket. You need to have a user name and password to get access. You may also be able to connect through a wireless connection.

What different types of hardware, software and connections can be used to connect to the Internet

At home, many people connect to the Internet through a 56K modem, a device for converting analogue signals to digital signals and back again (modulator/demodulator), which is connected to their telephone. The modem provides a relatively slow connection, which is fine for connecting to your e-mail and surfing the Internet, but is quite slow if you want to download files.

Most workplace connections, and many home ones, are now likely to be a broadband link, which is much faster than the modem, with speeds of up to 8Mbps (Mega bits per second). Your connection to the Internet at work may be through your LAN server, so all you may need to do is use your Internet software.

To connect to the Internet is usually through an internet service provider (ISP) and the system must use the standard rules and procedures for connecting – that is, TCP/IP (Transmission Control Protocol/Internet Protocol).

To access the World Wide Web you need to have a browser. This is software that can read the HTML files. The web browser will enable you to navigate the web (move around the pages), to download images and text, and to print. Microsoft Internet Explorer and Netscape Navigator are examples of web browsers.

What own connection will and will not do

You need to find out about your connection, provider and what your system will and will not do. If you are running on a 56K modem it will take a long time to download or send large files; there could be better ways of making files available to other users.

Browser facilities

What you need to know and understand

- How to reach useful information quickly
- How to send information from the browser to others via e-mail
- How to find the full web address for information
- How to download images and files
- How to complete online forms
- **Level 2** What methods can be used to exchange files
- **Level 2** How to download software patches
- **Level 2** How and when to delete temporary files
- **Level 2** How changing settings affects performance

How to reach useful information quickly

The information on the Internet is not organised, nor is it controlled or managed in any way. This means you need some assistance to find what you are looking for. To search effectively across this network of information you will often need to use one of the many *search engines* that are available. These are interactive services that have access to vast catalogues of hundreds of thousands of websites, which can be found through keyword searches. There is an ever-increasing number of search engines available and some of the more sophisticated 'learn' about responses to searches so that they can improve their search results.

You can spend a long time searching on the web and so it is important that you use more sophisticated search techniques to get the information you need. These techniques use Boolean logic to carry out the search. You can use the 'AND', 'OR', and 'NOT' operators to clearly define your criteria.

For example:

- Laser AND Printer – finds pages that include both the word laser and the word printer.
- Laser OR Printer – finds pages that include the word laser, or the word printer, or both.
- Laser NOT Printer – finds pages that include the word laser but not the word printer.

If you enter two or more words without a Boolean operator then the AND operator is used by default. Not all search engines fully support Boolean searches except through their advanced search screen menus.

Some search tips

• Use speech marks to search for an exact phrase	• Searching for **'Laser Printer'** will give you much better results than **Laser Printer**
• Use the + (plus sign) for words that must appear in the result	• Place the + sign directly in front of the important word, e.g. +laser
• Use the – (minus) sign to search for pages that do NOT include a particular word	• Place the – sign directly in front of the excluded word, e.g. –paper
• If you use more words in a search you will get more refined results	• For example, searching for printers will give you lots of results whereas searching for Laser Printers A3 will give you more precise results

Table 10.1 Tips for searching the Internet

When you have found what you are looking for, you can save a link to this site as a 'favourite' so that you can visit this site very quickly the next time you need it.

How to send information from the browser to others via e-mail

Some browsers let you send information using your e-mail. You can usually either send the content of a page or you can send the link. When the person receives the e-mail they can click on the link to open up the web page.

How to find the full web address for information

The full web address of a page of information is displayed in the address bar at the top of the browser. You can highlight the address and use Ctrl + C to make a copy of it; it is then easy to paste it into another document.

How to download images and files

Before downloading any files from the Internet it is important to remember that some files may contain viruses and be harmful for your computer. If you run a program or open a file directly from a website, which causes your computer or other programs to shut down, you could lose any unsaved work in your open files. It is better to save the file or program to disk, and then open it later. This way you can take security actions before you open the file:

- Check the file with a virus scanner.
- Save your work and close other programs.
- Disconnect from the Internet or any other network connections.

How to complete online forms

Many websites have forms that need to be completed, such as booking a journey, or completing an application to go on a course. On most forms some of the fields will be required fields, that is, they must be completed before the form can be successfully submitted.

You can usually move between the fields of the form by pressing the Tab key and there will be a submit or send button to click on when you have completed the form. Some browsers have an autocomplete facility which makes suggestions on frequently typed words to speed up the process.

What methods can be used to exchange files

The method used to transfer web pages to your computer is http (hypertext transfer protocol). Another method, ftp (file transfer protocol) is used to make files publicly available for transfer across the Internet. For example, if you needed a copy of the latest file to update your software from Microsoft, you could go to ftp://ftp.microsoft.com. To access some of these ftp sites you will need to have a user name and password.

How to download software patches

The provider of your web-browser software will sometimes release a patch. This will be a small update to the programs to fix a minor problem, quite often a problem that you were not even aware existed. You may receive a message from the provider to say that there is a patch to download; in your workplace this is more likely to be carried out by the technical support staff.

If you need to download a patch, step-by-step instructions will be provided; usually the patch will self-extract and install. You will usually need to restart your computer before the update becomes effective.

How and when to delete temporary files

When you view a web page it is stored on your hard disk as a temporary file. This speeds up the time it takes to view that page again and is particularly useful for frequently visited web pages. You can also view the web page without being connected to the Internet. However, these files take up space on your hard drive, so many of them will need to be deleted. You can quickly delete these files through your Internet Options.

How changing settings affects performance

Your Internet connection settings can be customised to suit how you use the system. You can change the settings so that a particular web page is opened when you make an Internet connection (Figure 10.1).

When you visit a website the URL (uniform resource locator) can be stored in a history folder so that you can quickly return to recently visited sites. The length of time to keep this information can be changed and you can also clear this information through your Internet options.

You can change the settings for keeping temporary Internet files and cookies. Cookies are small files that contain access information for a website. Your access to these sites is much quicker if the cookie is stored on your computer as

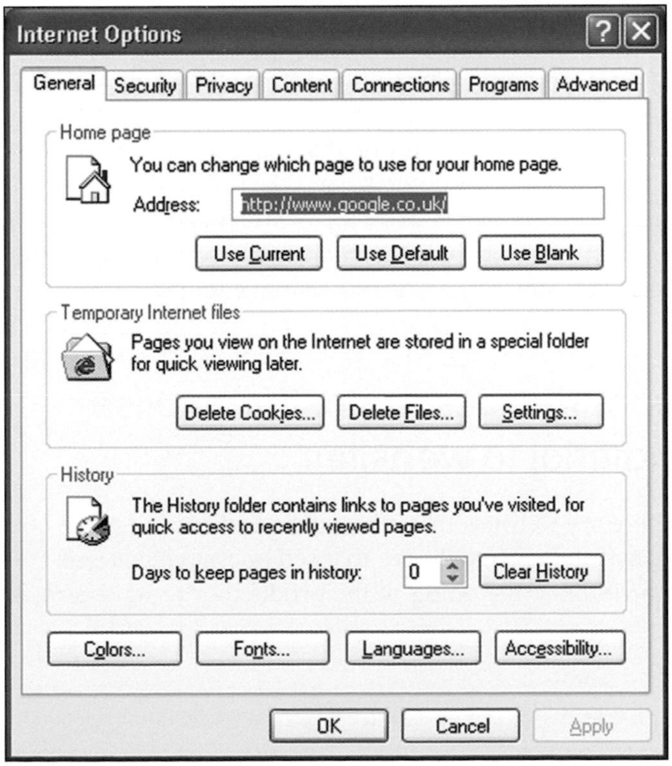

Figure 10.1 Internet Options

this is read automatically without you needing to supply the information each time you visit the site. You can manage these files through your settings; the more space allocated the faster the access time, but of course you need to have space on your hard drive.

Information and other opportunities

What you need to know and understand

- The different types of information
- **Level 2** What meta engines are and how to use them
- **Level 2** Opportunities to post or publish material to websites
- **Level 2** Opportunities to create websites

The different types of information

There are several different types of information that you will be able to use.

- Factual information, creative work, opinions and information that is continually updated (or live), and interactive information.
- Sources for finding information, such as guides and directories.
- Search engines to help you find information.

What meta engines are and how to use them

A meta search engine is one that searches several search engines simultaneously to find websites using the keywords provided in the search box. Meta search engines do not own a database of web pages; they send information to search to others. They are only as good as the search engines that they use and tend to work with smaller and/or free search engines.

Opportunities to post or publish material to websites

There are websites that invite their audience to make contributions to the site. Many interactive websites that sell books, videos and DVDs ask their visitors to contribute to the rating of the product, or to write a review to post on the site.

Opportunities to create websites

When you sign up to an Internet service provider (ISP) you will usually have access to a number of resources. This will often include the opportunity to create and set up your own website.

Internet security risks

What you need to know and understand

- What risks there may be in downloading documents and software
- Risks in sharing information
- **Level 2** Legal, ethical and economic risks
- **Level 2** Ways of protecting against risks

What risks there may be in downloading documents and software

See viruses in Unit 6: IT Security for Users, page 131.

Risks in sharing information

One of the problems of working on the Internet is knowing who you are communicating with. As anyone can have access to the Web, and can create and publish their own site, you need to take precautions to ensure that the site is safe. Digital certificates and signatures are used by many organisations to show that they are a genuine site.

You should always take particular care when disclosing personal information. This is not only about financial information and the problems of theft and fraud, but about your personal safety. Your personal address and telephone number should only be given when you are satisfied that it is safe.

Legal, ethical and economic risks

- Failure to properly protect personal data.
- Unauthorised access of information.
- Unauthorised and inappropriate use of the Internet by employees.
- Attack from viruses and spam.
- Financial transactions may be vulnerable to hacking.

Ways of protecting against risks

You Internet browser will have a number of security settings to help protect your computer. These can be set to manage the level of checking that is carried out and to prevent specified sites from being accessed.

Your computer will also, hopefully, be protected by a firewall. A firewall is a piece of software which blocks unwanted traffic from entering your computer.

User-access controls can also be used to protect your computer. As well as obvious physical controls such as locked doors, the computer system can be protected against risk through the use of passwords. Passwords are, however, only any good provided users don't let other people know what they are and also change them regularly.

Laws and guidelines

What you need to know and understand

- What laws and guidelines affect day-to-day use of IT
- **Level 2** What and how IT activities are affected by laws and guidelines

What laws and guidelines affect day-to-day use of IT

You will need to be aware of:

- Data protection – see Unit 6: IT Security for users, page 144.
- Disability – see Unit 6: IT Security for users, page 149.
- Health and safety – see Unit 3: Operate a computer, page 63.
- Copyright – see Unit 6: IT Security for users, page 149.

You also need to take into account the guidelines set by your employer or other organisation you work for.

What and how IT activities are affected by laws and guidelines

The copyright legislation is of particular relevance to this unit, for instance when considering downloading images from the Internet. See page 149.

Check it yourself

You need to demonstrate that you are competent in a range of skills for this unit. Complete the Internet and intranets skills checklist on page 198. You will need to make sure that you meet any gaps in your skills before you complete your evidence portfolio.

Skills checklist

Search	Level 1		Level 2	
	Use a search engine to find and select appropriate information	☐	Choose an appropriate search engine	☐
	Use bookmarks or favourites to make it easier to find useful information	☐	Use meta search engines	☐
	Send web pages via e-mail	☐	Use wild cards	☐
	Send web links via e-mail	☐	Use Boolean notation (AND or NOT)	☐
	Keep records of where useful information came from	☐		
	Save the results of searches	☐		
Find and evaluate	**Level 1**		**Level 2**	
	Choose a suitable source	☐	Choose an appropriate search engine	☐
	Locate information from various sources	☐		
	Choose information that is appropriate for what is needed	☐		

E-mail

What you need to know and understand

- E-mail facilities
- Problems with e-mail
- Laws and guidelines

E-mail facilities

What you need to know and understand

- E-mail messages
- **Level 2** Basic options for sending and replying
- How to send and receive attachments
- How to use an address book
- **Level 2** How to send e-mails to groups using a mailing list
- **Level 2** How to archive and compress e-mails
- **Level 2** What other resources may be provided by e-mail software

E-mail messages

E-mail is a communications system that enables you to send messages and information with the certainty that it has been placed in the recipient's mailbox. It is a way of carrying out rapid, text-based communication both inside and outside an organisation. In many organisations the use of e-mail has replaced the memo, and even letters to some extent.

To use e-mail your computer needs to be connected to a network and have the appropriate e-mail software on the system. The mail system, like any other system, has to be managed and supported. There will usually be a postmaster who has responsibility for setting up each mailbox, maintaining mailing lists and other network-wide features.

E-mail can considerably improve the internal communications of an organisation, particularly if it is introduced with an appropriate training programme to ensure it is used effectively. Unfortunately, like all communications systems, it is often used thoughtlessly.

Basic options for sending and replying

When you receive an e-mail it is stored in the **Inbox**. If you need to reply, choose the reply option to send your response; the e-mail address is automatically picked up from the sender's e-mail.

To create a new e-mail you need to enter the e-mail address of the recipient. Sometimes you will send a copy of the e-mail to another address; you enter this address in the **cc** box.

Every e-mail should be given a title, which is entered in the **Subject** box. Many users are suspicious of e-mails without a subject, and may delete these without opening them.

You then type the message in the **Message** box and send it. Many systems keep a copy of every outgoing message, these are stored in the **Sent** box.

How to send and receive attachments

You may need to send a file to someone. This can be sent as an attachment to an e-mail. All kinds of files can be attached to e-mails. E-mails will be received with attachments that can be opened and saved.

How to use an address book

E-mail systems have address books. Here you can store the e-mail addresses of all the people you need to contact regularly. These addresses, just as in paper-based address books, are organised in alphabetical order and can be organised into groups of people you want to contact. When sending an e-mail you can simply call up the e-mail address from the name of the person you want to contact.

How to send e-mails to groups using a mailing list

You may want to send e-mails to groups of people on a regular basis. For this, you can set up a mailing list group so that you can quickly select the list of recipients for an e-mail. Mailing lists should be updated regularly to ensure that the right people are receiving their messages.

How to archive and compress e-mails

If e-mailing is the standard way of communicating within an organisation, then it is important to manage the system. Copies of important e-mails need to be retained for some time, however they do not need to be kept online. There is a facility within e-mail programs to archive (remotely store) old but important e-mails.

What other resources may be provided by e-mail software

Many e-mail packages have a range of other tools. There will usually be a spellchecker tool so that you can check the spelling of words in the e-mail messages you send. You can set the priorities of your messages and request a delivery and read receipt to monitor the progress of your messages. You can also set up the system to send messages automatically – e.g. when you are not available you can set up an 'out of office' message to be sent to anyone contacting you by e-mail.

Some e-mail software also provides a calendar which can be used instead of a paper diary. You can use this to schedule events and to send e-mails to the other people involved to let them know what the schedule is; the system can also be set up so that you can add the event into their e-mail diary as well.

Problems with e-mail

What you need to know and understand

- Why some computer users may have difficulty in sending and receiving e-mails with attachments
- **Level 2** What limits there may be to the number or size of e-mails that can be received and stored
- **Level 2** How to keep the difficulties of sending and receiving large e-mails to a minimum
- What to do about e-mails from unknown users
- What viruses are and the problems they can cause
- How using anti-virus software can help to keep risks to a minimum
- **Level 2** What to do about e-mails intended to cause harm

Why some computer users may have difficulty in sending and receiving e-mails with attachments

There may be limits on the size of an e-mail that you send or receive. Many systems restrict you to e-mail attachments no greater than 5 MB in size. You may have a firewall protecting your computer against unwanted e-mail attachments. The firewall will block attachments containing certain types of files and will prevent you receiving or sending files containing rude words.

What limits there may be to the number or size of e-mails that can be received and stored

Most e-mail systems, whether a personal home e-mail system or a company's, will have size restrictions. Each mailbox has a maximum storage space for keeping messages online. Make sure you delete old messages that are no longer needed and archive those that you need to keep. The system will send you a warning message when your mailbox is too full.

How to keep the difficulties of sending and receiving large e-mails to a minimum

A file compression utility (e.g. WinZip) may be needed to send very large documents by e-mail. This reduces the size of the file to within the maximum size, so that it can be sent.

What to do about e-mails from unknown users

Be careful when you receive an e-mail from an e-mail address that you don't recognise; the contents could damage your computer or files. Some organisations advise staff to delete messages they don't recognise, or, at the very least, to place them in quarantine until they can be put through a virus scanner.

What viruses are and the problems they can cause

See Unit 6: IT Security for users, page 131.

How using anti-virus software can help to keep risks to a minimum

Computer systems are particularly vulnerable to attack from viruses that are inserted into attachments to e-mails. Most anti-virus software can be set up to automatically scan attachments as they arrive in the system, so that you can be sure that the attachments are safe to open.

What to do about e-mails intended to cause harm

Junk mail is sent through the post and by e-mail. In the case of e-mail it is also known as spam. It is usually companies trying to sell goods or services, and can be in the form of chain-mail, which encourages you to forward it to many other users. This type of mail can be a nuisance and is of concern because of the possibility of viruses embedded in the attachments, and a considerable inconvenience as it takes up time in dealing with them.

You can install a spam filter, or blocker, to restrict these unsolicited e-mails. The filter usually places all e-mails from unknown e-mail addresses into quarantine. You can then look through the list and decide which e-mails you wish to read and which to delete.

Laws and guidelines

What you need to know and understand

- What laws and guidelines affect day-to-day use of IT
- **Level 2** What and how IT activities are affected by laws and guidelines

What laws and guidelines affect day-to-day use of IT

You will need to be aware of:

- Data protection – see Unit 6: IT Security for users, page 144.
- Disability – see Unit 6: IT Security for users, page 149.
- Health and safety – see Unit 3: Operate a computer, page 63.
- Copyright – see Unit 6: IT Security for users, page 149.

You also need to take into account the guidelines set by your employer or other organisation you work for.

What and how IT activities are affected by laws and guidelines

You need to be particularly aware of the Data Protection Act 1998 and the Computer Misuse Act 1990 for this unit. The main issues are to do with sending and receiving information and inappropriate e-mails. (See pages 144–153 for these Acts.)

Check it yourself

- You need to demonstrate that you are competent in a range of skills for this unit. Complete the E-mail skills checklist on page 205. You will need to make sure that you meet any gaps in your skills before you complete your evidence portfolio.

Skills checklist

Send and receive	Level 1		Level 2	
	Send to individuals	☐	Add a signature to an e-mail	☐
	Send carbon copies	☐	Set the priority of the message	☐
	Reply to individuals	☐	Send messages to groups of people	☐
	Forward e-mails	☐	Send instant messages without attachments	☐
	Reply to all	☐	Send instant messages with attachments	☐
	Reply with history	☐	Receive instant messages without attachments	☐
	Delete e-mail	☐	Receive instant messages with attachments	☐
	Send e-mails with attachments	☐	Compress messages on sending	☐
	Open e-mails with attachments	☐	Uncompress messages that have been received	☐
	Save attachments to appropriate places	☐	Archive e-mails where necessary (folders and subfolders)	☐
	Find e-mails	☐		
	Follow any rules and guidelines for sending and replying	☐		
Use address books and other facilities	Level 1		Level 2	
	Maintain an e-mail address book	☐	Set up groups for sending e-mails to	☐
			Compress e-mail attachments	☐
			Decompress e-mail attachments	☐
Format e-mails	Level 1		Level 2	
	Change font	☐	Format e-mails using RTF	☐
	Change type size	☐	Format e-mails using HTML	☐
	Change colour	☐	Format e-mails using plain text	☐
	Format paragraphs – alignment			

(Continued)

Skills checklist (Continued)

Format e-mails	Level 1		Level 2	
	Format paragraphs – bullets	☐		
	Format paragraphs – numbering	☐		
	Format paragraphs – indents	☐		
Exchange information	Level 1		Level 2	
	Follow rules of 'netiquette'	☐	Use FTP to exchange information	☐
			Use HTTP to exchange information	☐
			Use interactive sites	☐

12
Word-processing software

What you need to know and understand

- Produce information
- Word-processing documents

Produce information

What you need to know and understand

- Know who or what the information is for, where it will be used (e.g. onscreen or hard copy) and when it is needed
- **Level 2** How to produce information that communicates clearly and accurately with the audience, where and when it is needed

See Unit 9: Artwork and imaging software, page 182.

Word-processing documents

What you need to know and understand

- How to produce simple word-processed documents that are accurate and well laid out
- **Level 2** How to produce professional-looking word-processed documents for a wide variety of uses

How to produce simple word-processed documents that are accurate and well laid out

Word processing is the generic term used to describe the computer-based production of text-based documents.

In most organisations letters, internal communications (such as memoranda (memos)), forms and reports are prepared using some form of electronic text-processing facility, usually a word-processing system. Modern word-processing facilities have features way beyond those that would have previously been carried out on a typewriter. Many documents are now produced in-house that would have been sent out to specialist designers and printers in the past, or may have been created through the use of more specialist software such as desktop publishing (DTP).

The basic text-processing facilities of wordwrap, editing, cutting and pasting, and tabulation have been greatly enhanced with a wide range of features such as the ability to carry out automatic numbering of paragraphs, use bullets, apply spelling checkers in a wide range of languages, look up words in a thesaurus to assist in the use of just the right word, and sophisticated line-drawing and text-presentation features.

At Level 1, the sorts of documents you will be working with will have a standard structure and style, and you may be using an existing template or creating a new document working from an existing example.

You will need to know how to use a range of layout and presentation features, including the use of headers and footers; page orientation (portrait and landscape); margins (left, right, top and bottom); fonts, colours and font sizes. You will need to know how to present tables of information. This may be achieved using tabulation or by inserting a table that can have lines, borders and shading to enhance the presentation. (See Quick Reference Guide, page 253.)

How to produce professional-looking word-processed documents for a wide variety of uses

Many documents, either for business or leisure purposes, can be improved or enhanced by the use of graphics or the inclusion of a set of data. A general newsletter distributed to all staff is more interesting to look at if it includes more than words; company reports are quicker to produce if the tables or figures do not need to be typed in again and can also be displayed as a graph;

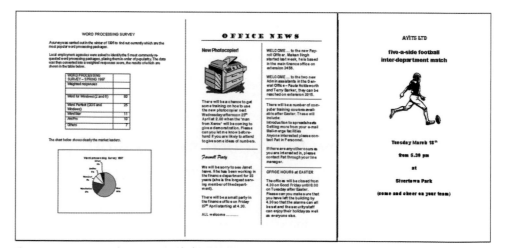

Figure 12.1 A word-processed document

the invitation for all staff to the interdepartmental five-a-side football match will be more inviting with some pictures in it.

Many of the uses of word processing, such as filling in forms, can be automated through the use of interactive macros which assist the user by prompting at each point in the process. Mail-merge facilities mean that standard mailings can easily be prepared for multiple recipients but each have the look and presentation of individual correspondence. (See Quick Reference Guide, page 253.)

Check it yourself

You need to demonstrate that you are competent in a range of skills for this unit. Complete the Word-processing software skills checklist on page 210. You will need to make sure that you meet any gaps in your skills before you complete your evidence portfolio.

Skills checklist

Handle files	Level 1		Level 2	
	Create files using the software	☐	Organise files	☐
	Open files using the software	☐		
	Save (As) files using the software	☐		
	Print files using the software	☐		

Combine information	Level 1		Level 2	
	Insert information	☐	Insert a spreadsheet graph	☐
	Resize inserted information	☐	Combine text with an image file	☐
	Position inserted information	☐	Insert a picture into a presentation slide	☐
			Simple information from a database on to a website	☐

Edit text	Level 1		Level 2	
	Insert	☐	Size and sort	☐
	Delete	☐	Use special characters and symbols	☐
	Cut	☐	Mail merge	☐
	Copy	☐		
	Paste	☐		
	Drag and drop	☐		
	Find and replace	☐		

Format text	Level 1		Level 2	
	Characters – size	☐	Columns – whole document	☐
	Characters – font	☐	Columns – part of a page	☐
	Characters – colour	☐	Styles – apply existing style to a word, line or paragraph	☐
	Characters – bold	☐	Pages – headers and footers	☐
	Characters – underline and italic	☐	Pages – insert page breaks	☐
	Paragraphs – alignment	☐	Files – change format of word-processed file to RTF	☐

(Continued)

Skills checklist (Continued)

Format text	Level 1		Level 2	
	Paragraphs – bullets	☐	Files – change format of word-processed file to HTML	☐
	Paragraphs – numbering	☐		
	Paragraphs – line spacing	☐		
	Paragraphs – borders	☐		
	Paragraphs – shading	☐		
	Paragraphs – tabs and indents	☐		
	Lines – spacing	☐		
	Lines – alignment and breaks	☐		
	Pages – size	☐		
	Pages – orientation	☐		
	Pages – margins	☐		
	Page numbers	☐		
	Date and time	☐		
Layout	**Level 1**		**Level 2**	
	Create simple tables and add data	☐	Tables – add columns	☐
	Enter text into existing templates – letters, faxes and web pages	☐	Tables – delete columns	☐
			Tables – modify column width	☐
			Tables – modify row height	☐
			Tables – add borders and shading	☐
Check text	**Level 1**		**Level 2**	
	Use spell check	☐	Proofread	☐
	Use grammar check	☐	Check line, paragraph and page breaks fall in appropriate places	☐
	Use word count	☐	Check headings and subheadings used appropriately	☐
Improve efficiency	**Level 1**		**Level 2**	
			Set up short cuts	☐

13
Spreadsheet software

Produce information

What you need to know and understand

- Know who or what the information is for, where it will be used (e.g. onscreen or hard copy) and when it is needed
- **Level 2** How to produce information that communicates clearly and accurately with the audience, where and when it is needed

See Unit 9: Artwork and imaging software, page 182.

Spreadsheets

What you need to know and understand

- Produce simple spreadsheets that are accurate and well laid out
- **Level 2** Produce more complex spreadsheets for a wide variety of uses

What is a spreadsheet?

One of the things that computers have always been used for is carrying out calculations. They are capable of carrying out vast numbers of calculations in a very short space of time. Many of these applications involve the use of special software which has been set up to perform specific functions such as accounting, complex engineering-design calculations, production forecasting or even putting humans on the moon. However, we all need to be able to do much simpler calculations, both in our daily lives and in our work.

Most spreadsheets look something like the grid below:

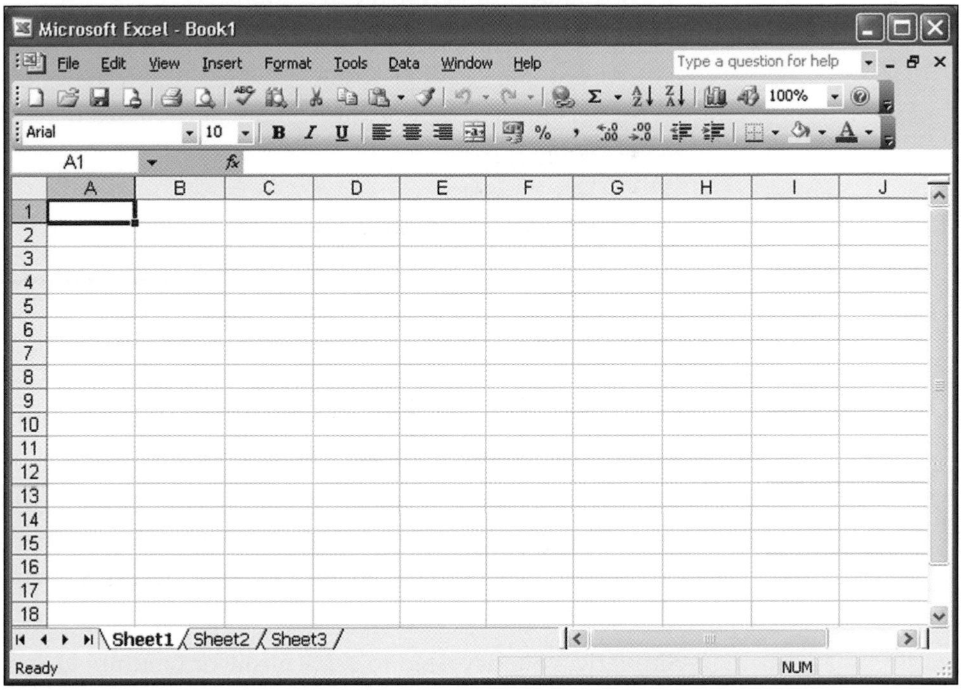

Figure 13.1 Spreadsheet grid

It is like a very large piece of paper that is divided into columns and rows. What you can see on the screen at any one time is just a small part of the complete spreadsheet available. The screen is like a small window on to the complete spreadsheet. If you try to move the cursor off the edge of the screen then a new portion of the spreadsheet comes into view but you do not lose the data in the part that is no longer displayed. When you scroll back, the data will still be there.

Each entry position in the spreadsheet is called a **cell** and you can reference any particular cell by giving its **column letter** followed by the **row number**, e.g. D4.

The selection border around the first cell on the worksheet tells you that this is the **active cell**. This cell will be affected by your next entry.

In the upper-left part of your screen the **cell reference** shows the number of the cell you are working in at the moment, the active cell. In Figure 13.1, it is A1 because the selected cell is located in column A, row 1.

Each cell can contain one item of data which will be:

- text – any character
- numeric – only real numbers should be entered as numeric
- formulae – to perform calculations.

Calculations, using **formulae**, can be entered into a cell. These may use the contents of other cells or absolute values. When the values in a cell are changed, all the formulae in the spreadsheet are automatically recalculated to give new results.

Produce simple spreadsheets that are accurate and well laid out

At Level 1, the sorts of spreadsheets you will be working with will have a simple structure, and you may be entering data into an existing spreadsheet or creating a new one working from an existing example.

You may need to *insert* an additional row or column in between existing ones. You may need the spreadsheet rows to move down and create an empty row or you may need the column to move across and create an empty column. (See Quick Reference Guide, page 261.)

Similarly, you may need to *delete* a row or column. Deleting means not only getting rid of the data but also closing up the rows or columns so that there is no space left. It is different from the command which leaves the cells in the layout but without any data in them.

Often when you are putting data into a spreadsheet, there is a lot of repetition. You can replicate, or copy, the contents of a cell to any other cell by the use of a *copy* command. You can also use the copy command to copy a formula from one cell to another. (See Quick Reference Guide, page 261.)

You can also use the *cut* and *paste* features of a spreadsheet package. However you must be extremely careful with this. It does not always work in exactly the same way as in other software. For example, if you wish to move the data from column A to column C and column C already has some data in it, the cut and paste facility will overwrite the contents of column C unless you insert an additional column to take the moved data. (See Quick Reference Guide, page 261.)

Spreadsheets contain large amounts of numerical data and, while accountants and financial wizards might like to see this information presented as columns of numbers, most people find it much easier to understand the situation at a glance if the figures are displayed graphically (Figure 13.2). You can use simple chart facilities within your spreadsheet package to display this information in the form of bar charts and pie charts. (See Quick Reference Guide, page 261.)

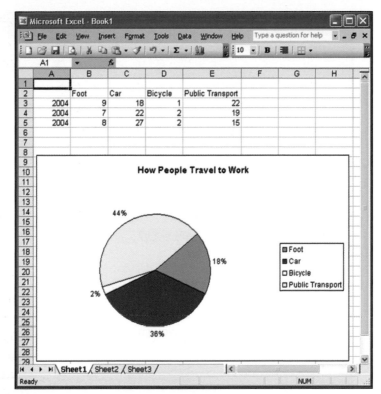

Figure 13.2 A pie chart produced from a spreadsheet

Produce more complex spreadsheets for a wide variety of uses

More complex spreadsheets may consist of more than one worksheet with links between the sheets. For example, the data for each quarter of the year can be held on a separate sheet and a summary sheet can then be included containing data extracted from the four quarters.

Quarterly Sales worksheet

Store	Jan-Mar	Apr-Jun	Jul-Sep	Oct-Dec	Annual Total
London	£6,489.00	£6,826.43	£7,150.68	£7,293.36	£27,759.47
Reading	£1,541.40	£1,621.55	£1,698.58	£1,732.47	£6,594.00
Cambridge	£1,801.80	£1,895.49	£1,985.53	£2,025.15	£7,707.97
Bristol	£3,578.40	£3,764.48	£3,943.29	£4,021.97	£15,308.14
Liverpool	£4,305.00	£4,658.01	£4,879.27	£4,976.62	£18,818.90
Glasgow	£4,145.40	£4,360.96	£4,568.11	£4,659.25	£17,733.72
Cardiff	£2,767.80	£2,911.73	£2,991.80	£3,110.89	£11,782.22
Total	£24,628.80	£26,038.65	£27,217.26	£27,819.71	£105,704.42

Figure 13.3a Quarterly Sales worksheet

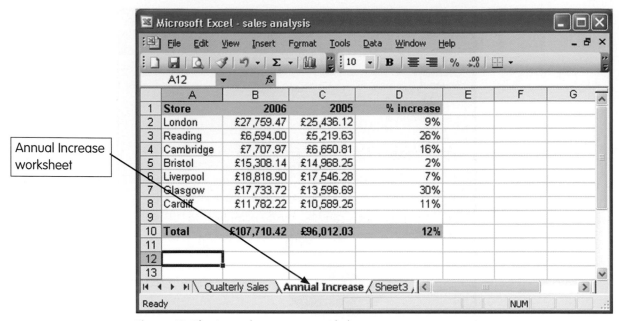

Annual Increase worksheet

Figure 13.3b Annual summary worksheet

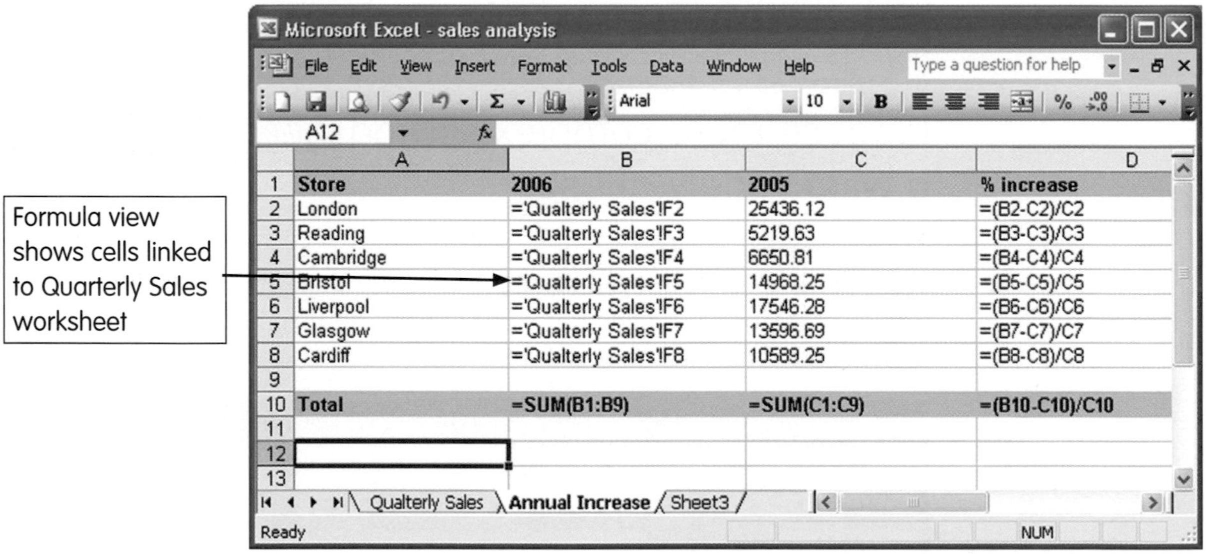

Formula view shows cells linked to Quarterly Sales worksheet

Figure 13.3c Formula view

Figures 13.3(a–c) shows a more complex spreadsheet consisting of two linked worksheets.

You will also need to know how to share data between software applications. You may need to copy data from your spreadsheet, or even a chart, and paste it into another type of document such as a word-processed report or on to a web page. Alternatively, you could import some data from a database into a section of the spreadsheet you are working on. (See Quick Reference Guide, page 261.)

Analyse and interpret

What you need to know and understand

- What methods can be used for simple data
- **Level 2** What methods are suitable for more complex data

What methods can be used for simple data

The primary reason for using spreadsheets to provide an information technology solution is that they are particularly useful for carrying out calculations. Calculations are achieved in a spreadsheet by placing *formulae* or *functions* into a cell. The results of the calculation are then displayed in the cell and, when any of the data used in the formula is changed, a new result will be calculated.

You will need to make sure that you know how to include formulae to carry out addition, subtraction, multiplication and division. The arithmetic operators use the following keys:

Addition	+
Subtraction	–
Multiplication	*
Division	/

Table 13.1 Arithmetic operators

Any formula can include reference to any cell or block of cells in the spreadsheet and it may also include absolute values.

Cell	Formula	What it does
B15	= B7+B12	Adds the value in B7 to the value in B12 and displays the result in B15
C15	= C10−C11	Subtracts the value in C11 from the value in C10 and displays the result in C15
D15	= D13*D14	Multiplies the value in D13 by the value in D14 and displays the result in D15
E15	= E8/E9	Divides the value in E8 by the value in E9 and displays the result in E15
F15	= F3*5	Multiplies the value in F3 by the absolute value 5 and displays the result in F15

Table 13.2 Formulae

The formulae that you use may look slightly different depending upon which software package you are using, but will be very similar.

Some of the calculations that are used most frequently in a spreadsheet will have a function pre-defined to make it easier and quicker to do. The mostly commonly used calculation in a spreadsheet is to add up a column or row of data. A function exists in your spreadsheet known as the SUM function (Figure 13.4). This function provides a formula that adds up the values in every cell within the range given. For example, = SUM(B2:B7) in the cell B9 will add up the values in B2, B3, B4, B5, B6 and B7 and display the result in B9. *Note*: The SUM function should only be used to add a continuous row or column of data. (See Quick Reference Guide, page 261.)

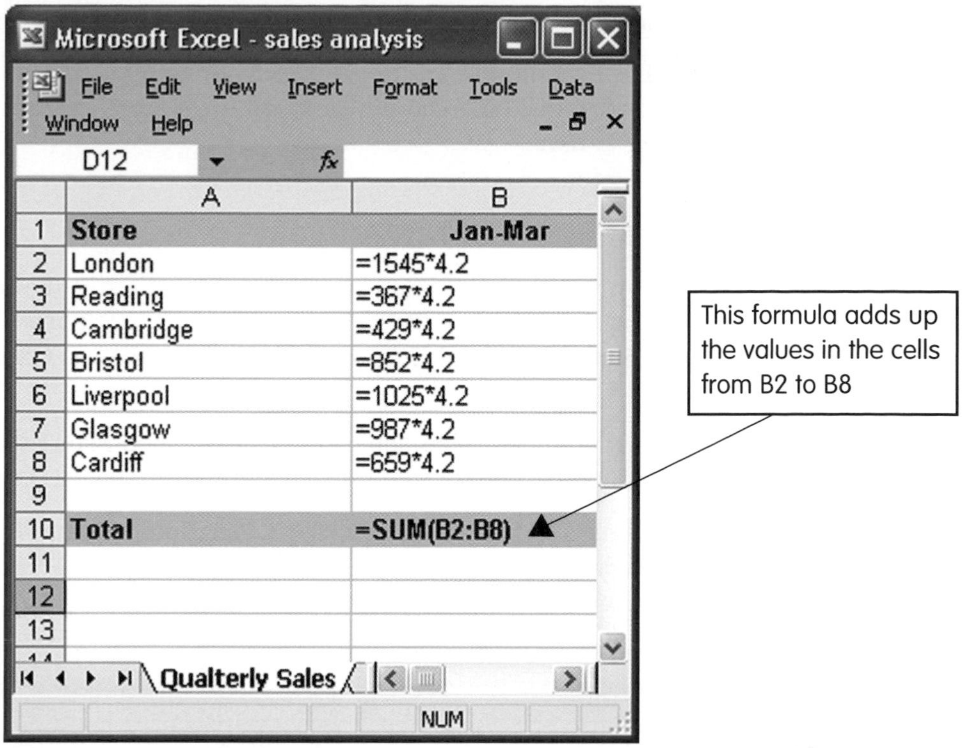

Figure 13.4 The SUM function

You may also need to present the data in your spreadsheet in a different order. You can use the sort command to reorganise your information, but make sure that you have all the cells to be reorganised highlighted before you start the process. With sorted data in your spreadsheet you can use the automatic sub-totals command.

What methods are suitable for more complex data

Function	What it does
= AVERAGE(B2:B8)	Calculates the arithmetic mean; i.e. the sum of the values from B2 to B8 divided by the number of values
= MIN(B2:B8)	Finds the minimum number (lowest) in the range of cells
= MAX(B2:B8)	Finds the maximum number (highest) in the range of cells
= COUNT(B2:B8)	Counts how many cells have a numeric value in the range of cells
= ROUND(B2,1)	Rounds the value in B2 to 1 decimal place
= IF(B2=5,Yes, No)	If cell B2 contains a 5 then the result is Yes, if it contains any other value then it is No

Table 13.3 Spreadsheet functions

There is a wide range of functions that are available in spreadsheet software.

Table 13.3 shows some of the more commonly used statistical, mathematical and relational functions available, although there are many others that you may need to use.

Absolute cell references

When you copy a formula from one cell to another, the cell references are modified relative to where they are going, i.e. if you copy the formula = SUM(B2:B6) from the cell B8 to the cell C8 it will be modified to = SUM(C2:C6).

However, there will be some instances when you don't want the cell reference to change.

In Figure 13.5 there is a column, B, containing the number of items in stock in each of the different stores. The next column, C, needs to have a formula to calculate the value of the stock.

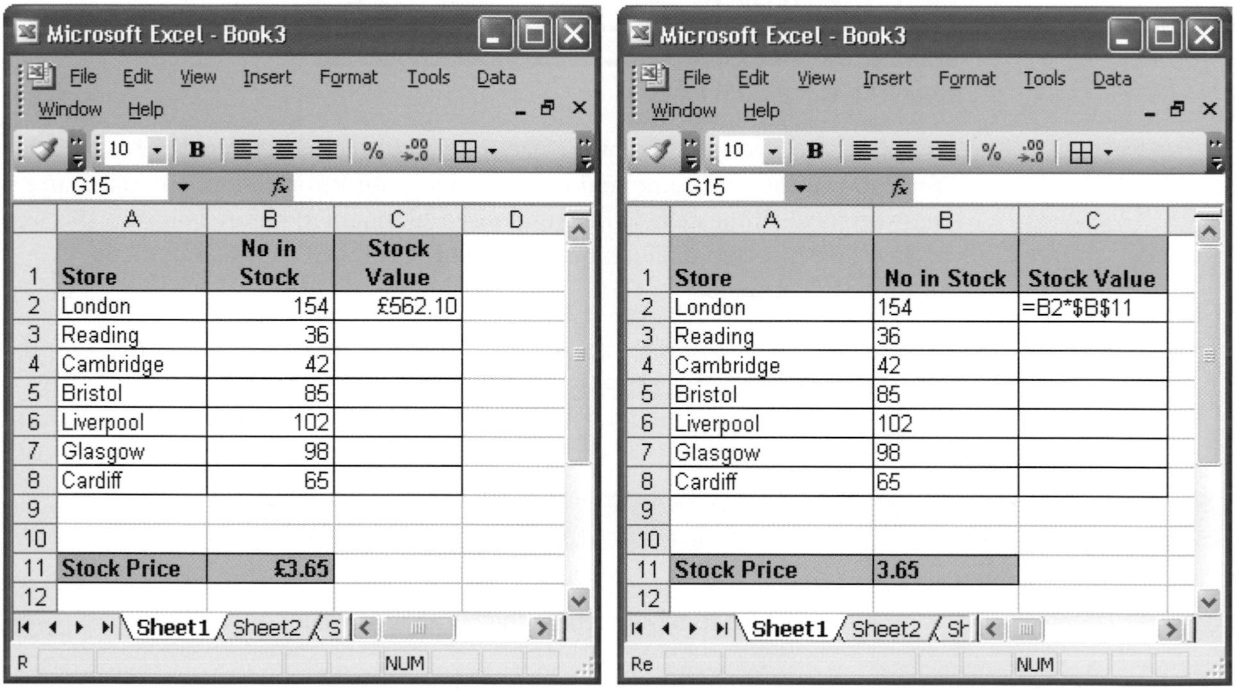

Figure 13.5 Cell B11 is an absolute cell reference

C2 contains the formula =B2*B11, but so that the reference does not change when you copy the formula to C3, the B11 reference has been made **absolute** – B11.

Complex spreadsheets will often contain large amounts of data. There will be occasions when only a selected part of the data needs to be viewed. Your spreadsheet software will have a facility to let you filter using the values at the top of the columns. This filter will only display those rows that match this value.

Check it yourself

You need to demonstrate that you are competent in a range of skills for this unit. Complete the Spreadsheet software skills checklist on page 222. You will need to make sure that you meet any gaps in your skills before you complete your evidence portfolio.

Skills checklist

Handle files	Level 1	Level 2
	Create files using the software ☐	Organise files ☐
	Open files using the software ☐	
	Save (As) files using the software ☐	
	Print files using the software ☐	

Combine information	Level 1	Level 2
	Insert information ☐	Insert spreadsheet graph into another application ☐
	Resize inserted information ☐	Link worksheets in a spreadsheet ☐
	Position inserted information ☐	Import data from another application ☐

Enter and edit spreadsheet data	Level 1	Level 2
	Insert data into single cells ☐	Insert data into multiple cells at once ☐
	Add and delete rows ☐	Use absolute cell references ☐
	Add and delete columns ☐	Add data and text to a chart ☐
	Clear cells ☐	Change the chart type ☐
	Cut ☐	
	Copy ☐	
	Paste ☐	
	Drag and drop ☐	
	Find and replace ☐	

(Continued)

Skills checklist (Continued)

Format spreadsheets	Level 1		Level 2	
	Cells – numbers	☐	Cells – colour	☐
	Cells – decimal places	☐	Cells – shading and borders	☐
	Cells – font	☐	Charts – move	☐
	Cells – alignment	☐	Charts – resize	☐
	Rows – height	☐	Pages – headers and footers	☐
	Columns – width	☐	Pages – adjust page setup for printing – fit to page	☐
	Rows and columns – borders	☐	Pages – adjust page setup for printing – margins	☐
	Rows and columns – shading	☐		
	Charts – titles	☐		
	Charts – labels	☐		
	Pages – size	☐		
	Pages – orientation	☐		
	Pages – margins	☐		
	Page numbers	☐		
	Date and time	☐		
Check spreadsheets	**Level 1**		**Level 2**	
	Check figures entered are correct	☐	Check page breaks in appropriate places	☐
			Check accuracy of results and correct formulae	☐

(Continued)

Skills checklist (Continued)

Functions and formulae	Level 1		Level 2	
	SUM	☐	Mathematical	☐
	Arithmetic operators: +, −, *, /	☐	Statistical	☐
	Fractions	☐	Financial	☐
			Relational	☐
Analyse and interpret	**Level 1**		**Level 2**	
	Use automatic sub-totals	☐	Use filters	☐
	Sort a cell range	☐		
Present spreadsheets	**Level 1**		**Level 2**	
	Tables	☐	The full range of graphs and charts available in the software	☐
	Bar graphs	☐		
	Pie charts	☐		
	Lists	☐		
Improve efficiency	**Level 1**		**Level 2**	
			Set up shortcuts	☐

14
Database software

Database design

What is a database?

A database is an organised collection of related data that is defined and accessed by a set of programs known as a database-management system (DBMS).

Each item of data, for example a name, is held in a field. The collection of related data fields are treated as a unit and are known as a record. The complete set of data records is held in a data file or table.

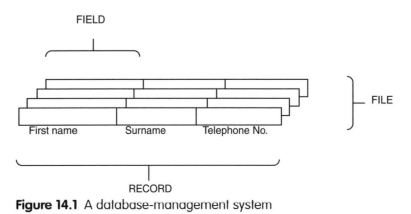

Figure 14.1 A database-management system

What types of information the database has been designed for

When you work with a database, either inputting data or extracting information, you need to know what type of data is held in the database. Unlike many other software applications, a database has to be set up to work with a specific set of data and there will be rules about what data is permitted to be put into the database. For example, when you type a date into a word-processing document you can decide what the date looks like, but when you put a date into a database it will be expecting it in a particular format, such as 23/05/2006, and it will not accept it in any other way.

How to find and retrieve information from a database

Many people keep simple, paper-based databases to assist with their work. This often takes the form of a card-index file or pages in a lever-arch file. How would you set up a simple filing system to keep the names, addresses, telephone numbers etc. for the staff in a large organisation or department? You might decide to have a record card for each person. The card could be divided up with spaces for the different items, the fields of data needed, and so might end up something like Figure 14.2.

Name:			
Address:			
City:		Post Code:	
Telephone No:		Fax No:	
Job Title:			
Department:			

Figure 14.2 Record card

These cards would be organised in a file, probably in alphabetical order of name with a divider card for each initial letter. Then, if you wanted to find the details of an individual, as long as you knew their name you could do so very quickly.

However, if you needed to find all the telephone numbers of the staff in a particular department, you would need to go through, card by card, checking the department and extracting the names and telephone numbers and then write out or word process a list with this information. This would be a very slow and time-consuming activity.

A simple, single-table database will do all of this for you, and quite a lot more.

Once accurate data is in the database, the key to successful use of that data is a good understanding of how to manipulate it to meet your needs. As you will need to make enquiries on the data, there will be some form of query language available. In many database packages this will be a simple query-by-example (QBE) screen that you fill in to specify the fields and the criteria for the selection required. This screen will also let you sort the data on one or more fields.

You would, for example, be able to select all the staff in a particular department and display their names in alphabetical order. To do this you would need to specify which fields you wanted. You would also need to specify the selection criteria. This may look something like this:

> Department = "S"   (to select all the records for the
>   Sales Department)

You would also need to specify which field, or fields, you wished to use to sort the data and whether this was in ascending (A to Z; 1 to 100) or descending (Z to A; 100 to 1) order. As you want this list in alphabetical order of name you would need to specify Surname followed by FirstName and in ascending order (Figure 14.3).

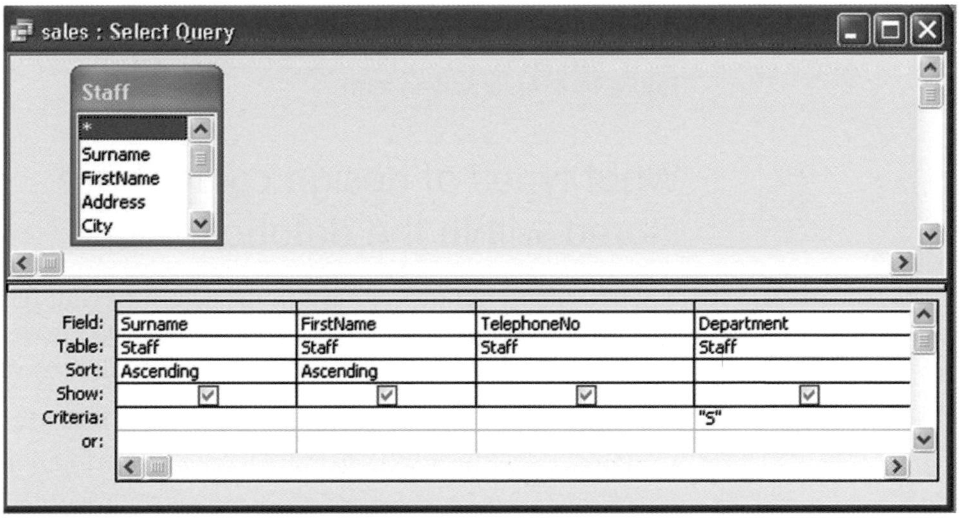

Figure 14.3 An example of a QBE screen in Microsoft Access

How to use a form designed for entering data into a database

To improve the quality of the input screens, you will usually be able to design onscreen forms; these can be laid out to suit your needs and, with appropriate use of colours, fonts and images, can reflect the organisation's house style. These will also be able to assist in controlling the quality of the input, for example you may be able to have 'pick-lists' to choose the data from, check boxes to select an option, and dates can be validated to make sure they are real dates. If the data is going to be input from a paper document it is usually a good idea to try to make the screen look like the form, that way fewer mistakes are likely to be made.

In your simple staff-information database, you could have a 'pick-list' for the department codes (Figure 14.4). This could be set up so that the list you choose from gives both the code and what it stands for. You could still choose the wrong department but you couldn't put in a code that did not represent any department.

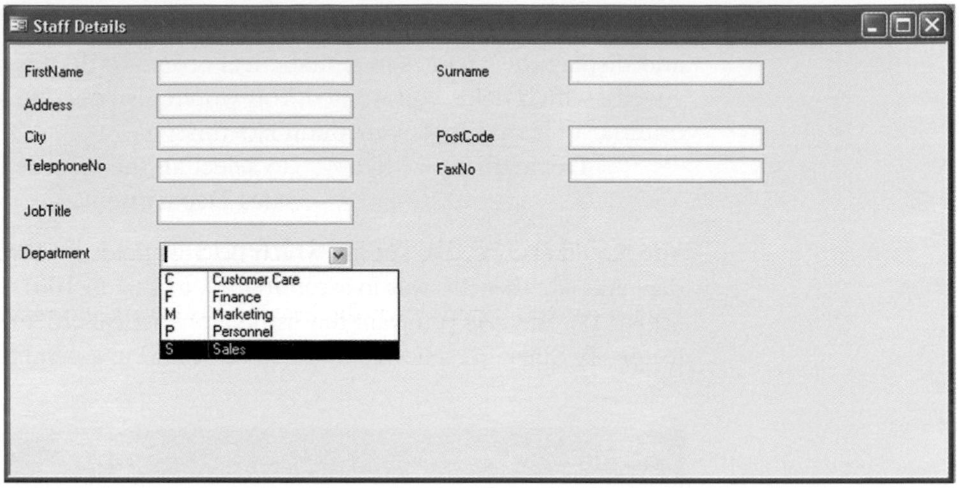

Figure 14.4 An onscreen form

What types of design content are stored within the database

There will be a number of parts to the design of your database. Some database packages, like Microsoft Access, store all the different design content of the database in the same file. An Access database will consist of:

- **Tables** – where the structure of the simple database is stored.
- **Forms** – where the design of the screens for input and output are held.
- **Queries** – these are the designs to retrieve information from the database.
- **Reports** – where the designs of printed reports for output to the printer are held.

How data is structured in a simple database

Most of the time when you use a database you will want to work with only selected parts of the complete file. To do this you need to know how the database has been structured.

A simple database will consist of a single table which is stored in a file. The data in this table will be organised into records. Each record contains one complete set of data, for example in a simple database about the staff in an organisation there will be one record for each member of staff. Each of these records will hold a number of items of data about the member of staff, for example their name, address, job title and the name of the department they work in. Each item of data is stored in a field.

Field characteristics

What you need to know and understand

- **Level 2** What characteristics fields may have
- **Level 2** How field characteristics can contribute to data validation

What characteristics fields may have

Each field is defined when the database is set up. For each field the following information needs to be given:

- **Field name** – this is how you refer to the field.
- **Data type** – this indicates the type of data that can be held (text or number).
- **Field size** – this defines the maximum number of characters allowed in the field (not used for numeric data).
- **Format** – this indicates how the data is to be displayed, for example the number of decimal places for a numeric field.

How field characteristics can contribute to data validation

- **Data type** – this can be used to restrict the data that can be input, e.g. only numbers. For example, if you tried to input letters into a field that has a data type of number you will get an error message to warn you (Figure 14.5).

Figure 14.5 Invalid value

- **Field size** – this can be used to make sure that only a certain number of characters can be entered, e.g. a national insurance number is 9 characters long. When you try to input more characters than that of the field size the extra characters are just ignored.

Data integrity

Why it is important to maintain data integrity

Integrity of data refers to the correctness of the data throughout its life in the system. Systems that do not ensure the integrity of data are of very limited value as the information extracted cannot be relied upon.

What methods can be used to maintain data integrity in a simple database

The primary point in ensuring the integrity is at the point of input. Most database packages have a wide range of facilities and features to assist and support you in this. Although each database package will be organised in a particular way, there will be a number of standard facilities available.

The structure of the database will be the first method used (see field characteristics above). In addition, you can set up validation rules to control the data as it is input.

To improve the quality of the input screens, you will usually be able to design onscreen forms; these can be laid out to suit your needs and, with appropriate use of colours, fonts and images, can reflect the organisation's house style. These will also be able to assist in controlling the quality of the input, for example you may be able to have 'pick-lists' to choose the data from, check boxes to select an option, and dates can be validated to make sure they are real dates. If the data is going to be input from a paper document it is usually a good idea to try to make the screen look like the form, that way fewer mistakes are likely to be made.

Check it yourself

You need to demonstrate that you are competent in a range of skills for this unit. Complete the Database software skills checklist on page 231. You will need to make sure that you meet any gaps in your skills before you complete your evidence portfolio.

Skills checklist

Enter data	Level 1	Level 2
	Open existing database files ☐	Create fields using correct characteristics – field name ☐
	Edit data in fields ☐	Create fields using correct characteristics – data type ☐
	Input new records ☐	Create fields using correct characteristics – field size ☐
	Deal with data that does not fit existing setup ☐	Create fields using correct characteristics – format ☐
	Save database files ☐	
Modify databases	**Level 1**	**Level 2**
		Modify field characteristics – name ☐
		Modify field characteristics – type ☐
		Modify field characteristics – size ☐
Format data	**Level 1**	**Level 2**
		Format – text data ☐
		Format – numeric data ☐
		Create report from single-table database ☐
		Format reports – page size ☐
		Format reports – page orientation ☐
		Format reports – page numbering ☐
		Format reports – headers and footers ☐
		Format reports – margins ☐

(Continued)

Skills checklist (Continued)

Check data	Level 1		Level 2	
	Check for completeness	☐	Use automated facilities – spell check	☐
	Check for accuracy	☐	Check report format and layout	☐
	Check for security	☐		
Database queries	**Level 1**		**Level 2**	
	Create queries with a single criterion	☐	Create queries with multiple-selection criteria	☐
	Create queries to sort data	☐		
	Save results of queries	☐		
Database reports	**Level 1**		**Level 2**	
	Produce predefined reports using menus or shortcuts	☐	Plan reports from single-table database	☐
			Create reports from single-table database	☐
Improve efficiency	**Level 1**		**Level 2**	
			Set up shortcuts	☐

15 Website software

Produce information

See Unit 9: Artwork and imaging software, page 182.

Websites

Pages are the basic documents of a website and are written using HTML (hypertext markup language). An HTML page contains **tags**; these are embedded codes that supply information about the structure and appearance of the page. This information is used by your web browser to determine how to display the page.

You do not need to know HTML to create web pages. There are several software packages that create the HTML code for you; you create the content as you would with a word processor. If you are familiar with HTML, you can also write and edit the HTML tags yourself.

Single-page websites

Simple, single-page websites are set up by many users. In small organisations, they are usually created so that they can have a web 'presence' with some simple information about what they do and how to contact them. Individuals may also set up this kind of site, again so that they can make their information available to the World Wide Web.

A simple website will include some text, usually very simple and factual, probably including details of how to make contact by telephone and by e-mail and a mail address. The page will have a background. This could be a simple colour or possibly a representative image texture. You would also expect the site to include at least one picture, quite often a photograph relating to the topic of the site.

Multi-page websites

More complex websites will have the information set out on different pages. The site will usually have a structure that makes it easy for the user to find the information they need, with buttons and other links to navigate around the site. It could include pages with contact details, interests, services or products.

Website features

What you need to know and understand

- What different features and design elements used on websites
- What features are used to help the user navigate
- **Level 2** How web pages and multi-page websites are structured
- **Level 2** What multimedia features are used
- **Level 2** What interactive features are used
- **Level 2** The benefits and drawbacks of different features for the user

What different features and design elements are used on websites

A website will consist of a number of basic features. The page will have a background; this may be a colour or could be a picture. The background will usually be consistent throughout the site, or could be themed for different parts of the site.

The website will obviously have content; that is, the information you wish to provide. This can be both text and images. You can further enhance your site with the use of sound – a sound might play when a page is opened or when a link is chosen.

The web page can be divided into a number of areas or frames. Each area consists of an independent web page. Frames are often used so that a web page is displayed in one frame when you click on a hyperlink in another frame (Figure 15.1).

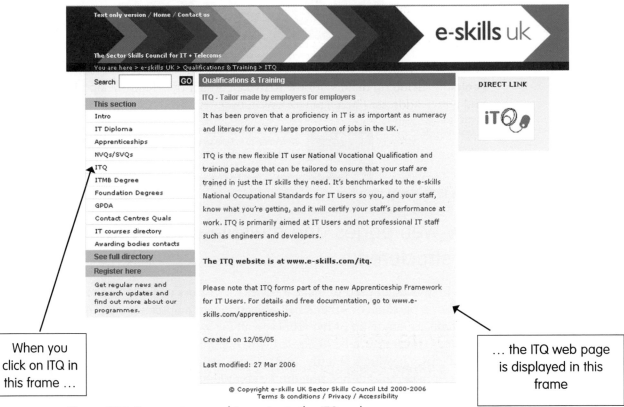

When you click on ITQ in this frame …

… the ITQ web page is displayed in this frame

Figure 15.1 Frames are used to navigate the ITQ web page

What features are used to help the user navigate

It is important that your web pages are easy to navigate around. On a single-page site you will need to provide links using buttons or hotspots to move to different parts of the page, and particularly to go to the top of the page from almost anywhere on the page.

Most multi-page websites will have a standard set of buttons, sometimes on a navigation bar, to go to parts of the site such as the home page, contents list, search facility, contact details etc (Figure 15.2).

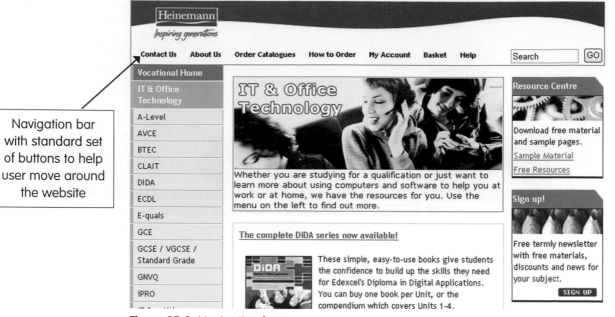

Navigation bar with standard set of buttons to help user move around the website

Figure 15.2 Navigation bar

How web pages and multiple-page websites are structured

A site map is often used to make it easier for visitors to find the pages they need. For a personal or other small website, a site map can be as simple as a contents list made up of hyperlinks to all the website's pages. For a large website, a site map will be organised with hyperlinks to categories or other logical group headings (Figure 15.3). These would then provide further levels of lists of hyperlinks depending on the complexity of the site. For example, if you sell holidays, your site map might have columns of hyperlinks for Short Breaks, Sun Holidays, Flights, and Last Minute Deals.

Site map

```
· London River Services
    ▸ London River home
    ▸ Journey Planner
    ▸ Maps
        ▸ Overview
        ▸ Route maps
        ▸ Local area maps
    ▸ Tickets and Oyster
    ▸ Travel information
        ▸ Departure boards
        ▸ Timetables
        ▸ Live travel news
        ▸ Lunch or dinner cruises
        ▸ Places of interest
        ▸ Hiring a boat
        ▸ Safety and security
        ▸ Accessibility
        ▸ Riverboat services guide
    ▸ News centre
    ▸ Careers at LRS
    ▸ Initiatives
    ▸ About LRS
        ▸ Company information
        ▸ History
        ▸ Piers
        ▸ Riverboat services
        ▸ Funding
        ▸ Legacy services
        ▸ Filming on the Thames
        ▸ Fares and ticketing
        ▸ Developing riverboat services
    ▸ Contacts and links
        ▸ Contact us
        ▸ Other contacts
        ▸ Local operators
        ▸ Online feedback form
        ▸ Useful links
        ▸ Lost property
```

Figure 15.3 A site map

Pop-ups are used to provide information while retaining the current information on the screen. A pop-up is a separate, usually smaller, window that will 'pop up' on your screen when you click on a link. They are frequently used for advertising information and can be an irritant to users. Most browsers will allow you to change the settings to block pop-ups from automatically appearing, giving the user the option of allowing a particular pop-up to be displayed.

What multimedia features are used

Websites can include a wide range of multimedia features. You may need to include sound, animation, or video files. All of these kinds of features require greater processing speeds to be available to the user, so you should use them appropriately, making sure that you do not create a website that is frustrating for many users who do not have high-speed connections. You should always ask the question – will the user benefit from having this feature included?

What interactive features are used

Many websites are not designed to just impart information but enable interaction with the user. This can be achieved through the use of:

- **Forms** – this is a collection of fields that are used to collect information from the user, for example when buying goods or services you will need to complete a form with delivery details. This information is then submitted and then processed by the website owner.
- **Discussion groups** and **message boards** – can be set up to enable the site users to communicate with each other; a computer-systems supplier may well set up such a feature for their user group.

On many sites the contact details will include an interactive link to an e-mail address where the users can send messages. A company selling clothes may have a number of different e-mail addresses for different types of messages; there may be an address for general enquiries, another for enquiries about outstanding orders and, quite commonly, an address to contact the webmaster for comments about the website and how easy or difficult it is to use.

Some sites will have an area that is only available to subscribers, people who have signed up to specific services and information. The website will have an area for these users to enter their registration login and password details.

The benefits and drawbacks of different features for the user

Many of the features that are used on websites have both benefits and drawbacks. The structure of a website may make it easier to manage but could make the navigation tedious if you need to go through many links to get to the information you are looking for. Table 15.1 lists the benefits and drawbacks of the features used on websites.

Feature	Benefits	Drawbacks
Colour	• Can make a site interesting and eye-catching • Can reflect an organisation's house style and image	• Colours and combinations of colours can be difficult for some users
Images	• Can be used to show the company's products, or to get the attention of the user	• Can make the web page slow to build, particularly for users who do not have a fast connection method
Sound	• Can get the attention of the user and make the site attractive to many users	• Users who are not in a private space or able to use headphones may cause annoyance to others around them
Frames	• The site has a very professional look and enables the user to navigate easily	• As several frames are on the screen at the same time the layout of the screen is more limited
Navigation bar	• The user can access the key sections of the site in the same way from any part of the site	
Site map	• This works like an index, so the user can find all the different parts of the site	• It needs to be well constructed to ensure users can find their way around
Pop-ups	• A small, extra piece of information can be displayed on the screen without loosing the main web page	• They can be very irritating as they appear on the screen you are working on, distracting you from what you are looking at
Animation	• Can make the site very interesting – particularly good for sites that show how something works, or a sequence of events	• Can make the web page slow to build, particularly for users who do not have a fast connection method
Video	• Can bring a site to life, providing opportunities to show short film clips of products, events and places	• Only really accessible to fast connections and so not all users will be able to see them
Forms	• Extremely useful for collecting information from the users of the site	
Discussion groups	• Can provide opportunities to discuss almost anything with almost anyone	• Need to be moderated, particularly when young people are using them, to protect vulnerable people

Table 15.1 Benefits and drawbacks of website features

Laws and guidelines

What laws and guidelines affect day-to-day use of IT

You will need to be aware of:

- Data protection – see Unit 6: IT Security for users, page 144.
- Disability – see Unit 6: IT Security for users, page 149.
- Health and safety – see Unit 3: Operate a computer, page 63.
- Copyright – see Unit 6: IT Security for users, page 149.

You also need to take into account the guidelines set by your employer or other organisation you work for.

What and how IT activities are affected by laws and guidelines

You need to be particularly aware of the Data Protection Act 1998 and the Disability Discrimination Act 1995 for this unit. The main issues are to do with access to information, particularly personal data. When designing websites you need to make sure that you create accessible web pages and refer to disability legislation. Some sites have the option to increase the text size to make it more accessible for visually impaired users; some text colours can be difficult for people who are colour blind; and there may be difficulties for those with some forms of dyslexia.

Check it yourself

You need to demonstrate that you are competent in a range of skills for this unit. Complete the Website software skills checklist on page 240. You will need to make sure that you meet any gaps in your skills before you complete your evidence portfolio.

Skills checklist

Handle files	Level 1		Level 2	
	Create files using the software	☐	Organise files	☐
	Open files using the software	☐		
	Save (As) files using the software	☐		
	Print files using the software	☐		
Combine information	**Level 1**		**Level 2**	
	Insert information	☐	Insert spreadsheet graph	☐
	Resize inserted information	☐	Combine text with an image file	☐
	Position inserted information	☐	Simple information from a database on to a website	☐
Plan and produce website	**Level 1**		**Level 2**	
	Use a web-design template to plan layout	☐	Choose content and features of website	☐
	Use a web-design template to plan format	☐	Plan layout of content and features	☐
	Use a web-design template to create simple website	☐	Create multi-page website	☐
			Create links to bookmark text within a page	☐
			Create links to other pages within the website	☐
			Create links to other websites	☐
			Alter simple code using programming language	☐

(Continued)

Skills checklist (Continued)

Edit, format and lay out content	Level 1		Level 2	
	Insert and delete	☐	Format – characters	☐
	Cut	☐	Format – lines	☐
	Copy and paste	☐	Format – paragraphs	☐
	Drag and drop	☐	Format – pages	☐
	Find and replace	☐	Format complex content – colour	☐
	Format – fonts	☐	Format complex content – fonts	☐
	Format – type style (bold or italic)	☐	Format complex content – size	☐
	Format – image	☐	Format complex content – background	☐
	Format – chart size	☐	Format complex content – pictures	☐
	Format – diagram size	☐	Insert and change text	☐
	Format – orientation	☐	Images – resize	☐
			Images – align	☐
			Images – rotate	☐
			Images – flip	☐
			Images – arrange	☐
			Layout – tables	☐
			Layout – frames	☐
Check text	**Level 1**		**Level 2**	☐
	Use spell check	☐	Proofread	☐
	Use grammar check	☐	Check line, paragraph and page breaks fall in appropriate places	☐
	Use word count	☐	Check headings and subheadings used appropriately	☐

(Continued)

Skills checklist (Continued)

Check images	Level 1		Level 2	
	Check size	☐	Check colour mode	☐
	Check alignment	☐	Check filters	☐
	Check orientation	☐	Check image resolution	☐
Upload	Level 1		Level 2	
	Upload content to web-page template	☐	Use file exchange (FTP or HTTP) to upload and publish a website	☐

16
Presentation software

What you need to know and understand

- Produce information
- Presentations
- Images, objects and sounds

Produce information

What you need to know and understand

- Know who or what the information is for, where it will be used (e.g. onscreen or hard copy) and when it is needed
- **Level 2** How to produce information that communicates clearly and accurately with the audience, where and when it is needed

See Unit 9: Artwork and imaging software, page 182.

Presentations

What you need to know and understand

- How to produce simple presentations that are accurate and well laid out
- **Level 2** How to produce complex presentations for a wide variety of uses

How to produce simple presentations that are accurate and well laid out

Simple presentations will usually consist of a number slides containing mainly text with some pictures and diagrams. A good presentation will be simply laid out with the slides following a consistent layout and colour scheme.

Text

As presentation materials are designed to be projected or displayed to a group of people, it is important to make sure that the text is clear and easy to read. Text size should usually be at least 24 point, and it is better to use simple fonts rather than fancy ones.

Colour

Make sure that the background colour does not interfere with the legibility of the text – some colour combinations are harder to read than others. Make sure you are consistent – a different colour background for each slide does not create the right impression.

Images

Images are used in presentations to enhance the information being given. Don't put too many images on a slide as they can distract from the information you are trying to get across.

How to produce complex presentations for a wide variety of uses

A presentation slide can contain many of the layout features of any document. You can include headers and footers and page numbers, you can use a range of fonts and can adjust the size of the text used. In a presentation, the other important layout consideration is the colour scheme and the background to be used. By setting up a master page, you can ensure that this layout is applied to all the slides in the presentation.

One of the most powerful aspects of presentation software is the ability to make it interactive. This is achieved using a range of techniques.

Animation

A presentation can be made to have a greater impact with the use of animation. Within the context of presentations, this means 'building' each slide one element at a time, as it is required. (See Quick Reference Guide, page 270.)

For each slide, the elements to be added are specified, and the order in which they are to appear is defined. The way in which they are added is then specified and may include effects such as *dissolve, zoom, flash, appear* and *fly*. Many of these effects will have further qualifying definitions such as whether they happen *fast, medium* or *slow*, or to specify the direction from which they will appear. When the element is displayed, it can be accompanied by an appropriate sound. There will usually be a number of predefined sounds available with the package, but you will also be able to add your own. (See Quick Reference Guide, page 270.)

Action buttons can be placed on to the presentation and have action settings assigned that will run when the button is 'clicked'. This may be to go to another slide within the presentation or to link to another application.

Slide transitions

You can identify different effects to be used to move from one slide to another. There will be a range of these transitions to choose from within your package and you should be able to choose the speed at which they take place. You can also assign a sound effect to accompany the change to a new slide. (See Quick Reference Guide, page 270.)

Timings

You can set up the slide show, for both the animation and slide-transition effects, to run whenever the left mouse button is clicked. However, you can also set it up so that it runs on pre-set timings. You can allocate a time delay as each element is added, and you can also define the time delay before the transition to the next slide. This means that you can set the show to run automatically. However, it is extremely important to get these timings right and there will be a tool available so that you can rehearse the timings and adjust the presentation to accommodate any required alterations. (See Quick Reference Guide, page 270.)

Images, objects and sounds

What you need to know and understand

- How to insert text and pictures and import other objects
- **Level 2** How to include still images and other objects

How to insert text and pictures and import other objects

The content of a presentation will be contained within a number of different objects placed on the slide. These may be text in text boxes, images, shapes and many other features (Figure 16.1). (See Quick Reference Guide, page 270.)

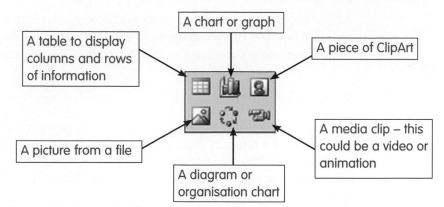

Figure 16.1 Types of objects in a Microsoft PowerPoint presentation

How to include still images and other objects

Images can be included from a wide range of sources. Pictures can be downloaded from digital cameras and inserted in your presentations. The organisation's presentation is more realistic if you use photographs taken within the company than if you use ClipArt or other generally available images. (See Quick Reference Guide, page 270.)

Links

Some of the information you want to include may be contained in another application. This may be a word-processed document, a set of data or chart that is held in a spreadsheet file. Sometimes you only need to present a 'snapshot' view of this information and then you can use the copy and paste features in the usual way. However, there may be occasions when you need to display the actual document and you will need to set up a dynamic link to the file.

Hyperlinks

A hyperlink is a connection to another element of the presentation. This link can be made from an item of text, a picture, a shape, a graph or by using a feature such as a button. You might use a hyperlink to go to another slide in the presentation, a different presentation altogether, a word-processed or spreadsheet document, an Internet, intranet, or e-mail address. (See Quick Reference Guide, page 270.)

Check it yourself

You need to demonstrate that you are competent in a range of skills for this unit. Complete the Presentation software skills checklist on page 247. You will need to make sure that you meet any gaps in your skills before you complete your evidence portfolio.

Skills checklist

Handle files	Level 1		Level 2	
	Create files using the software	☐	Organise files	☐
	Open files using the software	☐		
	Save (As) files using the software	☐		
	Print files using the software	☐		
Combine information	**Level 1**		**Level 2**	
	Insert information	☐	Insert spreadsheet graph	☐
	Resize inserted information	☐	Combine text with an image file	☐
	Position inserted information	☐	Insert a picture into a presentation slide	☐
Edit presentations	**Level 1**		**Level 2**	
	Insert and manipulate text	☐	Insert objects and other resources	☐
	Insert and manipulate pictures	☐	Resize images	☐
	Add lines to slides	☐	Change position of other objects	☐
	Add simple shapes to slides	☐	Change orientation of other objects	☐
Check presentations	**Level 1**		**Level 2**	
	Use spell check	☐	Proofread to check text and images	☐
	Use grammar check	☐	Check text formatting	☐
	Use word count	☐	Check images and other objects correctly positioned and edited	☐
	Check images – size	☐		
	Check images – alignment	☐		
	Check images – orientation	☐		

(Continued)

Skills checklist (Continued)

Format slides	Level 1		Level 2	
	Align text	☐	Change colour scheme for slides	☐
	Use bullets	☐	Use organisational house style	☐
	Use numbering	☐		
	Use line spacing	☐		
	Adjust colour	☐		
	Adjust fonts	☐		
	Adjust size	☐		
	Adjust background	☐		
	Adjust pictures	☐		
	Adjust other objects	☐		
Produce presentations	**Level 1**		**Level 2**	
			Choose appropriate presentation style to suit audience	☐
			Choose suitable templates	☐
			Use suitable templates	☐
			Adjust suitable templates	☐
Present slides	**Level 1**		**Level 2**	
	View slides	☐	Save presentation as a slide show	☐
	Reorder slides	☐	Print speaker's notes	☐
	Present as slide show	☐		
	Print presentation as handout	☐		

Use IT to exchange information

What you need to know and understand

- E-mail facilities
- Problems with exchanging information
- Laws and guidelines

E-mail facilities

What you need to know and understand

- E-mail messages
- **Level 2** Basic options for sending and replying
- How to send and receive attachments
- How to use an address book
- **Level 2** How to send e-mails to groups using a mailing list
- **Level 2** How to archive and compress e-mails
- **Level 2** What other resources may be provided by e-mail software

See Unit 11: E-mail, page 199.

Problems with exchanging information

What you need to know and understand

- Why some computer users may have difficulty in sending and receiving e-mails with attachments
- **Level 2** What limits there may be to the number or size of e-mails that can be received and stored
- **Level 2** How to keep the difficulties of sending and receiving large e-mails to a minimum
- **Level 2** What to do about e-mails from unknown users
- What viruses are and the problems they can cause
- How using anti-virus software can help to keep risks to a minimum
- **Level 2** What to do about e-mails intended to cause harm
- What risks there may be in downloading documents and software
- Risks in sharing information

See Unit 11: E-mail, page 201, and Unit 10: Internet and intranets, page 195.

Laws and guidelines

What you need to know and understand

- What laws and guidelines affect day-to-day use of IT
- **Level 2** What and how IT activities are affected by laws and guidelines

What laws and guidelines affect day-to-day use of IT

You will need to be aware of:

- Data protection – see Unit 6: IT Security for users, page 144.
- Disability – see Unit 6: IT Security for users, page 149.
- Health and safety – see Unit 3: Operate a computer, page 63.
- Copyright – see Unit 6: IT Security for users, page 149.

You also need to take into account the guidelines set by your employer or other organisation you work for.

What and how IT activities are affected by laws and guidelines

You need to be particularly aware of the Data Protection Act 1998 and the Computer Misuse Act 1990 for this unit. The main issues are to do with sending and receiving information and inappropriate e-mails. (See pages 144–153 for these Acts.)

Check it yourself

You need to demonstrate that you are competent in a range of skills for this unit. Complete the Use IT to exchange information skills checklist on page 251. You will need to make sure that you meet any gaps in your skills before you complete your evidence portfolio.

Skills checklist

Send and receive	Level 1		Level 2	
	Send to individuals	☐	Add a signature to an e-mail	☐
	Send carbon copies	☐	Set the priority of the message	☐
	Reply to individuals	☐	Send messages to groups of people	☐
	Forward e-mails	☐	Send instant messages without attachments	☐
	Reply to all	☐	Send instant messages with attachments	☐
	Reply with history	☐	Receive instant messages without attachments	☐
	Delete e-mail	☐	Receive instant messages with attachments	☐
	Send e-mails with attachments	☐	Compress messages on sending	☐
	Open e-mails with attachments	☐	Uncompress messages that have been received	☐
	Save attachments to appropriate places	☐	Archive e-mails where necessary (folders and subfolders)	☐
	Find e-mails	☐		
	Follow any rules and guidelines for sending and replying	☐		
Search	**Level 1**		**Level 2**	
	Use a search engine to find and select appropriate information	☐	Choose an appropriate search engine	☐
	Use bookmarks or favourites to make it easier to find useful information	☐	Use meta search engines	☐
	Send web pages via e-mail	☐	Use wild cards	☐
	Send web links via e-mail	☐	Use Boolean notation (AND or NOT)	☐
	Keep records of where useful information came from	☐		
	Save the results of searches	☐		

Supporting texts

The following is a list of software-specific texts published by Heinemann supporting each of the applications units of the ITQ.

Unit 9: Artwork and imaging software
Learning to Pass New CLAiT 2006 Unit 6 (0435082671)
Learning to Pass CLAiT Plus 2006 Unit 6 (0435463470)

Unit 10: Internet and intranets
Learning to Pass New CLAiT 2006 Unit 7 (043508268X)
e-Quals Level 1 Office XP Using the Internet (0435462733)
Learning to Pass CLAiT Plus 2006 Unit 7 (0435463489)
e-Quals Level 2 Office XP Using the Internet (0435462520)
Learning to Pass ECDL Syllabys 4.0 Using Office 2003 (0435463411)

Unit 11: E-mail
Learning to Pass New CLAiT 2006 Unit 8 (0435082698)
e-Quals Level 1 Office XP E-mail (0435462768)
Learning to Pass CLAiT Plus 2006 Unit 8 (0435463497)

Unit 12: Word-processing software
Learning to Pass New CLAiT 2006 Unit 1 (0435082574)
e-Quals Level 1 Office XP Word Processing (0435462709)
Learning to Pass CLAiT Plus 2006 Unit 1 (043546342X)
e-Quals Level 2 Office XP Word Processing (0435462539)
Learning to Pass ECDL Syllabys 4.0 Using Office 2003 (0435463411)

Unit 13: Spreadsheet software
Learning to Pass New CLAiT 2006 Unit 2 (0435082604)
e-Quals Level 1 Office XP Spreadsheets (0435462717)
Learning to Pass CLAiT Plus 2006 Unit 2 (0435463438)
e-Quals Level 2 Office XP Spreadsheets (0435462555)
Learning to Pass ECDL Syllabys 4.0 Using Office 2003 (0435463411)

Unit 14: Database software
Learning to Pass New CLAiT 2006 Unit 3 (0435082620)
e-Quals Level 1 Office XP Databases (0435462725)
Learning to Pass CLAiT Plus 2006 Unit 3 (0435463446)
e-Quals Level 2 Office XP Databases (0435462490)
Learning to Pass ECDL Syllabys 4.0 Using Office 2003 (0435463411)

Unit 15: Website software
Learning to Pass New CLAiT 2006 Unit 7 (043508268X)
e-Quals Level 1 Office XP Using the Internet (0435462733)
Learning to Pass CLAiT Plus 2006 Unit 7 (0435463489)
e-Quals Level 2 Office XP Using the Internet (0435462520)

Unit 16: Presentation software
Learning to Pass New CLAiT Unit 5 (0435082663)
e-Quals Level 1 Office XP Presentation Graphics (0435462741)
Learning to Pass CLAiT Plus Unit 5 (0435463462)
e-Quals Level 2 Office XP Presentation Graphics (0435462512)
Learning to Pass ECDL Syllabys 4.0 Using Office 2003 (0435463411)

Unit 17: Use IT to exchange information
Learning to Pass New CLAiT 2006 Unit 8 (0435082698)
e-Quals Level 1 Office XP E-mail (0435462768)
Learning to Pass CLAiT Plus 2006 Unit 8 (0435463497)
Learning to Pass ECDL Syllabys 4.0 Using Office 2003 (0435463411)

All titles can be purchased direct from www.heinemann.co.uk or ordered from your local bookstore.

Quick Reference Guides

Desktop-publishing software

This guide shows commands and functions using Microsoft Publisher. Other DTP software packages will have similar commands and functions available.

Any drop-down menu can be displayed by holding down the Alt key as you press the key for the letter that is underlined in the menu name. For example, Alt + f displays the File menu. Many commands in the menu have an underlined letter. Type the letter to carry out the command.

Right-clicking on a slide, selection or object will produce a pop-up menu of available commands.

Action	Button	Menu	Keyboard
Handle files			
Open a DTP document		File – Open	Ctrl + O
New DTP document		File – New	Ctrl + N
Save		File – Save	Ctrl + S
Save As		File – Save As	F12
Print		File – Print	Ctrl + P
Print to file		File – Print. Click on Print to file.	
Close or Exit	× or ×	File – Close or Exit	Alt + F4
Create a new folder		Starting from the Publisher: File – Save As dialogue box – click the Create New Folder button and name the folder. Starting from a folder on the Windows desktop: File – New – Folder. Name the folder and press Enter.	
Create drawings, artwork and images			
Use a template		File – New – Template. Select from list.	
Line			
Arrow			
Oval			
Rectangle			

(Continued)

Action	Button	Menu	Keyboard
Autoshapes			
Fill – colour/patterns		Format – Picture – Colours and Lines	
Line colour		Format – Picture – Colours and Lines	
Transparent fill			Ctrl + T
Columns		Arrange – Layout Guides – Grid Guides	
Gutter		Format – Text Box	
Margins		Arrange – Layout Guides – Margin Guides	
Paper size/orientation		File – Page Setup	
Insert, manipulate and edit artwork and images			
Cut		Edit – Cut	Ctrl + X
Copy		Edit – Copy	Ctrl + C
Paste		Edit – Paste	Ctrl + V
Undo		Edit – Undo	
Redo		Edit – Redo	
Insert ClipArt		Insert – Picture – ClipArt	
Insert picture		Insert – Picture – From File	
Insert from scanner or camera		Insert – Picture – From Scanner or Camera	
Insert WordArt		Insert – Picture – WordArt	
Crop		From the Picture toolbar, select crop tool and drag handles.	
Rotate or Flip image		Arrange – Rotate or Flip – select Free Rotate Rotate Left 90° Rotate Right 90° Flip Horizontal Flip Vertical	
Align objects		Arrange – Align or Distribute Align Left Align Center Align Right Align Top Align Middle Align Bottom Distribute Horizontally Distribute Vertically Relative to Margin Guides – select	
Line/Border style		Format – Picture – Colours and Lines	

(Continued)

Action	Button	Menu	Keyboard
Bold	**B**	Format – Font – Font style	Ctrl + B
Italics	*I*	Format – Font – Font style	Ctrl + I
Underline	U	Format – Font – Underline	Ctrl + U
Font	Times New Roman	Format – Font	
Font colour	A	Format – Font – Colour	
Font size	12	Format – Font – Size	
Left align		Format – Paragraph	Ctrl + L
Centre align		Format – Paragraph	Ctrl + E
Right align		Format – Paragraph	Ctrl + R
Justify		Format – Paragraph	Ctrl + J
Character spacing		Format – Character spacing	
Line spacing		Format – Line spacing	Ctrl + 1, Ctrl + 2, Ctrl + 3 (1.5 line space)
Rotate text		Format – Text Box – Text Box	
Ruler guides		Hold Shift down, drag from ruler.	
Select All (in a text frame)		Edit – Select All	Ctrl + A
Greyscale, whiteout		Format – Object – Picture	
Adjust contrast		Format – Object – Picture	
Adjust brightness		Format – Object – Picture	
Go to background/ foreground		View – Master Page	Ctrl + M
Bring to front		Arrange – Order	Alt + F6
Send to back		Arrange – Order	Alt + Shift + F6
Group		Select objects – click on group icon	
Ungroup		Select grouped objects – click on ungroup icon	
Edit template		Save As – set Save Type as Publisher Template	
Check text and images			
Spellcheck	ABC	Tools – Spelling	F7
Check image size, alignment		Tools – Design checker	

(Continued)

Select objects	
To select:	**Method**
An object	Click anywhere on object
Several objects	Ctrl + click on each object OR Drag selection tool

Select text	
To select:	**Method**
Start of line	Home
End of line	End
One word	Double-click on word (also selects the following space).
Several words	Press and drag the I-beam across several words and release.
A line	Click alongside line in left margin (mouse pointer changes to an arrow pointing right).
A paragraph	Double-click alongside paragraph in left margin.
A sentence	Hold down **Ctrl.** Click anywhere in sentence.
A block of text	Click cursor at start point, hold down **Shift.** Click cursor at end point.
To deselect	Click anywhere off the text.

Word-processing software

This guide shows commands and functions using Microsoft Word. Other word-processing packages will have similar commands and functions available.

Any drop-down menu can be displayed by holding down the Alt key as you press the key for the letter that is underlined in the menu name. For example, Alt + f displays the File menu. Many commands in the menu have an underlined letter. Type the letter to carry out the command.

Right-clicking on a document, selection or table will produce a pop-up menu of available commands.

Action	Toolbar	Menu	Keyboard
Handle files			
Create a new document		File – New, then click OK in the dialogue box.	Ctrl + N
Open an existing document		File – Open, then navigate to the file in the Open dialogue box, select the file and click Open.	Ctrl + O
Save		File – Save	Ctrl + S
Save As		File – Save As	F12
Print		File – Print	Ctrl + P
Print preview		File – Print Preview	Ctrl + F2
Close or Exit	× or ✕	File – Close or Exit	Alt + F4
Create a new folder		Starting from the Word File: File – Save As – dialogue box – click the Create New Folder button and name the folder.	
		Starting from a folder on the Windows desktop: File – New – Folder. Name the folder and press Enter.	
Combine information			
Insert ClipArt		From Drawing toolbar	Insert – Picture – ClipArt	
Insert hyperlink		Insert – Hyperlink	Ctrl + K
Chart		Insert – Object – Microsoft Graph Chart	
Compare and merge documents		Tools – Compare and Merge Documents	
Edit text			
Cut		Edit – Cut	Ctrl + X
Copy		Edit – Copy	Ctrl + C
Paste		Edit – Paste	Ctrl + V
Drag and drop		Highlight text to be moved and then click and drag to new position.	
Find		Edit – Find	Ctrl + F
Replace		Edit – Replace	Ctrl + H

(Continued)

Action	Toolbar	Menu	Keyboard
Cancel			Esc
Undo		Edit – Undo	Ctrl + Z
Redo		Edit – Redo . . .	Ctrl + Y
Select all		Edit – Select All	Ctrl + A
Symbol		Insert – Symbol	
Convert table to text		Table – Convert – Table to Text	
Convert text to table		Table – Convert – Text to Table	
Mail merge		Tools – Letters and Mailings – Mail Merge	
Format text			
Font size	12	Format – Font – Font	
Font	Times New Roman	Format – Font – Font	
Font colour	A	Format – Font – Font	
Bold	B	Format – Font	Ctrl + B
Italics	I	Format – Font – Font	Ctrl + I
Underline	U	Format – Font – Font	Ctrl + U
Subscript/Superscript		Format – Font – Font tab, select as required.	
Left align		Format – Paragraph – Indents and Spacing	Ctrl + L
Centre align		Format – Paragraph – Indents and Spacing	Ctrl + E
Justify		Format – Paragraph – Indents and Spacing	Ctrl + J
Right align		Format – Paragraph – Indents and Spacing	Ctrl + R
Bullets		Format – Bullets and Numbering – Bulleted	
Numbering		Format – Bullets and Numbering – Numbered	
Character spacing		Format – Font – Character spacing	
Line spacing		Format – Paragraph – Indents and Spacing – Line Spacing	Single: Ctrl + 1 1½: Ctrl + 5 Double: Ctrl + 2
Space before/after a paragraph		Format – Paragraph – Spacing Before or After	
Hanging indent		Format – Paragraph – Indents and Spacing – Special	
First line indent		Format – Paragraph – Special	
Borders		Format – Borders and Shading	
Shading		Format – Borders and Shading	
Tabs	Select tab type and click on ruler	Format – Tabs	
Page number	(from Header and Footer Toolbar)	Insert – Page Numbers or View – Header and Footer	

(Continued)

Action	Toolbar	Menu	Keyboard
Page setup		File – Page Setup	
Paper size/orientation		File – Page Setup – Paper Size	
Margins		File – Page Setup – Margins	
Header/Footer		View – Header and Footer	
Page break		Insert – Break – Page Break	Ctrl + Return
Add Automatic Date and Time	[icon] and [icon]	View – Header and Footer	
Increase indent	[icon]	Format – Paragraph – Indents and Spacing	Ctrl + M
Decrease indent	[icon]	Format – Paragraph – Indents and Spacing	
Demote	[icon]	Format – Paragraph – Indents and Spacing	
Promote	[icon]	Format – Paragraph – Indents and Spacing	Ctrl + M
Section break		Insert – Break – Continuous (or Next Page) Section Break	
Columns	[icon]	Format – Columns	
Column Break		Insert – Break – Column Break	
Styles and Formatting	[icon]	Format – Styles and Formatting	
Styles and Formatting, applying existing style	Header ▼	Format – Styles and Formatting	
Save as different document type		File – Save As – Save as type: such as web page	
Text wrapping	[icon] from Picture toolbar	View – Toolbars – Picture or Format – Object – Layout	
Layout			
Table	[icon]	Table – Insert – Table	
Table, insert rows or columns		Table – Insert – Rows above or below, or Columns above or below	
Table, delete rows or columns		Table – Delete – Rows or Columns	
Table, change row height or column width		Table – Table Properties – Row or Column	
Check text			
Spellcheck	[icon]	Tools – Spelling and Grammar	F7
Grammar Check	[icon]	Tools – Spelling and Grammar	F7
Word count		Tools – Word Count	
Improve efficiency			
Macros		Tools – Macro – Macros	Alt + F8
Customise toolbars		View – Toolbars – Customize	
Drawing toolbar	[icon] or [icon]	View – Toolbars – Drawing	

(Continued)

Action	Toolbar		Menu	Keyboard
Normal view	☰	left above status bar	View – Normal	
Print layout view	▣	left above status bar	View – Print Layout	
Ruler			View – Ruler	
Show/Hide	¶			
Shrink to fit	🔍 and 🗐		File – Print – Zoom: Scale to Paper Size	

Select text

To select:	Method
Start of line	Home
End of line	End
One word	Double-click on word (also selects the following space).
Several words	Press and drag the I-beam across several words and release.
A line	Click alongside line in left margin (mouse pointer changes to an arrow pointing right).
A paragraph	Double-click alongside paragraph in left margin.
A sentence	Hold down **Ctrl.** Click anywhere in sentence.
Whole document	Hold down **Ctrl** and click in left margin **OR** choose Select All from Edit menu.
A block of text	Click cursor at start point, hold down **Shift.** Click cursor at end point.
To deselect	Click anywhere off the text.

Drawing toolbar

Group objects	D̲r̲aw ▾	– On Drawing toolbar then Group
Ungroup objects	D̲r̲aw ▾	– On Drawing toolbar then Group
Bring to front (graphics)	D̲r̲aw ▾	– Order – Bring to Front
Order (graphics)	D̲r̲aw ▾	– On Drawing toolbar – Order
Send to back (graphics)	D̲r̲aw ▾	– On Drawing toolbar – Order – Send to Back

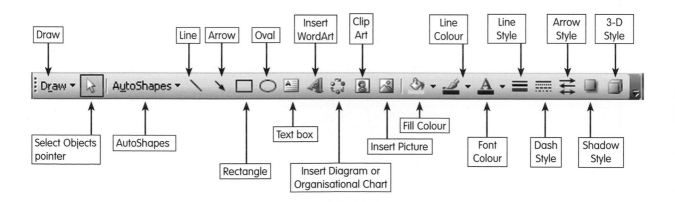

Spreadsheet software

This guide shows commands and functions using Microsoft Excel. Other spreadsheet packages will have similar commands and functions available.

Any drop-down menu can be displayed by holding down the Alt key as you press the key for the letter that is underlined in the menu name. For example, Alt + f displays the File menu. Each command in the menu has an underlined letter. Type the letter to carry out the command.

Right-clicking on a cell, selection or object will produce a pop-up menu of available commands.

Action	Toolbar	Menu	Keyboard
Handle files			
Create a new workbook file		File – New, then click OK in the dialogue box.	Ctrl + N
Open a workbook file		File – Open, then navigate to the file in the Open dialogue box, select the file and click Open.	Ctrl + O
Save a workbook file		File – Save	Ctrl + S
Save a second copy of a workbook with another name or in another place		File – Save As… Choose the folder, name the file, click Save.	
Switch between open workbooks		Click on the workbook's button on the taskbar at the bottom of the screen. **Or** Window menu and select the name of the workbook.	Ctrl + Tab (Repeat as required)
Switch between worksheets in a workbook		Click on the worksheet tab near the bottom of the window.	Ctrl + Page Up Ctrl + Page Down.
Close a workbook	✕	(This is the lower X if there are two. The upper X is the button to close Excel.) File – Close	Ctrl + W
Print a worksheet	then	Preview first. File – Print Preview. Click the Print button in the Preview window. File – Print	Ctrl + P
Create a new folder		Starting from the Excel, File – Save As dialogue box – click the Create New Folder button and name the folder. Starting from a folder on the Windows desktop, File – New – Folder. Name the folder and press Enter.	
Move a worksheet		Drag the worksheet tab to its new position in the same or another workbook. **Or** right click the worksheet tab, select Move or Copy and choose the new position.	
Copy a worksheet		Hold down the Ctrl key as you drag the worksheet tab to its new position. **Or** right click the worksheet tab, select Move or Copy, tick the Create a Copy box and choose the new position. Click OK.	
Print a selected area		As a one-off, File – Print, Choose the Selection option, click OK. For long-term use, File – Print Area – Set Print Area. Print as usual.	

(Continued)

Action	Toolbar	Menu	Keyboard
Combine Information			
Paste cells into Word document		Select and copy cells required. Switch to the Word file and Paste where required.	Ctrl + C and Ctrl + V
Link cells		Select cells, Copy, move to new position. Edit – Paste Special – Paste Link.	
Import a data file		Start Excel and then File – Open and then change the Files of type: box to either txt files or csv files and navigate to the folder where the file is. Select the file and click Open. The Text Import Wizard will start in the case of text files. csv files will open in Excel. File must be saved as Excel file.	
Enter and edit spreadsheet data			
Enter cell contents		Select the cell with the mouse or cursor (arrow) keys. Key in the data. Press Enter to complete entry and move down. **Or** press Tab to complete entry and move right. **Or** press Shift + Enter to complete entry and move up. **Or** click the green tick in the formula bar to complete entry and stay in the same cell. To cancel an entry before completion, press Esc or click the red cross in the formula bar.	
Edit cell contents		To replace an existing entry, select the cell and key in the new entry. To alter the existing entry, double click in the cell to place a cursor and edit in the cell. **Or** click the formula bar and edit the active cell there. **Or** use the F2 function key to place a cursor and edit the active cell as before.	
Delete cell contents		Edit menu, Clear, the choose Contents to clear contents but leave formatting, or choose All to clear both contents and formatting. The Delete key clears the content but not the formatting and completes the action. The Backspace delete key clears the content but leaves the cursor in the cell instead of completing the action. When editing cell contents, Backspace deletes to the left and Delete deletes to the right.	
Cut command	✂	Edit – Cut	Ctrl + X
Copy command	📑	Edit – Copy	Ctrl + C
Paste command	📋	Edit – Copy	Ctrl + V
Move cell contents	✂ and 📋	Select cells, Cut, move to new position, Paste. **Or** point to cell border, hold down the left mouse button and drag to new position.	
Copy cell contents	📑 and 📋	Select cells, Copy, move to new position, Paste. **Or** point to cell border, hold down the left mouse button and hold down Ctrl key as you drag to new position.	
Insert a row or column		Insert – Rows or Columns. If a whole row or column is selected then the insertion will happen at once. If several rows or columns are selected then that number of rows or columns will be inserted.	Ctrl + Shift + + (plus key)

(Continued)

Action	Toolbar	Menu	Keyboard
Delete a row or column		Edit menu, Delete. Choose to delete a whole row or column or to shift cells up or left. If you select a whole row or column before using Edit, Delete then the whole row or column will be deleted.	
Search for text in a cell		Edit – Find. Key in text, set options and click Find Next.	Ctrl + F
Replace text in a cell		Edit – Replace. Key in text to find and replace, set options and click Find Next, then Replace.	Ctrl + H
Undo actions		The arrow by the button gives a list of actions so that you can undo several at once. **Or** Edit – Undo… The most recent action will be shown.	Ctrl + Z
Copy values only		Select cells, Copy, move to new position. Edit – Paste Special – Values.	
Enter data into more than one cell at same time		Select the cells that are to have the same data by highlighting and using the Ctrl key to highlight non-adjacent cells, type the entry and then press Ctrl + Enter.	
Insert Picture		Insert – Picture – ClipArt or From File	
Relative and absolute references		When formulas are copied, relative references change to suit their new position, absolute references do not change. Absolute references are shown by dollar signs, e.g. \$A\$4.	F4
Names cells and ranges		To name a selected cell or range, click the Insert menu, select Name, then select Define. Key in the name. OK. Named cells in formulas are unchanged when copies, like absolute references.	
Formats			
Number formats	% ,	Currency and percent can be set using toolbar buttons or just by keying in a number as currency or percent. Number of decimal places can be increased or decreased using toolbar buttons. To set other number formats, Format menu, Cells, Number tab.	
Date formats		Date formats are set automatically if you key in a date. To set Date formats, Format – Cells, Number tab. Date formats can be used for medium and long dates. Short dates have the month first. Use the Custom format dd/mm/yy to put the day first.	
Font, size and enhancements	Times New Roman 12 **B** *I* <u>U</u>	Use the toolbar lists and buttons for font, size, bold, italic or underline. **Or** click the Format – Cells then click the Font tab and select the options from the dialogue box. Ctrl + 1 (number one, not letter L) shows the Format cells dialogue box.	Ctrl + B Ctrl + I Ctrl + U

(Continued)

Action	Toolbar	Menu	Keyboard
Alignment		Select cells click Format – Cells – then click Alignment tab for options.	
Borders		Select cells click Format – Cells then click the Border tab for more options.	
Background fills and patterns		Select cells Format – Cells then click the Patterns tab for more options.	
Change Row height or Column width		Format – Row – Height or Format – Column – Width. **Or** position mouse pointer over the column headings dividing line and click and drag to desired width etc.	
Page orientation		File – Page Setup – Page tab, Portrait or Landscape.	
Show/Hide formulas		Tools – Options – View tab. Click in Formulas checkbox.	Ctrl + ' (backwards quote)
Copy formats only		Select cells, Copy, move to new position. Edit – Paste. Special – Formats.	
Show/Hide objects		Tools – Options – View tab. Objects row, choose show all or hide all.	
Add headers and footers		View – Headers and Footers. **Or** File – Page Setup – Header/Footer tab. Choose Custom Header or Custom Footer.	
Automatic Date		In Header and Footer, click on the icon for the calendar and today's date will be inserted.	
Automatic filename		In Header and Footer, click on the File icon and the filename will be inserted.	
Fit on one page		File – Page Setup – Page Tab. Fit to 1 page wide by 1 page tall.	
Conditional Formatting		Format – Conditional Formatting… and then choose options.	
Hide columns or rows		Format – Row or Column – Hide	
Unhide columns or rows		Select rows or columns either side of hidden rows or columns, then Format – Row or Column – Unhide.	
Locking and protection		Click the Format – Cells then click the Protection tab and unlock selected cells. Then click the Tools menu, Protection to protect the sheet. A password is optional.	
Functions and formulae			
Basic arithmetic operations		Start formula with =. Use the operators + (add) – (subtract) ∗ (multiply) / (divide).	
Mixed operations		Brackets first, then multiply and divide, then add and subtract.	
SUM()	Σ ▾	Adds the contents of cells and ranges in its brackets. Key in the formula.	Alt + =
AVERAGE()		Finds the average (mean) or cells and ranges in its brackets.	
MAX()		Finds the largest value in the cells and ranges in its brackets.	
MIN()		Finds the smallest value in the cells and ranges in its brackets.	

(Continued)

Action	Toolbar	Menu	Keyboard
TODAY()		Returns the current date.	
ROUND()		Needs two numbers in its brackets: the number to be rounded and the number of decimal places to keep.	
COUNT()		Finds how many of the cells in the brackets contain numbers.	
IF()		Has three entries (arguments) in its brackets. A condition that may be true or false, the actions to take if true, the action to take if false.	
Analyse and interpret			
Sort data	A↓Z Z↓A	Select range of cells to sort. Data – Sort and set options.	
Choosing test data		Use representative data, extreme data and rogue data. Also use marginal values to text formulas containing IF functions.	
Filter	Y=	Data – Filter – AutoFilter or Advanced Filter	
Present spreadsheets			
Create a chart		Select the data. Insert – Chart.	
Format a chart		Double click on area required. **Or** right-click and select Format… Select required options from dialogue box.	
Change Chart type		Chart – Chart Type	
Print a chart		To print chart alone, select chart before printing. Deselect chart to print whole sheet.	
Move and resize a chart on a worksheet		Point to outer area and drag to move. Use resize handles to make larger or smaller.	
Add text to chart		Use Text box from Drawing toolbar and type required text.	
Show gridlines, row numbers and column letters for printing		File – Page Setup – Sheet tab, click Gridlines and Row and Column headings check boxes	
Repeat selected cells on each page		File – Page Setup – Sheet tab, choose rows or columns to repeat.	
Split window		Select position to split. Window – Split.	
Freeze panes		Select position to freeze. Window – Freeze Panes.	
Arrange windows (for 2 or more workbooks)		Window – Arrange. Choose horizontal or vertical.	
Improve efficiency			
Macros		Tools – Macro – Macros to see list of macros in workbook. Tools – Macro – Record new Macro to add a new macro to the workbook.	

Database software

This guide shows commands and functions using Microsoft Access. Other database packages will have similar commands and functions available.

Any drop-down menu can be displayed by holding down the Alt key as you press the key for the letter that is underlined in the menu name. For example, Alt + f displays the File menu. Many commands in the menu have an underlined letter. Type the letter to carry out the command.

Right-clicking on a cell, selection or object will produce a pop-up menu of available commands.

Action	Toolbar	Menu	Keyboard
Enter data			
Open an existing database			Ctrl + O
Either:		Start Access. (Use Start button, All Programs, MS Access.) Choose to open an existing database. Select More Files, OK. In the Open dialogue box, find the file you want, click Open. The database window appears.	
Or:		Search in My Documents or its sub-folders for the file you want. Double click on the file to start Access and open the file. The database window appears.	
Enter and edit data in table		Do this in datasheet view of a table. Click into the field and key in the data. A record is automatically saved when you move out of it. Widen columns if necessary to show all the data.	
Delete a record		Select the row. Click Delete Record button on toolbar or use Edit menu and choose Delete Record. You will see a warning that the record will be deleted.	Ctrl + (minus sign)–
Add a record		Add new records at the bottom of the table.	Ctrl + (plus sign)+
Find and replace data in a table		Select the field to search. Edit – Replace.	Ctrl + H
Close a database, table, form, report or query	✕ or ✕	File – Close. It is automatically saved when you close it.	Ctrl + F4
Close Access	✕	File – Exit. The file is automatically saved when you close it.	Alt + F4
Create a new database		Start Access. (Use Start button, All Programs, MS Access.) Choose to create a blank Access database. OK. Enter the name, choose the folder, click Create. The database window appears.	Ctrl + N
Create a database table		Write down the fields, types and lengths before you start. Have the database window open, Tables tab in front. Double-click Create table in design view. Enter field names and data type in top of design window. For each field, enter size and any other details in lower half of window. F6 key swaps from upper to lower half and back. Save design and give table a name.	
Data types		Text can hold any characters, letters, numbers, or punctuation. Maximum size 255.	

(Continued)

Action	Toolbar	Menu	Keyboard
		Number. Use Long Integer or Integer for whole numbers. Use Single or Double for numbers with decimal places.	
		Currency. Use this for money. Format to 0 or 2 decimal places.	
		Date/time. Use for dates and times and format as required.	
		Logical (Yes/No). Use where there are only two possible values, true and false.	
Primary key		Choose a field that will have a different entry for every record. In design view of the table, select the field and click the Primary Key button on the toolbar.	
Design view and datasheet view		Tables and queries have both these views. Design view is for creating or altering the structure. Datasheet view is for entering or viewing data. Swap between the views by using the leftmost toolbar button or use the View menu.	
Index a field		In design view of the table, click Indexes button. Enter index name and choose field(s) to index.	
Modify databases (L2 only)		You can change the structure and characteristics of the fields.	
Copy table structures	and	Within the same database, select the table (unopened). Copy, Paste, choose Structure Only and name table. To a different database, select the table (unopened). File menu – Export. Select the database. Choose Definition only.	Ctrl + C and then Ctrl + V
Copy a complete table with data	and	Similar to copying structure, but choose Structure and Data or Definition and Data.	Ctrl + C and then Ctrl + V
Copy data from one table to another		Select complete rows and use Copy and Paste Append from the Edit menu. Alternatively use an Append query.	
Import table from other database		File – Get External Data – Import. Navigate to folder containing file, select file and click Import. Choose the table to import and click OK.	
Import data from Excel or csv files		File – Get External Data – Import. Navigate to folder containing file, change file type to Excel or text files, select file and click Import. the Import Text Wizard will start. Choose appropriate options, especially if first row contains field names.	
Export data to Word		In Print Preview, Tools – Office Links – Publish It with Microsoft Office Word.	
Export data to Excel		In Print Preview, Tools – Office Links – Analyze It with Microsoft Office Excel	
Check Data		The data in the database is only useful if it is accurate. You should always proof read the data that you enter.	
Spell check		Tools – Spelling	F7

(Continued)

Action	Toolbar	Menu	Keyboard
Database queries		Queries do not save data, but use data taken from tables. Use queries to sort records and to select records and fields for display.	
Create a query		With the database window open, click the Queries tab. Double-click 'Create query in design view'. Add the table you need. Close the Show Table window. The lower part of the design window is the design grid where you set up the query. Put in the fields you want by dragging down from the table or double clicking.	
Sorting		In the sort row of the design grid, click in the field (column) you want to sort by. Choose ascending or descending from the drop-down box.	
Displaying or hiding fields		In each column of the design grid is a tick box. Tick to show the field, no tick to hide the field.	
Selecting by one criterion		In the Criteria row of the design grid, click in the field you want to use. Type in your search criterion. This can be: The exact data entry you are looking for, e.g. Oxford. A criterion using relational operators, e.g. >10 Relational operators are: >greater than, <less than, >=greater than or equal to, <= less than or equal to, =equal to, <> not equal to.	
To see the query results	or	Query – Run	
Save a query		Click the save button and give the query an informative name starting qry...	
Use an existing query		In the database window, with the Queries tab in front, select the query. Either click Design to see design view or click Open to see datasheet view.	
Selecting by multiple criteria using logical operators		Put criteria in the same row to link them using AND. All criteria must be true for the record to show. Put criteria in different rows to link them using OR. Only one of the criteria need be true for the record to show.	
Use wildcards in query criteria		? stands for any single character. * stands for any number of characters.	
Action queries		There are four types: Update, Append, Make-table and Delete. Create a select query first then change it to the action query you want, using the Query menu. You have to run an action query using the run button. Update and Delete queries act on the table on which they are based. Make-table and Append queries copy data to another table in the same or a different database.	
Forms		A form is for display on a screen. Forms can be used for data entry.	
Use an existing form		In the database window, with the Forms tab in front, select the form. Either click Design to see design view or click Open to display the form.	
Print a form		Print button to print all records one after another. File – Print, Selected Records to print just the current record.	Ctrl + P

(Continued)

Action	Toolbar	Menu	Keyboard
Create a form	📇!	Start in the Forms section of the database window. Choose to create a form using the wizard, or click the New button and choose an Autoform. Select a table or query on which to base the form. Work though the wizard or let the Autoform run.	
Add/delete a field on a form	📄	To add a field, show the field list (View, Field List) and drag the field on to the form. A text box and label will appear. To delete a field, select and delete its text box and label.	
Image on a form	🖼	To put in an image from a file, place an image box on the form, then locate the file. Use the image box property list to select Zoom instead of Clip. To use Clipart, place an Unbound OLE object box, and choose Microsoft Clip Gallery. Alternatively use the Insert – Object.	
Move/resize/format labels and text boxes on a form		Work in design view. Select the control so that the handles show. Drag the handles to resize. Point to the control edge (grasping hand) to move linked controls together. Point to top left handle (pointing finger) to move a control by itself. When a control is selected the formatting toolbar is active, allowing you to change font, size, colour etc.	
Properties of a control	📋	Select the object you want to alter, the form, an area of the form or a control. Right-click and choose Properties. Find and edit the property.	
Header and footer		View – Form Header/Footer to add to form design. Drag the header or footer area to the required size. Use the toolbox to select a control and place it on the form. Use a label for normal text such as headings.	
Database reports		Simple reports can be produced from the Table. Database reports are for printing out selected data. They allow a choice of layout and formatting.	
Print a table	🖨	Open the table in datasheet view. Preview first. (File, Print Preview or use Preview button.) Then File, Print. To change landscape, File, Page Setup, Page tab, click on Landscape, then OK. You have to do this every time – Access will not remember that you want landscape.	Ctrl + P
Sort in a table	A↓ Z↓ Z A	(Quick and temporary – also see sorting in query.) Click in the field (column) you want to use for sorting. Click Sort Ascending or Sort Descending button on toolbar.	
Use an existing report	🔍 then 🖨	In the database window, with the Reports tab in front, select the report. Either click Design to see design view or click Preview to view the report before sending to the printer.	
Print selected records		Open the table. Select the records. File – Print. Click Selected Records option button. OK.	
Create a report	📋	Start in the Reports section of the database window. Use the wizard, or click the New button and choose an AutoReport. Base a report on a query so that you can select records for printing. The wizard lets you select fields. It also lets you set up grouping, sorting and totals.	

(Continued)

Action	Toolbar	Menu	Keyboard
Sort a report		Click the sorting and grouping button on the toolbar. Use the dialogue box to select the field(s) you want to use for sorting.	
Add/delete fields		Show the field list as you do for a form, and drag a field on to the report. To delete a field, select and delete its label and text box.	
Totals	abl	You can set up totals in a grouped report using the wizard. To set your own total, place a text box in the report footer and enter the formula =SUM([field name]). You can also put subtotals in group footers in the same way. You cannot put a total in the page footer.	
Add an image to a report		The method is the same as adding an image to a form.	
Move/resize/format labels and text boxes on a report		Work in design view. Select the control so that the handles show. Move, resize or format as for a form.	
Margins		File – Page Setup – Margins tab	
Headers/footers		The report header appears once, at the top of the first page. The report footer appears once below the last record on the last page. The page header and footer appear on every page. A grouped report also has group headers and footers that appear at the beginning and end of each group of records.	
View menu		If the toolbox, field list, headers or property window are needed but are not visible, use the View menu in design view and select them.	

Presentation software

This guide shows commands and functions using Microsoft PowerPoint. Other presentation software packages will have similar commands and functions available.

Any drop-down menu can be displayed by holding down the Alt key as you press the key for the letter that is underlined in the menu name. For example, Alt + f displays the File menu. Many commands in the menu have an underlined letter. Type the letter to carry out the command.

Right-clicking on a slide, selection or object will produce a pop-up menu of available commands.

Action	Button	Menu	Keyboard
Handle files			
Open a presentation		File – Open	Ctrl + O
New presentation		File – New	Ctrl + N
Save		File – Save	Ctrl + S
Save as		File – Save As	F12
Print		File – Print	Ctrl + P

(Continued)

Action	Button	Menu	Keyboard
Close or Exit	× or ✕	File – Close or Exit	Alt + F4
Create a new folder		Starting from PowerPoint: File – Save As – click the Create New Folder button and name the folder. Starting from a folder on the Windows desktop: File – New – Folder. Name the folder and press Enter.	

Combine information

Insert ClipArt	from Drawing toolbar	Insert – Picture – ClipArt	
Insert picture		Insert – Picture – From file	
Insert sound		Insert – Movies and Sound – Sound from Clip Organiser (or from File)	

Edit presentations

Insert new slide	New Slide	Insert – New slide	
Cut		Edit – Cut	Ctrl + X
Copy		Edit – Copy	Ctrl + C
Paste		Edit – Paste	Ctrl + V
Change case		Format – Change case	
Cancel			Esc
Undo		Edit – Undo	
Redo		Edit – Redo	
Text box		Insert – Text Box	
Select All (in a text box)		Edit – Select All	Ctrl + A
AutoShapes	AutoShapes ▾ on Drawing toolbar	Insert – Picture – AutoShapes	
Copy a slide		In Slide Sorter view – select Slide – Copy- paste in new position **Or** Insert – duplicate slide	
Sound		Insert – Movies and Sound	

Check presentations

Spellcheck		Tools – Spelling and Grammar	F7
Grammar check		Tools – Spelling and Grammar	F7
Word count		Tools – Word Count	

Format slides

Font	Times New Roman ▾	Format – Font	
Font size	12 ▾	Format – Font	
Bold	**B**	Format – Font	Ctrl + B

(Continued)

Action	Button	Menu	Keyboard
Italics	*I*	Format – Font	Ctrl + I
Underline	U	Format – Font	Ctrl + U
Shadow	S	Format – Font	
Left align		Format – Alignment	Ctrl + L
Centre align		Format – Alignment	Ctrl + E
Justify		Format – Alignment	Ctrl + J
Right align		Format – Alignment	Ctrl + R
Line spacing		Format – Line Spacing	
Bullets		Format – Bullets and Numbering	
Numbering		Format – Bullets and Numbering	
Demote (Indent)			Tab key
Promote			
Format objects		Format – Object/AutoShape/Text Box/Picture	
Produce presentations			
Change slide layout		Format – Slide Layout	
Chart effects		In Normal view select the chart – select Slideshow menu – Custom Animation – Add Effect – select chart object in task pane – dropdown arrow – Effect options	
Design template		Format – Apply Design Template	
Footer		View – Header and Footer	
Master slide		View – Master – Slide Master	
Present slides			
Slide Sorter view		View – Slide Sorter	
Slide order (change)	In Slide Sorter view – drag slide to new position On Slide/Outline tab – drag slide icon to new position		
Slideshow view	on status bar	View – Slideshow	F5
Hide a slide	in Slide Sorter view	Slideshow – Hide Slide	
Slide transition	Transition (in Slide Sorter view)	Slideshow – Slide Transition	
Animation		Slideshow Custom Animation (not Slide Sorter view)	
Custom animation		In Slide or Normal view – select Slide – Slideshow menu – Custom Animation. Check each object to be animated	
Rehearse timings	in Slide Sorter view	Slideshow – Rehearse Timings	

(Continued)

Action	Button	Menu	Keyboard
Summary slide		In Slide Sorter view – select Slides first (use Control and click the slides whose titles you want to use).	
Guides		View – Guides. Ctrl and drag for a new guide.	
Normal view	⊞	View – Normal	
Paper size/orientation		File – Page Setup	
Ruler		View – Ruler	
View options		View menu – Select	

Select text

To select	Method
Start of line	Home
End of line	End
One word	Double-click on word (also selects the following space).
Several words	Press and drag the I-beam across several words and release.
A sentence	Hold down **Ctrl.** Click anywhere in sentence.
A block of text	Click cursor at start point, hold down **Shift.** Click cursor at end point.
To deselect	Click anywhere off the text.

Drawing Toolbar

Rotate	Draw ▼ – Rotate	Format – Object/AutoShape/Text Box/ Picture	
Order	Draw ▼	Drawing toolbar – Draw – Order	
Group		Drawing toolbar – Draw – Group	
Ungroup	Draw ▼	Drawing toolbar – Draw – Ungroup	
Flip	Draw – Rotate or Flip (For ClipArt – Ungroup and Group first)		

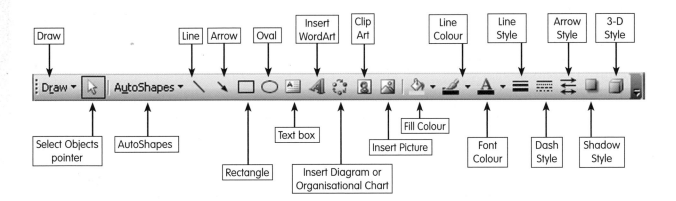

Index

Page numbers in italics indicate tables or figures.